EXPOSURE

VICTIMS OF RADIATION SPEAK OUT

The Chugoku Newspaper

Foreword by
Robert Jay Lifton

KODANSHA INTERNATIONAL
Tokyo • New York • London

NOTES TO THE READER

For reasons of privacy, names of some interviewees have been changed.
Chinese, Japanese, and Korean names appear in traditional order, with the family name first.
Conversion of yen figures to dollars is as per the rate prevailing at the time of first printing in 1992.
The Chugoku Newspaper carried out their investigations in the period from 1988 to 1989; the name "Soviet Union" has thus been retained throughout the book.

ACKNOWLEDGMENTS

The Chugoku Newspaper would like to thank the Research Institute for Nuclear Medicine and Biology at Hiroshima University, the Radiation Effects Research Foundation and the Hiroshima Red Cross and Atomic Bomb Survivors Hospital for their assistance in preparing the articles in this book.

Originally published in Japanese as *Sekai no Hibakusha* by Kodansha Ltd. in 1991.

Distributed in the United States by Kodansha America, Inc., 114 Fifth Avenue, New York, N.Y. 10011, and in the United Kingdom and continental Europe by Kodansha Europe Ltd., 95 Aldwych, London WC2B 4JF. Published by Kodansha International Ltd., 17-14 Otowa 1-chome, Bunkyo-ku, Tokyo 112, and Kodansha America, Inc.

LCC 92-15044
ISBN 4-7700-2065-1

CONTENTS

FOREWORD

Robert Jay Lifton

Director of the Center on Violence and Human Survival,
John Jay College of Criminal Justice

The end of the cold war enables us to look more clearly at the world. We need no longer be blinded by the strange polarization that so consumed and distorted international perceptions. New openings bring confusions, but also the possibility of new insight.

What becomes immediately evident is the absurdity of our long-standing relationship to nuclear technology. We can view with retrospective detachment the specter of two morally mad superpowers threatening to exterminate one another, and the rest of the world into the bargain. Indeed each, according to the rules of that bizarre arrangement, had to be *willing* to do so under certain conditions in order to maintain its "credibility" for what we used to call "nuclear deterrence."

But we are just now beginning to tabulate the human costs of those nuclear weapons policies, and, by extension, the technology of nuclear power as well. A key to understanding these costs comes from a phenomenon that impressed me profoundly in my study of Hiroshima survivors: their experience of what I came to call "invisible contamination." The *hibakusha* (victims of radiation) encountered a weapon that could not only destroy on an unprecedented scale but leave behind in the bodies of those exposed a potentially fatal poison they could not see, feel, or smell. That poison, stemming from irradiation, could either reveal itself very quickly or else remain quiescent for months, years, or decades. Survivors have been haunted by a lifelong fear of invisible contamination, a fear that could extend over the generations. During recent trips to Hiroshima, people would tell me of their relief that studies show no significant increase in abnormalities in the next generation, but would sometimes add that they are still worried about what could happen to the third generation and the ones after that. This book represents the broadest documentation of the effects and fears of this "invisible contamination" as experienced by people exposed to radiation in one way or another throughout the world.

Our self-destructive pursuit of this technology is propelled by our distorted psychological relationship to it, by the spiritual disease I call nuclearism. By nuclearism I mean a form of exaggerated dependency on the technology to the point of near worship. Nuclear weapons can become virtual deities, embraced as a means of protecting us from danger and evil, of keeping the world going, of providing salvation.

Perhaps this is not surprising, as the weapons can represent a combination of ultimate technology and ultimate power. They can do what in the past only God could do, destroy the world, and therefore, we assume, they can create wondrously as well. These distortions did not begin with the appearance of the weapons; they were part of the original mythology of radiation, dating back to Marie Curie and before, attributing to it a life-enhancing magic and even a capacity to endow immortality.

That mythology takes its latest and most grotesque form in a contemporary projection of a superweapon of unprecedented explosive power, not to be used on earth but only against "killer asteroids" or "doomsday comets" threatening from the outer atmosphere. That advocacy was dramatically put forward by Edward Teller at a recent meeting of nuclear scientists held at Los Alamos, the laboratory at which the Hiroshima bomb was constructed. In the middle of the proceedings there came a cry of "Nukes forever!" from the back of the room. Uttered by one of Teller's leading disciples, it suggests the religious fervor with which the very agents of our potential annihilation can be rendered immortal objects.

This book reveals the weapons and the technology for what they are, and in the process contributes greatly to our struggles to extricate ourselves from nuclearism. Its stance is steady and even-handed as it examines radiation effects everywhere—at Three Mile Island or on a Navajo reservation in the United States, or in Chernobyl and surrounding areas, the disease of nuclearism; the lure of the weapons and the technology affects all.

A virtue of this book is its exclusive concern with human beings. It avoids the pseudoscientific rhetoric of technical achievement and risk assessment in favor of straightforward description of what the various phases of the technology have done to people, and of the resulting fear, anger, and frustration. The book wisely includes effects of both weapons production and nuclear power. While these are separate social and political issues, the poisons and the physical and psychological responses to them are all too similar. When I interviewed people at Three Mile Island in Pennsylvania, their fear of invisible contamination was directly reminiscent of what I had encountered in Hiroshima. That kind of fear is in no way pathological, but represents the mind's equivalent of what the great American physiologist Walter Cannon once called "the wisdom of the body."

There is compelling appropriateness in the project's being undertaken by concerned journalists from Hiroshima. From the time the bomb was dropped, the *Chugoku Newspaper*, as Hiroshima's leading paper, has been a prime source of information about the experiences and feelings of the people of that city over subsequent decades. Its editors and writers have taken on what I call a "survivor mission" on behalf of the city's victims, a commitment to transforming the fear, conflict, and pain of the survivors into an active exploratory enterprise of profound significance.

Their contribution goes even beyond their descriptions of the human effects of radiation. In the way they have approached their study, they have demonstrated what I call a species mentality, a commitment that transcends immediate group or nationality and extends to all of humankind. They evoke in us a sense of shared fate, of universal susceptibility to a technology that knows no boundaries, geographical or temporal. We are all in this together, as potential victims and potential perpetrators as well. (Groups everywhere, when responsible for radiation effects, are strikingly similar in their patterns of false reassurance, denial, and encouragement of psychic numbing or diminished inclination to feel.)

The simple truth this book forces us to recognize is that nuclear technology endangers our species. That is so for two decisive reasons: the uncontrollable dimensions of accidents or detonations (whatever the claim of limited risk), and the ineradicable existence of human error. Whatever the brilliance of the technology, it must be managed by fallible human hands. Hence, whatever the assumed needs for weaponry and power sources, there are better ways.

More than that, the mentality that follows upon our recognition of shared fate can prod and expand our capacity for what I call a species self. The term refers not to a distant, noble ideal but an actual sense of self importantly related to one's connection to all other selves on the planet. This does not mean that one ceases to be an American or a Japanese or a Nigerian, or for that matter a mother or husband or physician or working person. Rather than surrender one's more immediate identifications, one subsumes them to the larger human identity.

As we travel around the world with the authors of this book, we come to realize that species mentality and species self are principles virtually imposed upon us by our own deadly nuclear technology. In renouncing and replacing this technology, we assert our capacity to function collectively on behalf of the human future.

INTRODUCTION

More than forty-five years have passed since Hiroshima and Nagasaki were destroyed by atomic bombs. Since the end of the Second World War, nuclear weapons have not been used in warfare once. Unfortunately, it cannot be said with the same certainty that man and his environment have not been in any danger from exposure to radiation from nuclear materials. In reality, unregulated nuclear testing, the manufacture of nuclear weapons, uranium mining, and accidents at nuclear power plants have caused a steady increase in the number of victims of radiation, or *hibakusha*, during the postwar period.

It is a common mistake to believe that radiation poses a threat only to those who come into direct contact with it. In fact, the environment the world over is beginning to feel the effects of radioactive contamination. Although the dangers of global warming, ozone depletion, and acid rain have been well publicized over the last few years, the issue of radioactive contamination has, for some reason, not played any major role in discussions on the environment so far, despite being an essential element of the debate.

Recognizing that radioactive contamination was rapidly becoming a global problem, the *Chugoku Newspaper* sent a team of reporters from its base in Hiroshima to all corners of the world to gather information concerning the many unknown victims of radiation. By publicizing their stories, the newspaper hoped that their suffering would be somewhat alleviated and that attention would be drawn to the extensive damage done to the environment.

The reporters' investigations took them to fifteen countries in all, including the Soviet Union, Brazil, the United States, French Polynesia, India, Namibia, and South Korea. Much of the material they unearthed had never been reported before, or only in a very superficial manner. The leaking of radioactive material used in medical equipment in Brazil; thorium contamination from a Japanese refinery in Malaysia; radioactive contamination from a nuclear power plant in India; high incidences of disease caused by uranium mining in Namibia; the tragic effects of nuclear weapons testing in the Semipalatinsk region of the Soviet Union: all these incidents caused great suffering, yet they have received little attention from the press.

The publication of this series of articles brought a widespread response from the paper's readership in Japan. Correspondence poured in from readers expressing shock at the existence of so many radiation victims other than those in Hiroshima and Nagasaki, anger at the irresponsibility of governments that violate the human rights of their own citizens in such a blatant manner, and yet more anger at the continued destruction of the environment. The articles were pasted up in libraries and public halls and used in peace studies classes in schools all over the country.

Largely as a result of the articles' success in bringing the public's attention to the dangers of radiation, a number of victims of radioactive contamination from areas as far-flung as Chernobyl and Bikini Atoll were able to participate in a conference held in Hiroshima by the International Physicians for the Prevention of Nuclear War in October 1989. In addition to demands for a nuclear-free world and appeals for aid for victims of radiation, the conference heard details concerning the damage caused by nuclear testing in Kazakhstan, which until then had been shrouded in secrecy. In turn, this disclosure of widespread destruction of the environment prompted the *Chugoku Newspaper* to instigate the first-ever investigation of the testing area.

At the same time, the articles served to emphasize the role that Japan could play to help radiation victims around the world. The fact that the articles have prompted the exchange of information concerning the treatment of radiation victims in Japan to help those in a similar plight in other countries is a great source of satisfaction to us at the *Chugoku Newspaper*. We hope that, in the future, Japan will become known as an information center for radiation victims and the treatment of their illnesses.

The series "Hibakusha of the World," which started on May 21, 1989, and continued through to May 29, 1990, totaled 134 articles in all. The series went on to win the 1990 Japan Newspaper Publishers and Editors Association award, the third received by the paper for work relating to nuclear power. The paper had previously been recognized for the articles "Hiroshima Twenty Years On" in 1965 and "Hiroshima Forty Years On" in 1985.

Responsible for the series were the following journalists: Shimazu Kunihiro, Tashiro Akira, Yabui Kazuo, Nishimoto Masami, Okatani Yoshinori, Tochiyabu Keita, and Kawamoto Kazuyuki.

We will be very happy if this book contributes in some way to a greater awareness and understanding of radioactive contamination and the detrimental effects of radioactive substances on the environment. We also hope that the publication of these articles may in some way be instrumental in bringing relief to those *hibakusha* who continue to live in fear and uncertainty about their futures.

Ogata Yukio
Executive Editor
Chugoku Newspaper
November 1990

PART 1

THE UNITED STATES

HANFORD'S HIDDEN PAST

*I*n 1942, under the code name of The Manhattan Project, development of the atomic bomb began in America, heralding the dawn of the nuclear era. Three years later, the bombings of the Japanese cities of Hiroshima and Nagasaki marked the beginning of the desperate race for nuclear supremacy. Prominent in the American effort in the arms race over the next forty-five years was the town of Hanford in Washington State. However, it is only recently that the residents of Hanford have begun to uncover the hidden past of the nuclear weapons facility with which they coexisted all those years.

Previous page: Hanford Nuclear Reservation, Washington State: A monument to the folly of the race for nuclear supremacy.

A CURSE ON THE PEOPLE OF HANFORD

Despite driving into the hills and using roads long fallen into disuse, we appeared to have missed the turning for the Hanford nuclear complex. Eventually, we decided to rent a small plane with the idea that we might have more luck from the air.

The scene below us changed from one of green fields to a vast expanse of rock and desert. Low, rolling hills revealed a desolate plain of almost five hundred square miles stretching away into the distance. Along the banks of a river, smokestacks and clusters of buildings came into view—in all, we counted nine reactors. The area was surrounded by steep mountain ranges. This had been the reason why Hanford was chosen as one of the first sites for the development of nuclear weapons, the others being in Oak Ridge, Tennessee, and in Los Alamos, New Mexico.

Originally a town of twelve hundred people, Hanford was commandeered by the U.S. Army in 1943, following which work was begun on the construction of a plutonium manufacturing facility. All this took place under a thick veil of secrecy.

At the western end of the complex we could see the B reactors. The two towers shone brightly in the sunlight, and around their bases nestled a collection of gray buildings. "Those are the reactors that produced the plutonium for 'Fatman,' the Nagasaki bomb," our pilot, farmer Tom Bailie, pointed out. The uranium used in the process was imported mainly from Canada. In 1944 these reactors reached critical mass; the resulting plutonium was then transported to Los Alamos, where Fatman was put together. "People say that Nagasaki's most terrible nightmares were born here," commented Bailie.

Hanford's role did not finish with Fatman. After the end of the Second World War, the advent of the Cold War increased the demand for plutonium, and the complex expanded rapidly to become the mainstay of America's nuclear program. In 1968, when the supply of plutonium at Hanford was judged to be sufficient, the B reactors stopped producing plutonium and the others were gradually shut down. The remaining plants, the N reactors, were finally taken out of operation in 1986.

No smoke, nothing—there wasn't a single sign of human habitation. The Hanford complex is now nothing more than a hideous monument to the nuclear era. Our pilot, however, did not agree with this observation. "A monument?" he snorted. "No way. This place is a curse on us." With that he started to tell us about the radioactive contamination which had only come to light three years previously, and which was causing panic among the local residents.

In the thirteen-year period from 1944 when the B reactors first went into operation, 530,000 curies of iodine-131 were released into the atmosphere. Buried for decades in secret files, this fact was only made public in 1986, along with the equally shocking revelation that in 1949, as an experiment, radioactive material had deliberately been released into the surrounding area.

Six years of hard work on the part of one reporter lie behind the disclosure of these facts. Karen Steele, environment and special projects reporter for the *Spokesman Review* of Spokane, first investigated the situation at Hanford in 1984. She had just published an article pointing out the illegality of the construction of a nuclear power plant for a private company within the complex, when she received a phone call. The caller told her there were issues more important at stake in Hanford than the mere misuse of funds. The woman, a worker at the plant, told her that, since Reagan had come to power, there had been a sudden increase in the production of plutonium for military use. She added that the health of employees was being ignored, and that the disappearance of over twenty pounds of plutonium, ample for a bomb, was being investigated by the FBI.

From this unexpected beginning, Steele's interest in Hanford increased to include not only incidents in the complex itself, but also those in the surrounding areas. Women told her about the prevalence of thyroid diseases and cancer in the area; farmers testified that, on the nearby farms, it was not unusual for cows and goats to be born with deformities. Steele concluded that the nuclear complex must be giving off some kind of harmful substance.

At the same time, environmental protection groups such as the Hanford Education Action League (HEAL) were conducting their own inquiries into Hanford. The groups had been negotiating with the Department of Energy (DOE) ever since 1984 for the release of relevant documents concerning the nuclear complex. In response to numerous requests from Steele's newspaper, HEAL, and the Environmental Policy Institute of Washington D.C., the DOE decided to release the material in

February 1986. The documents contained the shocking information that, over a period of thirteen years during the 1940s and 1950s, a total of 530,000 curies of iodine-131 had been released into the atmosphere; an amount certain to cause serious contamination.

Steele got the story on the front page of the *Spokesman Review*, and larger papers all over the United States soon followed up with their own articles about radioactive contamination in Hanford.

Steele and the league members next focused their attention on a single sentence buried in the mass of papers which seemed to indicate that an important experiment, codenamed Green Run, was carried out in 1949. For reasons of national security, the DOE refused access to material giving further details about the experiment. Using the Freedom of Information Act, Steele went to court to demand publication of the documents. The result of her year-and-a-half battle was 126 pages of material, the contents of which were more incredible than any the campaigners had ever imagined. The documents proved clearly that radioactive material taken from nuclear fuel extracted from the reactors had been deliberately released into the atmosphere as part of an experiment. On May 4, 1989, with her account of the experiment known as Green Run, Steele's revelations hit the headlines yet again.

This tenacious pursuit of the facts finally spurred the federal government into action. Starting in 1987, officials decided to allocate an annual budget of $5 million for a health survey of residents in the vicinity of the nuclear complex to investigate radiation-related illnesses and assess the residents' eligibility for compensation.

What had started with a single phone call turned into a six-year crusade for Karen Steele. During that time she was the target of abuse from many who opposed her persistent investigations. However, as she told us herself, she was determined to find out the truth for the sake of all the people who had been kept in the dark for so long.

"I realize that secrecy is an essential part of military operations," she said. "But in the case of Hanford it was taken too far. The DOE still has thirty thousand pages of relevant documents in its possession which it refuses to release." The reasons behind the experiments have never been explained; only when the results of the medical survey are obtained in full will the true extent of the damage done in the name of nuclear development become known.

THE TRUTH ABOUT GREEN RUN

What was the purpose of the Green Run experiment exactly, and how was it carried out? A study of the top-secret material released by the DOE on court order answered some of our questions and enabled us to trace the sequence of events making up Green Run:

December 2: Uranium fuel rods extracted from the cooling tank after sixteen days, a fifth of the usual cooling time. Later the same night experimental dispersal of radioactive material was carried out.

December 3: End of experiment at 5:00 A.M. Reports come in from the area surrounding the nuclear complex of radiation levels higher than those that would normally result in an emergency alert if detected inside the complex. (Quantities released—xenon: 20,000 curies; iodine-131: 7,780 curies. Dispersed over an area 1,200 by 400 miles.)

One of the scientists who took part in Green Run agreed to speak to us on condition that we did not stray from the material which had already been released. "The purpose of Green Run," Robert told us, "was to get a clearer picture of Soviet nuclear capability."

"The Soviet Union conducted its first successful atom bomb test in August 1949, bringing an end to the American monopoly of nuclear weapons," Robert said. "America needed to know what stage of development the Soviets were at. To do this, we had to use the same methods as they did. At the time, the usual cooling period for uranium fuel rods was approximately ninety days, which was thought necessary to minimize the release of iodine-131 (half-life: eight days). After ninety days the rods were moved to the plutonium manufacturing plant. In the Soviet Union, however, the cooling time was a mere sixteen days.

"We think they shortened this in an effort to speed up development time," Robert replied. "The experiment was called Green Run because green fuel was used—fuel that had not been adequately cooled."

We found it difficult to understand why local residents were not warned of the impending danger even though scientists had predicted the release of vast quantities of radioactive material.

"Well, it seems ridiculous these days when just about anyone can make an atomic bomb," Robert said, "but at the time the Soviets were desperate for any information they could lay their hands on concerning our nuclear program. Spies were on constant alert. What do you think

THE UNITED STATES 23

would have happened if it had all been made public?"

We spoke to Martin, another scientist who had been involved in Green Run. He had been in charge of measuring the levels of radioactivity in the surrounding area.

"Of course we worried about the environmental effects of the experiment. But the military had complete authority, so we had no choice."

Martin, now retired, lives in Oak Ridge, Tennessee, the birthplace of the Hiroshima bomb, "Little Boy." Since leaving, he has continued to maintain a strong interest in Hanford. "There's no doubt that the method of conducting Green Run has serious implications for the people's trust in government nuclear policy," he continued. "But what's more worrying is all the other radioactive material that has been released into the atmosphere since the 1940s."

According to Martin, the total amount of radioactive material released into the atmosphere over the thirteen years from 1944 almost reaches Chernobyl proportions. The total for 1944 and 1945 represents sixty percent of the whole amount, or 340,000 curies. During this period the Nagasaki bomb was being constructed at Hanford.

"At that time we were using sand filters to get rid of radiation—we had to make things up as we went along," Martin said. To us, it sounded as if the sand filters were more for peace of mind than anything else.

The testimony of these two scientists clearly demonstrates that safety was of secondary importance in the race to produce atomic weapons.

VICTIMS OF RADIATION IN HANFORD

The full extent of the damage to the health of nearby residents through radioactive contamination from the Hanford nuclear complex is uncertain.

In February 1989, a public hearing of a congressional committee concerning energy and commerce was held in Washington. The topic under discussion was radioactive contamination. June Casey of Oakland, California, stood up to give testimony. The gathering was silenced by the powerful words of condemnation that sprang from the lips of this mild-mannered woman.

"My body has been subjected to radiation released by the Hanford nuclear complex for a long time, yet I only found out three years ago. I find it impossible to contain my anger at the government's abuse of my trust."

Two months later June received some news which added fuel to her fury—Karen Steele's disclosure of the Green Run experiment of December 1949. The figure 1949 leaped off the page at her.

Born and raised in Portland, Oregon, she entered Whitman College in Walla Walla, Washington, in the fall of 1949. Her joy at being able to study at one of the most prestigious colleges on the West Coast did not last for long, however. Around Christmas the same year the long brown hair that was her pride and joy began to fall out. Worried, she consulted a doctor. He merely laughed and told her she had been studying too hard. When June graduated two years later, she had hardly any hair left and she had begun to wear a wig.

About the time she started teaching, her former roommate at college gave birth to a physically disabled child. June herself eventually married, and after two miscarriages gave birth to a boy. She left work to look after her son, and led a quiet and peaceful life with her husband, a high school principal.

Her life was disrupted when she saw the article detailing how radio-active material had been discharged from the Hanford complex over a period of thirteen years. At the time the world's eyes were focused on the disaster at Chernobyl. "I'll never forget that day," she said. "It was May 11, 1986—Mother's Day." It was not the kind of present she had expected. Shocked, she read on to find that as much radioactive material had been released from Hanford as had leaked from Chernobyl, a month earlier.

Her hair loss, the miscarriages, her roommate's disabled child—all these incidents corresponded with the history of the release of radioactive substances at Hanford. She recalled when she had started to lose her hair; the date was roughly three weeks after the Green Run experiment. Her college was situated only fifty miles southeast of Hanford, well within the affected area, according to the secret documents released by the DOE. "I did some research and found that iodine-131 causes dysfunction of the thyroid gland and miscarriages, as well as birth defects—that made me even more conscious of the radiation in my own body."

June became a member of the National Association of Radiation Survivors, an organization set up to help victims of radiation. This gave her access to a large volume of information which the association had gathered on the effects of the Hiroshima and Nagasaki bombs, and the tests at the Bikini and Nevada sites. Studying this material only served to increase her anxiety: "The damage caused by Hanford is just starting to come out into the open—the government has a lot to answer for."

Millie Smith, aged forty-two, of Olympia, Washington, was another who testified to the effects of radioactive contamination. Her emaciated form lay stretched out on a sofa; cancer was eating its way through her body. "If only I had known about Hanford earlier," she began.

Millie was born in 1947 just south of the Hanford nuclear complex in the town of Pasco. She first began to feel there was something not quite right with her body while at high school, at about the age of sixteen, when she often felt too ill to do gym. She was diagnosed as having a dysfunction of the thyroid gland, and was put on medication.

The years went by, and Millie got married and had a daughter. "My health didn't get any better, though. I still had very little energy—I thought that it was just the way my body was," she said.

In the spring of 1986 Millie read about the contamination in a Seattle newspaper for the first time. The connection between exposure to radiation and her constant lethargy did not occur to her at first. Then came the accident at Chernobyl. "I found out that similar amounts of radiation had been released at Hanford . . ." Millie was shocked to see reflections of herself in the victims of radiation from Chernobyl pictured on television. Her general feeling of ill health showed no signs of going away, and, believing that she might be suffering from some radiation-linked illness, Millie decided to see a doctor. The news was not good. "We can remove the cancer from your chest, but . . . ," he said, his voice trailing off. Millie was told that it was too late to arrest the progress of the cancer.

Concerned about the effects of being exposed to large doses of radiation, she decided to write to some of her classmates from high school. Of the forty-eight who wrote back to her, twenty-five had thyroid conditions. She found out that a further nine had died of cancer or leukemia.

"It didn't take an expert to realize there was something strange going on—I mean, for that number of people of the same age brought up in the same town to suffer from the same illness . . ." Her expression hardened. "Nuclear fallout from Hanford is the only possible cause."

The main contaminant released into the atmosphere from Hanford was iodine-131. Once this substance enters the body it accumulates in the thyroid gland, hindering hormone secretion, sometimes also causing cancer. The human body from birth to puberty is particularly vulnerable to its effects. The period up until 1957, when great quantities of radioactive material were being discharged from Hanford, coincides exactly with the childhood and adolescence of Millie and her classmates. Millie expressed grave doubts about a government which deliberately allows the release of dangerous materials and then covers it up. "I can understand the need to keep information secret in the interests of national security," she said. "But if I'd known that I'd been exposed to such large amounts of radiation, I would have had a checkup earlier and been treated earlier. The way things are going at the moment, I'm losing my life to government secrecy."

The experience of Hanford would seem to indicate that national security and the welfare of the people can be mutually exclusive. If Millie Smith and her fellow sufferers have their way, however, the government will not be able to ignore the rights of its citizens for much longer.

THE TRI-CITY: CITIES GETTING RICH FROM THE BOMB

In stark contrast to the bare earth and rocks of the nuclear complex, the residential areas to the south of Hanford are a lush green. The towns of Richland, Pasco, and Kennewick, which have a total population of eighty thousand, are together known as the Tri-city.

Before the war, they were small, sleepy towns consisting of a railroad station and not much else. However, the construction of the nuclear complex brought a sudden prosperity to the region, and they became three of the wealthiest towns in America.

It was no easy task to find people in the Tri-city willing to discuss the effects of radioactive contamination with us. Responses to our inquiries were along the lines of "What do you want to know about that kind of thing for?" and "Illnesses? Anyone can get sick, you know." One family in Kennewick told us that the people in the Tri-city couldn't say anything. They added, however, that if we went to Seattle their daughter would speak on their behalf.

The Jurji family moved to the Tri-city from California in 1949, the same year that Green Run was carried out in response to developments in the Soviet Union's nuclear weapons program. The father was a welder who had come to work on extensions at the Hanford site. After his daughter Judith had graduated from high school, she left Hanford for Seattle and only found out about the nuclear contamination in 1987.

Just to be on the safe side she went to a doctor, only to be told that she had a thyroid condition. She had often felt so ill that it was an effort to go to work, but she had never known the cause.

Judith was not the only one ill in the family. Six of her relatives including her mother and sisters were plagued with the same condition. When she told them what she had heard, however, her family was shocked. The local papers had made no mention of any radioactive contamination; it was the first time they had heard such a story. Judith was warned not to talk about the article in the town. Everyone in the Tri-city area knew the consequences of speaking out against goings-on at the nuclear complex: Most of the residents are connected to the plant in some way or another, and any accusations of misconduct or incompetence, even if confined to within the site, would mean the loss of one's job and possibly further harassment from the management.

The fact that a high school in the Tri-city area has a mushroom cloud for its emblem illustrates the people's dependency on the Hanford nuclear complex. The local people's suspicion of strangers can perhaps be explained by the knowledge that their lives are tied to the future of the plant. At the same time, the people have grown up in constant awareness of the arms race with the Soviet Union, leaving them with strong anti-Soviet and anti-Communist tendencies. In the daughter's opinion, the combination of these two factors has allowed the people to accept without question whatever the government tells them—or does not tell them.

"Those of us on the outside must stand up for the rights of those in the Tri-city area to speak freely," she said. At present in the process of organizing the sufferers into a support group, she has found seventy people so far in Seattle alone. Their first meeting was held in May 1989 in Spokane. "Forty-four years after the end of the war, I can finally understand what the survivors of Hiroshima and Nagasaki must be going through," she concluded.

THE 'MILE OF DEATH'

Northeast of the Tri-city, beyond Hanford's cluster of reactors, lies the vast agricultural belt of the Columbia Basin. The town of Mesa is the center of the region; a typical small town consisting of a couple of diners and three general stores, home to three thousand people. It was in Mesa that we were able to gauge for the first time the true feelings of those living near the plant. There we spoke to Robert and Betty Perkes, who own a farm in the region. After the conspiracy of silence in the Tri-city towns we were amazed at their frankness: "Go ahead and tell the world. America has created nuclear weapons. At the same time it's also created thousands of victims." The couple, both born in Idaho, married and came to Mesa in 1953. Robert was an ex-serviceman; the area had been recommended by the army. The Perkes worked hard to build a new life for themselves. They got rid of the weeds, bulldozed the rocks away, and planted wheat, potatoes, and beets. Betty gave birth to six children on the farm.

Their second son died two days after he was born; his lungs had not developed properly. The Perkes's three daughters all suffer from thyroid conditions, and Betty has had a tumor removed from her breast. Robert himself is also on medication for a thyroid problem. It was 1986 when they first made the connection with Hanford, thanks to Karen Steele's article. As Betty Perkes told us, the article "solved the mystery of all those strange incidents over the years."

Deformed cows and goats had been born on neighboring farms. A DC-3 had flown over every two or three days with a large bag hanging from it. Someone from the military came round to survey the family's health, giving no name or rank.

"He must have been checking whether the radiation had had any effect," Betty said with a shiver. "At the time Robert and I were busy with work and bringing up the kids—we didn't have a moment to think about it. We didn't even know they were making atomic bombs there, and naturally it had never occurred to us that land recommended by the army would be contaminated by radiation." When Robert Perkes found out about the contamination, he teamed up with Tom Bailie, a fellow farmer who had at one time run for a seat in the state legislature. The two men conducted a survey of their own, visiting the twenty-eight homes in the square mile around the Perkes's farm. Most were owned by ex-servicemen. They were profoundly shocked by what they discovered. One woman had had seven miscarriages, another had lost her daughter to bone cancer. There was a mother who had killed her deformed baby and then herself; a home deserted when the father had died of cancer . . . the list went on. Of the twenty-eight families surveyed, only one had no health problems. The area became known as the "mile of death."

The Mesa region, stretching from the east to the northeast of the Hanford nuclear complex, lies directly in the path of a westerly wind that often blows through the Columbia Basin. "There's no doubt we were on the receiving end of a lot of fallout," Perkes said. "We had no idea that our milk, meat, and vegetables were riddled with radiation. If only we'd known, we'd never have let them get away with this careless disregard for our lives for so long." The relaxed expression left Robert Perkes's face as he spoke these bitter words.

According to investigations carried out by a number of groups, radioactive material was not only discharged from the plant into the atmosphere, but was also found to have leaked out of underground tanks, threatening contamination of the water table. "The nuclear contamination is not something that happened in the past. It's happening now, with the groundwater, the river, the soil—if we were to look into other areas around here, I know we would find a host of other places that deserve the name 'mile of death' . . . the tragedy is just beginning to unfold."

COMPENSATION FOR VICTIMS OF HANFORD

In Seattle we met Tom Foulds, the lawyer representing the victims of Hanford in a case to be brought before the Spokane Federal Court. Foulds's days were filled with finding witnesses to give evidence, the aim being to obtain compensation for suffering caused by exposure to radiation. In his office in central Seattle, the files on Hanford are steadily piling up.

Since the fall of 1988 the *New York Times* and a number of other major papers had published several articles dealing with the issue of contamination caused by nuclear weapons factories across the United States, such as those at Rocky Flats, Colorado, and Savannah River, South Carolina. Foulds's interest in the articles at that time was mainly of a personal nature: his wife, Jackie, died of leukemia in 1976 at the age of forty-eight. The couple had lived in Nevada at one time, in a region which, unbeknown to them, was contaminated by radiation from nuclear testing. The thought that his own wife may have been a victim of radiation is a driving force in his efforts to help the people of Hanford. At the beginning of 1989, when a patient from Hanford suffering from a radiation-linked illness asked if it would be possible to sue the complex and obtain compensation, he decided to take on the case.

Foulds was surprised at the number of people he encountered in the Hanford area with thyroid conditions, cancer, and leukemia. His surprise soon turned to anger. The authorities seemed oblivious to the extent of the suffering; there was no specialized medical treatment provided, and of course no compensation of any kind. "Even if nuclear weapons are essential for national security, as the army would have us believe, there is no possible justification for sacrificing the people of the nation just for some military aim. Willful neglect is the order of the day here—there's no regard for democratic principles whatsoever."

There was one major hurdle to overcome before the case could be heard, however. By law, the U.S. government cannot be taken to court over a matter of national security or foreign policy, forcing Foulds to search for a means of avoiding this legal obstacle. After a careful examination of the documents made public by the DOE, he found a loophole. Hanford operated by contracting out to private businesses. One of these contracts contained a clause which forbade "any injury to the local residents." Foulds therefore made the subcontractors the target of his demands for compensation.

"The complex poured out at least 530,000 curies of radiation over a thirteen-year period, and I have proof that it is still doing this. The plant is clearly liable for the damage it has caused by continuously discharging dangerous substances into the environment."

Part of Foulds's task has been to gather statements from experts to support the case. Professor Allen B. Benson, of Spokane Falls Community College, an expert on iodine-131, told Foulds that "the effects of iodine-131 on children and pregnant women were well known at the time of the experiment." Dr. Thomas Hamilton of Seattle, known for his research on the problems faced by victims of radiation in the Marshall Islands, stated that "the consequences of exposure to iodine-131 are being felt in Hanford, but the contamination was kept secret for so long that there is a huge vacuum in the medical records there." According to Foulds, the plaintiffs number over ten thousand. At present there is no law in the United States which provides financial relief for suffering caused by exposure to radioactive substances from a nuclear facility. The residents of Hanford are pinning their hopes on this case, as are victims of radiation in other parts of the country.

THREE MILE ISLAND
TEN YEARS AFTER

*I*t is over ten years since the worst commercial nuclear accident in the United States occurred at the Three Mile Island nuclear power plant in Pennsylvania on March 28, 1979. Following the accident it was seven years before the company publicly acknowledged that there had been a partial meltdown of the reactor core, and ten years before it became known that this meltdown had reached a level of fifty-two percent. Since the accident, the construction of additional atomic power facilities has been shelved. This may be interpreted as proof that not only has the myth of safety surrounding nuclear power generation been destroyed, but also that the myth that nuclear power is cheap appears to be on shaky ground.

Previous page: Three Mile Island, the site of the worst commercial nuclear accident in the United States.

COUNTING THE COST OF CORE MELTDOWN

Over 125 miles west of New York, in the middle of Pennsylvania's agricultural belt on the outskirts of Harrisburg, we found what we had been looking for. The four cooling towers looked just the same as they had ten years previously when the cameras of the world were focused on the unfolding saga at Three Mile Island. Our own cameras were taken from us at the gate before we entered the precincts of the plant.

The two northern towers were belching out steam—this was the Unit 1 reactor, which began operations in 1974. It had stood silent for seven years after the accident involving the Unit 2 reactor, but operations had begun again in 1986 after getting the all-clear from the Nuclear Regulatory Commission. The cooling towers for the Unit 2 reactor were no longer in operation. Beside them was a cylindrical building in which was housed the reactor that had sent the nearby residents into a panic in 1979. It glistened in the bright sunlight, giving no hint of the disaster which had taken place there.

We walked through a gate into Unit 2's barbed wire–enclosed compound, where our luggage was searched. We were not given any of the film badges generally used for detecting radiation. According to our guide, the public information manager for the plant, thirty thousand people had used badges there, and as zero readings were taken every time, the company had stopped issuing them. Of course, it also means that if for any reason someone was exposed to radiation, there would be no way of proving it.

Inside the control room for Unit 2 the core area was monitored on five television screens. This was where the core was uncovered just before dawn on March 28, 1979. As we watched, five workers in protective clothing stood above the core, removing the highly radioactive fuel rods, an operation which had been continuing for four years. A total of 150 tons of material was being removed from the reactor: 100 tons of fuel and 50 tons of parts and equipment. According to our guide, the work was due to be completed by fall 1989, with the decontamination of the core scheduled to be finished by spring the following year.

One headache for the staff at the plant is what to do with over two million gallons of contaminated water stored on the site. The current plan is to heat the waste water and reduce it to a more manageable volume of solids before disposing of it. "This operation will produce 1,020 curies of tritium—that's about one teaspoonful. There will be no effect on the atmosphere whatsoever," our guide assured us. The local residents have little confidence in the company's assurances, and there is fierce opposition to the plan from environmental groups.

As the cleanup operations continue at Three Mile Island, investigations are being carried out in an attempt to piece together a total picture of the accident. After three years of outright denials, in 1982 it was finally acknowledged that meltdown of the core had occurred. The first figure given as the percentage of core meltdown was 20%. This grew with each check, first to 35%, then 45%, until the final figure was put at 52%. Finally, in August 1989, cracks were found in the pressure tank, which proved that the reactor had really only been a hairsbreadth away from a disaster even more catastrophic than the accident in March 1979.

The construction cost of the Unit 2 reactor was $700 million. The cost of the cleanup operation will be $1 billion by the time it is finished. Taking into account the drop in share prices, the total loss to the company is likely to be in the region of $40 billion. We strained to look up at the tower, which may as well have been constructed of solid gold for what it had cost, and marveled at the mind-boggling price of nuclear accidents.

NO CHANCE OF A QUIET RETIREMENT

After a tour around the plant we visited some of the local residents. Right in front of us on the opposite bank of the Susquehanna River, we could see the four cooling towers of the nuclear complex. We spoke to local resident Bill Whittock, aged eighty-three, about his feelings toward his imposing neighbors.

"I came close to being killed countless times during the Second World War, but that accident in 1979 made me more scared than I've ever felt before," he told us, gesturing toward the silenced Unit 2 reactor. "I heard a roar like a plane taking off—it was just before dawn, about four o'clock." Whittock had leaped out of bed and been greeted by the sight of two of the four towers opposite belching steam high up into the sky. This stopped after ten minutes, then started again after another five had passed.

"The same kind of thing had happened twice before," Whittock continued. "But not on this scale. It was obvious something had gone drastically wrong." At this stage of events, the staff of Three Mile Island had a real crisis on their hands; there was every possibility that the core might melt and sink into the ground as depicted in the movie *The China Syndrome*. The condenser pumps and water supply pumps stopped one after the other, leaving the inside of the reactor to boil dry, as it were, and the temperature was rising rapidly.

Whittock had an odd metallic taste in his mouth, unlike anything he had ever tasted before. His wife, Irene, was in Alaska at the time visiting her family. Three days later the state government issued an evacuation order and Whittock left town carrying the couple's two cats. He saw the familiar cooling towers on television at the home of a friend and was shocked to hear the announcer describing the complex as the scene of the world's first major accident involving nuclear power.

After the accident, five years passed without incident for the Whittocks, although they never stopped feeling uneasy about the possibility of being exposed to radiation. Then in 1986, Bill found a growth on his neck. On his doctor's advice he had a thorough examination at the Temple University Hospital in Philadelphia; he was told he had skin cancer. A piece of skin about an inch square was removed from his neck immediately.

"No doctor could tell me if it was caused by the accident or not. But there's no doubt that radiation would have been released with the steam that came out of there. You can see why I can't help thinking that my illness has something to do with that accident, can't you?" Whittock added that the elderly couple two doors down were also suffering from cancer; the husband had cancer of the pancreas and the wife breast cancer.

"We moved here twenty years ago because we wanted to spend our retirement quietly in the country. Of course there wasn't a nuclear power plant here then." Five years later two ugly concrete towers went up in front of their house. The Unit 2 reactor was built, and the view from their garden was completely blocked. The local residents were told that once the plant was up and running, their power bills would be next to nothing. "So we didn't complain about it," said Whittock. "But then there was the accident, and the value of our property dropped by forty percent."

The Whittocks are typical of their generation: willing to put up with a certain amount of personal inconvenience for the sake of the community as a whole. But after Bill's cancer was diagnosed and the value of their property dropped, they started to lose patience with the authorities.

"Well, wouldn't you?" he asked us. "First they told us that nuclear power was safe, and then there was that disaster. Now they're telling us that our health won't be affected—do they really expect people to believe them? Human beings invented nuclear power, now they've lost control over it. It's a crime."

COMPENSATION FOR 'PSYCHOLOGICAL STRESS'

Bradley Baker, aged nine, knows nothing about the accident at Three Mile Island. He was born nine months after it, with Down's syndrome. Bradley is a slow learner, but he loves movies and enjoys reading picture books. At his home in an apartment block seven miles from the power plant, Bradley's mother, Debbie, aged thirty-three, told us about the trials of the last nine years.

Bradley was Debbie's second child; their other child is a girl.

"My husband was thrilled when Bradley was born," she continued. "He was looking forward to playing football with him when he got older." The joy at the birth of a son was short-lived, however. The Bakers were plunged into despair when they found out Bradley was a Down's syndrome child. Refusing to believe that nothing could be done for her son, Debbie went to the local library and did some research on his condition. From the medical encyclopedias she learned that radiation could cause genetic damage to offspring.

"It had never occurred to me that there could be some connection between that accident and Bradley's condition." Debbie was carrying Bradley at the time of the accident. Three days later, when children and pregnant women within a five-mile radius of the plant were advised to evacuate, she collected her daughter, who was at a friend's house, and the family went to stay at the home of another friend thirty miles to the north.

"Harrisburg was in a panic. My friend told me they had known about the accident on the second day—those of us who actually lived there didn't find out until the evacuation order came on the third day. We were in danger for three days and they didn't even tell us. And I was carrying Bradley."

Spending every waking moment watching her son who could never have a normal life, Debbie's resentment toward the power company began to grow. She consulted a lawyer and took the owners of the plant to court, seeking compensation on the grounds that her son's condition had been caused by the Three Mile Island accident. In the end she settled out of court in 1985. She was unwilling to reveal the amount, but the company is rumored to have paid her $1,090,000 in compensation.

The two parties remain in disagreement about the nature of the settlement, however. The GPU Nuclear Corporation, which has taken over the management of the complex, insists that the payment was made for psychological stress caused by the accident and denies that the payment acknowledges any connection between Bradley Baker's condition and the accident. Debbie Baker interprets the decision in a different manner.

"There's no way they would pay out that kind of money if they didn't feel responsible," she said. "As far as I'm concerned they're acknowledging that Bradley's condition is their fault."

According to the corporation, three hundred suits filed against them have been settled out of court. The company has so far paid out over $14 million in compensation. Another two thousand suits are pending. It looks like being many years before all the cases are settled. "The fact that we were able to get compensation means I don't have any financial worries," Baker told us. "But Bradley will never be normal, and I know the rest of my life will be spent looking after him." When we pointed the camera, Bradley, who was perched on his mother's knees, rewarded us with a cheerful grin.

A FARM IN RUINS

Walking toward Paul Holowka's farm, we stopped dead in our tracks. Piled haphazardly on a wagon next to the gate were the heads of three wild deer. On closer inspection we found that the left and right antlers of the deer did not seem to match, and they looked extremely brittle. "Hi! I see you've noticed!" our host called out as he came over to greet us. "They've all been like this recently, you know. The environment around here has been pretty screwed up lately," he added, with a resentful glance toward the steam pouring out of the nuclear power plant a couple of miles to the east.

Holowka, aged sixty-three, owns 160 acres of land on which he used to grow wheat, corn, and a variety of vegetables, besides keeping dairy and beef cattle, poultry, horses, and goats. Now he has only forty head of cattle and fifty chickens. The roof of the shed is falling down, the machinery inside rusty with lack of use. "I've had to sell off the cattle one by one to keep going," he told us frankly. Holowka has been ill since the accident at Three Mile Island ten years previously. "I've just lost all my energy—the farm's really gone to the dogs." His unshaven face showed no sign of animation.

On the morning of the accident at Three Mile Island, Holowka and his elder sister, Marie, were busy with the milking. Suddenly there was a tremor that felt as if it had originated in the very bowels of the earth. Barely had the word earthquake left their lips when the air around them turned a bluish black and they experienced a strange taste in their mouths which left a burning sensation in their throats. Three days later, they were advised to evacuate along with other local residents, but, not wanting to abandon their livestock, they stayed on the farm. When Holowka heard the newscaster talk about possibilities of extensive damage to the environment, the true gravity of what had happened struck home. "They stopped coming round to collect milk, of course. You can't expect people to drink contaminated milk." The farm was right in the center of the contaminated area, so not only Holowka's milk but also his carefully nurtured crops had to be sold so cheaply he might as well have given them away.

The family's worries did not stop there. Five months later, Marie came down with a thyroid condition. Three years later she was found to have lung cancer as well, and she went into hospital for an operation. Holowka's other sister began to have problems with her legs, and for the last five years has been unable to walk without the aid of a stick. Holowka himself often suffers from a sore throat and is concerned that he too may have a thyroid condition. The corporation flatly denies any connection between illnesses such as the Holowkas' and the accident. Management has stated that a small quantity of radiation was released but not enough to cause cancer or have any damaging effect on the environment. "So how do they explain what's been happening here since the accident? That's what I'd like to know."

Holowka has little confidence in the corporation's assurances and went on to recount several stories of other odd incidents that had happened on the farm in the last ten years. Corn with white leaves; cattle bleeding to death; low birth rates, not to mention the illnesses of himself and his sisters. "Nothing like this happened before that damned accident over there; they can keep saying that the plant has nothing to do with it, but I don't believe them for a moment."

Holowka's distrust of the corporation has been deepened further by the announcement of plans to dispose of the huge tank of waste water stored inside the plant's compound. "When they get rid of that water, radiation is bound to be spread over the surrounding areas once again, isn't it?" he said, the vision of further ruination of his farm only too clear.

THE NEED FOR INDEPENDENT SURVEYS

During our investigations in the vicinity of Three Mile Island, we often heard the name Dr. Tokuhata mentioned.

George Tokuhata was sixty-five years old, and had been living in the United States ever since he first came as a Fulbright scholar to study preventive medicine after the Second World War. After studying at a number of institutions, including Johns Hopkins University, he was invited to head the Epidemiological Research Division at the Pennsylvania Department of Health. "Since the accident, the focus of my work has been on nuclear power," he told us. We sat in his office, its walls decorated with Japanese *ukiyo-e* prints, while the doctor talked about his research over the previous ten years, which included a survey of the effects of the accident at Three Mile Island on the surrounding area.

The first news of the accident had arrived three hours after the initial breakdown of the water supply pumps. Tokuhata had rushed to his office before any other details were released, and had stayed there for two days without sleep to answer the inquiries of the media and the public concerning the possibility of exposure to radioactive material, and the time it would take for the situation to stabilize.

Tokuhata also met with experts from the DOE who had rushed up from Washington to deal with the crisis. At lunchtime on the third day they advised the governor to issue an evacuation warning. However, Tokuhata's real work started after the crisis had died down, when he was given the responsibility of conducting a survey of residents' health in the surrounding area. Unfortunately, the state government had taken no precautions such as preparing emergency funds or a skeleton staff to be made available in the event of a nuclear accident, so Tokuhata started his two surveys with the help of a grant from the federal government. The aim of one survey was to monitor the outward migration of the thirty-seven thousand people who lived within five miles of the plant, while that of the other was to monitor the condition of the four thousand pregnant women within ten miles of it. A year after the accident, twelve percent of the residents were found to have moved away from the area. According to Tokuhata this is a normal figure for a highly mobile society such as the United States. Of the pregnant women surveyed, six hundred or fifteen percent were found to have suffered miscarriages. Again this was not seen by Tokuhata or his survey team to be a significant figure, as it corresponded with the rate of miscarriage outside the survey area. The radiation level within a ten-mile radius was found to be only 10 millirems on average. Tokuhata claimed that, as levels of 100 millirems per annum occur in areas of natural background radiation, it was impossible to imagine that any harm had been done to residents' health.

The results of these surveys have been heavily criticized by environmental groups. A team headed by one local resident, Jane Lee, carried out an independent survey which showed that in one section of the neighboring city of Middletown, the incidence of cancer had increased sixfold in the ten years since the accident. In response to the criticism, Tokuhata widened the scope of his survey to include areas within a twenty-mile radius of the plant; but his team found no evidence of an increase in the number of cancer cases. Expressing mounting irritation at such different results, residents' groups have accused Dr. Tokuhata of being in league with those wishing to promote nuclear power. Their next move may be to take him to court on accusations of falsifying data. When asked about the breakdown in communication between himself and the local people since the accident, Tokuhata replied calmly:

"As a scientist, my duty is to carry out investigations rationally and accurately for future reference, and that's exactly what I've done." His furrowed brow spoke eloquently of the trials and tribulations of the last ten years.

* * *

In the years since the accident at Three Mile Island, forty-six nuclear reactors have been put into operation. Five have been closed down, the construction of another sixty-nine has been canceled or delayed, and plans to build new reactors have been shelved. This seems to be America's only answer to the disaster.

URANIUM MINING ON THE NAVAJO RESERVATION

*I*ndian reservations stretch from Arizona into New Mexico, across an expanse of land famous for its part in the history of the old West, as illustrated in countless Westerns. But the area also has another story to tell, one which has never been made into a movie: the story of uranium mining and radioactive contamination. We visited some forgotten villages in this area where native Americans are yet again facing upheavals in their lives.

Previous page: A Navajo woman mourns the death of her husband, a former uranium miner.

THE RADIOACTIVE FLOOD

The dancing started as the sun began to sink toward the west. Men and women linked arms, chanting as they danced with stately grace. We were in Church Rock, New Mexico, at the source of the Puerco River, a tributary of the Colorado. An Indian prayer meeting had just begun. The people were asking the gods to bring back the pure, fresh water they had once enjoyed. Mingled with their prayers was resentment toward those who were responsible for the contamination of the river and their wells ten years previously.

On July 16, 1979, just after five o'clock in the morning, a dam holding waste material from the neighboring uranium refinery burst, causing a huge mass of mud to pour into the hundred-foot-wide Puerco River. Johnny Arviso, a local farmer, recalled that "the mud came at us in waves." However, the real horror started after the filthy waters had receded.

"The bottom of the river was turned to mud—it stank like a mixture of oil and acid," Arviso continued. Naturally the mud was radioactive. The company mobilized its employees in an effort to clean up, but the scale of the accident was too large. Over ninety thousand gallons of mud and eleven hundred tons of tailings had escaped. Following the accident, high concentrations of radium, uranium, and other substances were detected in river and well water, making it too dangerous to drink. Since then a pipe has brought water from a lake twenty-five miles away, and from the outlet it is carried in buckets to the seven hundred households in the river valley. However, this does not guarantee total safety; livestock has become contaminated by drinking water from the river, posing a considerable risk to local consumers.

Uranium mining began at Church Rock in the late 1940s, and the hills in the area are dotted with abandoned mine shafts. The dam accident in the mountains, which the tribal elders described as "a desecration of the home of the gods," was one of the worst in the history of American nuclear development. The reservoir was found to have been overloaded in defiance of warnings from the state government.

A recent geological survey revealed that radiation levels are still from ten to one thousand times higher than the "safe" limit. "Because we're Indians they thought they could get away with not looking after that dam properly," the deputy mayor of the locality, Ted Silversmith, told us angrily. "The United Nuclear Corporation closed the refinery, but that won't bring our water back." He added that although the area had got attention because of the accident, there were places much worse off. He was referring to a region known as the Four Corners, where the desert is a maze of abandoned mines.

CONTAMINATION OF THE FOUR CORNERS

The Four Corners is where the states of New Mexico, Utah, Arizona, and Colorado converge. Its main residential center is Shiprock, and it was there that we met Perry H. Charley, a Navajo Indian. Charley is presently investigating the emission of radioactive substances from the old uranium mines that are scattered around this vast area of rocks and sand.

It was hard for us to believe that such a danger could exist in a place where nature appears to dominate completely. "I'd like to think that, too," Charley said in reply. "But I'm afraid I can't." He took us across the border into Arizona for about twenty miles until we reached the village of Tsee Tah. There we left the highway and turned onto a gravel road that wound up into the mountains. The car crawled precariously up to a height of over three thousand feet, where we stopped and got out.

Studding the mountainside were holes six to ten feet in diameter. Our guide walked around slowly, holding a geiger counter. Near the holes were piles of rocks heaped haphazardly on top of each other. As Charley approached one of the holes, the counter began to emit a beeping sound. The needle pointed to fifteen microroentgens. He walked a little closer. The needle reached 250 next to a pile of rocks, which looked as if a yellow powder had been sprinkled over them.

"It's quite safe if you only walk around here from time to time," Charley said. "But if you lived here it would be pretty bad." He showed us a hole surrounded by wooden railings—the locals sometimes used the disused holes as sheep pens.

The uranium mines dug into the side of the mountains are still full of radon gas. Charley has confirmed this to be the case for 176 of the mine shafts he has surveyed since October 1988. This figure is over five times the official number of thirty registered by the DOE. "I shudder to think what the figure would be for the whole of the Four Corners region," he told us.

Originally, radium was mined in this region for use in pottery glazes. However, things started to change in the latter part of the 1940s. In 1949 the Soviet Union staged its first successful atomic bomb test, signaling the start of the arms race. The desperate search for uranium was on.

Uranium was found in Four Corners, right in the center of the Navajo reservation. The area was swamped in a "uranium rush" the likes of which had never been seen before. Mining companies dug out the uranium, starting with that easiest to reach, and transported it to seven refineries built close by, where it was processed. At its peak, the Four Corners region is said to have accounted for twenty-five percent of the uranium used in the production of nuclear weapons.

In the early 1970s, however, the price of uranium plunged on the world market, and Four Corners lost any competitive edge it previously had. One by one the mines were closed. All that was left were countless holes in the mountainsides and huge heaps of tailings. Most of the mines were simply abandoned, as we had seen, with no measures taken to prevent damage to the environment.

The village of Tsee Tah is home to twenty-seven families, who make a living at the foot of the mountains by raising sheep, horses, and cattle. When the wind blows the village is covered with radioactive dust from the disused mines. At the base of the mountains is a spring which the villagers rely on for their water supply. "We knew nothing about radiation until very recently," said Francis Clah, father of ten children. "I'm worried enough about myself, but even more so about my children and any future grandchildren I might have."

As a result of Charley's investigations, decontamination of the disused mines has finally started. There are so many holes, however, that nobody knows how long the operation will take to complete. "If this had been a white town, you can be sure that they would have got on to it a lot more quickly." Charley's face hardened. "Some things never change: they trampled all over us before, and now they're doing it again."

VICTIM OF THE URANIUM RUSH

Behind Charley's determination to investigate radioactive contamination in the abandoned uranium mines lies a personal tragedy—the death of his father, Harris Charley, who died of a chest ailment in 1986 at the age of sixty-five. His widow showed us a photo of her husband; a strong, powerfully built man totally suited to the ten-gallon hat he was wearing. Mrs. Charley looked sadly at the picture. "Harris lost a lot of weight after he got sick. I reckon it was the mines that got him, you know . . ."

Charley's father was wounded and discharged from the navy around the time that uranium mining began in the nearby mountains in 1948, three years after the end of the war. The village had no other industries, so there was plenty of competition for jobs at the mines. Harris Charley, with eight children to support, went to work as soon as he recovered from his wounds.

At the beginning, his days were spent underground from morning till night. First the side of the mountain was dynamited, then the uranium was dug out of the resulting rubble. Harris was strong and popular with the other workers, so in time he was made a foreman, and he spent his days traveling around the mines. His chest ailment was discovered in 1964 when he had a medical after transferring to the Colorado mines. His widow confided to us that he had been complaining of shortness of breath for two or three years prior to the checkup. Following advice from his doctor, Harris gave up the mines and started work as a carpenter. His new trade was short-lived, however. Soon the Charley children, by this time grown-up, were doing their father's work for him. His condition worsened as time passed, until he had wasted away to two-thirds of his former weight, his powerful chest sunken by disease. Eventually he was taken to a Utah hospital.

Unbeknown to Harris, he had spent seventeen years digging up not only uranium but a number of other radioactive substances. Radon gas is particularly liable to accumulate in uranium mines, and is a well-known cause of lung ailments. The uranium dug out of the ground at Four Corners was first sent to a local refinery and then on to Oak Ridge, Tennessee, the home of the Hiroshima bomb. There the uranium was enriched and used in the manufacture of plutonium, which was then placed in a nuclear warhead.

"I don't think my father realized that what he was digging up was going to be used for making atomic bombs," Charley said. "As far as he was concerned it was just a funny-looking rock they were dealing with."

Charley consulted a lawyer and has recently managed to obtain official recognition that his father's death was caused by his work environment.

According to the lawyer, Earl Mettler of Albuquerque, there have been approximately thirty similar cases to date. However, even though exposure to radiation was recognized as the cause of death, Charley will only be entitled to receive ordinary industrial accident compensation which only amounts to four or five hundred dollars a month. Charley explained why the ruling was unfair: "The benefit for work accidents is calculated on the salary at the time of the accident, in this case at the time of death. When you think of the length of time between when the person leaves work and when they die, the amount is meaningless. The Navajo are too proud to take a trifling allowance like that—we will demand proper compensation." In a low voice, the turquoise pendant around her neck quivering slightly, his mother added, "If they had made the environment safer to work in, Harris would be alive today."

Here was a family that had in a sense been sacrificed to the military ambitions of its leaders. In spite of this, a miniature Stars and Stripes still occupies pride of place in their living room.

DROPPING LIKE FLIES IN RED VALLEY

Stretching out in all directions, the brick-red plains and the distant mountains stood out in breathtaking contrast to the cloudless blue sky. The set of numerous Westerns, Red Valley is a Navajo reservation located to the south of Monument Valley National Park. In this valley, we heard, the men were dropping like flies from lung cancer.

Raymond Joe, a former miner whom we met at the local town offices, spoke to us about conditions in the mines. His face was swollen, his skin a sickly pallor. "When the mining of uranium was at its peak, those mountains were lit up at night like Christmas trees. We were working day and night to get the stuff out of the ground. And this is the result," he said, showing us a scar on his back—Joe had had an operation to remove a tumor from his lung at a Shiprock hospital.

Joe first became a miner in 1952, the year the United States exploded its first hydrogen bomb, ushering in a new phase of the nuclear arms race. The mines moved from a system of two eight-hour shifts to three, so that uranium could be dug out of the ground twenty-four hours a day. The uranium rush was in full swing, and the earth shook with explosions, filling the mines with suffocating clouds of dust.

"The white foreman would give us the order to go down. We had no protection like masks or anything—just a helmet."

Once inside, the miners would load the rubble onto wagons and move them outside, where the yellow ore was removed and loaded onto a truck. The men worked with bare hands, and were constantly covered in a thin coat of dust. The reward for this backbreaking work was ninety cents an hour. "There was no other work," Joe continued. "We knew that the rock was used for making atomic bombs. But we never suspected that the yellow stuff itself was dangerous. We never worried about our health, either."

Joe traveled around Utah and Colorado, working a total of nineteen years in the mines. He left in 1975 after a medical check in Shiprock indicated that he may have cancer. His benefit of $283 per month was insufficient to bring up seven children, so his wife Dorothy went to work in a textile factory to make ends meet.

At the peak of the rush, two hundred uranium mines were to be found in the mountains of Red Valley. One hundred and eighty households were clustered in three small villages, and 150 people from them worked at the mines. In the late 1970s, lung cancer began to occur frequently in this group; fifty men have died so far, others are in hospital. The figures tell the story only too plainly. Of the thirty-two Navajo males diagnosed as having lung cancer between 1969 and 1982, twenty-three worked in the uranium mines. None of them smoked. According to Dr. John Samet of the University of New Mexico, who conducted the survey, the connection between their cancer and the radon gas in the mine is irrefutable. Moreover, Dr. Samet believes that "the number of lung cancer patients will continue to grow." Ventilation equipment to reduce the concentration of the gas was only installed in the mines in the early 1970s. Joe and his fellow miners had worked for all those years with no protection whatsoever.

RADIOACTIVE HOUSES

Traveling around the Navajo reservations that stretch from New Mexico into Arizona, we were struck by the unusual style of housing there. Some houses were shaped like inverted bowls, while others were built in hexagonal form. These were the traditional Navajo houses, known as *hogan*, which recently caused great consternation in the community when they were found to be contaminated by radiation. Fornic Yazzie, aged sixty-eight, is one of those who lives in a "radioactive house" in Red Valley. In July 1989 her home was checked by an employee of the local Navajo council, who detected radiation in two places: the chimney of the main building and the foundations of the outbuildings. Fornic's husband, Clifford, passed away eighteen years ago and since then she has lived alone. When we visited she was spinning wool to make into traditional Navajo carpets. She keeps about a hundred head of sheep for the purpose, spinning the wool and then weaving it on a mechanical loom. One small rug takes her two months. Every day she sits with her back to the fire, spinning and weaving. "They told me that radiation was detected in this chimney," she confided. "But there hardly seems any point in pulling it down and putting up a new one at this late stage, does there?"

From the front of the house we could see holes scattered over the face of the steep, red mountains nearby. These were the remains of the uranium mines in which Fornic's husband had worked for twenty years. The rubble discarded after the uranium had been sorted was left to pile up around the entrances to the mines. Most of these rocks were a foot square and about three inches thick; the perfect material for building foundations, walls, and chimneys.

From the 1950s on into the early 1960s, Clifford brought the rubble home after work and used it to slowly build up the main building and the storehouse. The chimney was constructed at the same time.

Clifford Yazzie later died of lung cancer.

A quarter of a mile up the road to the north of Fornic Yazzie's house were other *hogan* made of mud and stone. Every house we asked at had, without any qualms at all, used the rubble from the mines as a building material. As the residents put it, "everyone did it, and no one told us it was dangerous." We wondered if it was really safe to be exposed constantly to radiation day in, day out.

"There's no way that could be safe," commented Linda Taylor of the Southwest Research and Information Center in Albuquerque, which is involved with assisting victims of radiation among the Navajo.

According to Taylor, the reason nothing has been done for the uranium workers is because not enough is known about the effects of low doses of radiation and that it was too easy for the government to sit back and take advantage of the locals' lack of education.

The radioactive houses are now being pulled down one by one. Yet in Mrs. Yazzie's case, even if the contaminated material were removed from her home, she would still be unable to escape the dust from the abandoned mines that is stirred up every time the wind blows. A note of irritability crept into her voice at the suggestion of moving.

"This is our land. We can't just run away from it like that."

A LETHAL LEGACY

The work carried out by Navajo men was not confined to the mines— they were also the main source of labor for the uranium refineries, where solvents were used to extract the ore. We were sitting in a diner in Shiprock, the former center of the "uranium rush," when a tanned Navajo man called out to us:

"You Japanese? Whaddya doing in a place like this?"

When we replied that we were looking for people who had worked at the uranium refineries, he told us that we had come to the right place, and that he would gladly talk to us.

Russen Tohdacheeny, now an employee of the Indian Affairs Bureau, had started work at the Kerr-McGee uranium refinery in Shiprock in 1954, after three years in the navy. His first work at Kerr-McGee was adding sulfuric acid to the excavated rock to extract the uranium. Soon after he was moved to the last stage of the refining process, where his job was to pack the yellowcake into large drums. The doors and windows of the buildings were closed to prevent the humidity level from rising. "We had these small masks," Tohdacheeny continued, "but it was far too hot to wear them. We used to give the drums a whack so that the stuff settled: when we did that, clouds of it would rise up in the air—we were covered in yellow powder all day."

After work the men would go home without changing, and wear the same clothes the next day. The dust that gathered on the roof of the refinery alone was said to be worth $100,000. These were the abominable conditions under which Tohdacheeny and 120 fellow workers had to work. Tohdacheeny could not recall ever having a medical checkup.

He stayed at the refinery for four years before leaving to join the police force, where the pay was better. "But I've heard lately that some of my friends who stayed on have got lung cancer," he said with obvious concern.

At one time there were as many as twenty-five refineries in operation in the Midwest uranium mining belt, seven of those located in the Four Corners region. The four refineries of Shiprock, Monument Valley, Tuba City, and Mexican Hat were located on Navajo reservations. All the refineries began operations in the late fifties or early sixties, and all closed down in the seventies when the American uranium mining industry lost out to competition from Canada and Africa. They left behind a lethal legacy, however: piles of tailings loaded with radioactive byproducts of the refining process.

Only two pounds of uranium can be extracted from each ton of ore. The rest is waste. According to information supplied by the DOE, there are nine million tons of this waste in the reservation areas alone, and thirty million tons in all on abandoned refinery sites in the Midwest. The residents recently became aware of the danger of the dust from this conveniently forgotten waste blowing down onto the reservations and began to demand that steps be taken to prevent their villages from becoming covered in radioactive dust. In 1982 this resulted in attempts to clean up the environment. The DOE's strategy has been merely to cover the piles of rubble with earth to stop the dust flying around. Operations were completed at Shiprock in 1987 and the cleanup at the other three reservations was to be finished by 1991.

We found the site of the former Shiprock refinery covered in rocks. Although the site was only three hundred yards from the center of town, waste material was buried under these rocks. Until 1987, the exposed dust from the abandoned tailings was frequently blown through the city, which has a population of thirty-five thousand.

"It's just a damn crime, that's all there is to it," were Tohdacheeny's parting words.

FIGHTING FOR THE RESTORATION OF JUSTICE

The Navajo Indians have begun to rebel against long years of oppression by demanding assistance for the victims of uranium mining among their people.

"We want to bring justice back to the United States," said Phillip Harrison, launching into his speech at a meeting in Red Valley, Arizona. Harrison is one of many who have lost a relative to the mines—in this case his father. It is ten years since Harrison formed a committee to support the mine workers and decided to devote himself to alleviating the suffering which has come to the surface in the Four Corners region over the last few years. He sees the movement also as "a fight for the restoration of Navajo rights," and in his speech he recounted the history of the cruel repression of the Indians, and their demands for self-determination.

Until the eighteenth century, the Navajo were found in the region northwest of what is now Albuquerque, near the Mexican border. They were forced west by European settlers, and were finally rounded up into the barren Four Corners area because it had little value to the white settlers. Apart from using it as a backdrop for Westerns, white Americans showed little interest in the Four Corners region of rocks and sand until the wilderness was suddenly transformed into a treasure trove with the coming of the nuclear age. They dug up all the ore they could find, but it was mainly the Navajo who did the digging.

Harold Tso is a former member of the Navajo council which worked to improve working conditions at the mines. He told us about the lengths the government went to in order to deceive the Navajo. "Before mining started, the government told the Navajo that they would be mining copper. The word *uranium* is nowhere to be seen in the contract. They leased the land for a dollar per acre—the government's lies have caused tragedy here."

Safety measures were not taken in the mines or at the refineries until the 1970s, when the number of white workers increased and complaints about working conditions began to be made. No general survey of the damage caused to the health of local residents has been carried out to date, but the effects of exposure to radioactive substances are gradually coming to light. For example, the infant mortality rate and the incidence of congenital diseases in the Four Corners region are twice the national average. Cancer in children is also common. Harrison had harsh words to say about white domination of the region.

"They worked our people as hard as they could, and under terrible conditions, then threw them out when the mines were no longer profitable. The companies and the government that condoned it are no better than thieves. They never think about the Navajo except as a means for making money." We noticed there were no paved roads in the Navajo reservation, very little farmland, and no irrigation projects like those we had seen in California. Telephones are still a rarity. There are areas which have only got electricity in the last two years. In short, the area suffers from an almost total lack of public amenities. It is little wonder then, that, according to Harrison, sixty percent of the people depend on welfare.

He and his fellow committee members are pressing for a law to provide aid for people suffering from illnesses caused by working at the uranium mines. The reasoning behind their demands is that the Navajo workers became victims of the nation's nuclear policy, so it is only just that the government should provide compensation. Unfortunately, Harrison explained, it would take over $100,000 to organize a campaign to get a new law created.

"There's no way Navajo can raise that kind of money," Harrison said. "But we can't stay silent about this. We're going to do our best to draw Washington's attention to the situation here." He paused, then added, "Don't forget to tell the people in Hiroshima that there are *hibakusha* over here, too."

RADIOACTIVE CONTAMINATION IN GREENLAND

On January 21, 1968, an American B-52 strategic bomber carrying four hydrogen bombs crashed into the ice near Thule Air Base in northwest Greenland. The explosives used to ignite the bombs detonated on impact, causing the dispersal of plutonium and other radioactive materials over a wide area. Twenty years after the accident, the high incidence of skin cancer detected among Danish workers who were employed in the cleanup operation serves as a reminder of the danger of exposure to radiation.

Previous page: The contaminated U.S. Air Base at Thule, Greenland.

CONTAMINATED SNOW

Ole Markussen, aged fifty-one, is the leader of the former workers at Thule Air Base. We spoke to him at his apartment in a Copenhagen suburb, where he lives with his wife, Sally, without whose care he would be forced to stay in a hospital. Quietly he launched into an explanation of what had happened on that day in 1968.

"I was taking a nap in the barracks when I was woken by a terrific boom. I rushed outside to see what had happened and found the area lit up by pillars of fire shooting up into the sky." He returned to the barracks and switched on his radio. "After half an hour or so, the news came over that there had been a plane crash, but there was no mention of any hydrogen bombs," he continued.

The accident occurred at 5:40 in the afternoon. Being winter in the Arctic Circle, it was dark all day. A few of the truck drivers got together and drove out into the pitch darkness to see if they could rescue any of the crew. Markussen and most of the other workers stayed in their rooms. Six hours after the accident there was a fierce blizzard which blew contaminated snow from the accident site into the barracks seven miles away. Markussen believes that the plutonium made its way into his system via this snow.

"The U.S. Air Force has never made public the amount of radioactive material that was released that day. There's no way they should be able to get away with that." By this time our host was shaking with rage.

The plane wreckage, along with the shattered bombs, was disposed of in just over a month. Until the sun appeared in spring, however, nothing could be done about the twenty-two square miles of contaminated snow and ice, and it wasn't until March that the cleanup was begun in earnest. This operation also took about a month. Markussen's work in the transport division involved supervising the men who were repairing the heavy vehicles contaminated by the radiation. He continued to work at the base for four years after the crash, and during that time experienced no health problems. It was at the beginning of 1980 that he first began to notice changes in his body.

"The skin on my legs turned black and they swelled up," he told us.

"The doctor had never seen anything like it before."

Markussen experienced a constant feeling of tiredness and in 1984 collapsed with a brain hemorrhage while at work. He has since been in hospital eight times. His left leg is paralyzed from the knee down and he has also developed a speech impediment.

The couple knew that a number of Markussen's friends from his days at the base were suffering from the same kind of ailments. In February 1986 they went on television to tell the public about the terrible effects that exposure to radiation had had on their lives.

"I got in touch with the people I worked with in those days, and together we demanded that the government conduct an investigation," Markussen said. Including the widows of some of his former acquaintances, the couple received almost four hundred replies. Skin conditions, loss of sense of balance, mental illnesses . . . the situation was far more serious than they had ever imagined. At the time of the accident, there were 1,202 Danish workers at the Thule Air Base. By July 1989, 214 had died. In the case of six of the fourteen who passed away in the first half of 1989, the cause of death was cancer.

We interviewed Hugh Zuchariae, head of the Department of Dermatology at Marselisborg Hospital in Aarhus. Zuchariae is involved in the treatment of Thule's former workers. His twenty-seven patients suffer from skin diseases that include rashes on their hands, arms, and the soles of their feet; he has diagnosed two as having skin cancer. Of the twenty-seven, five were involved directly in cleaning up the radioactive contamination at the base.

"As there's no data concerning the amount of plutonium that was scattered and the extent of exposure to radiation, it's impossible to say for certain that their skin diseases have any connection with radiation. But it's clear that men who have worked at Thule do show a higher rate of skin disease than normal," said Dr. Zuchariae, choosing his words carefully.

WORKERS ADVISED NOT TO HAVE CHILDREN

We met the widow of Arleng Hogsted, one of Markussen's former colleagues, at a Copenhagen hotel. Her husband had died at the age of forty-three, leaving her with four handicapped daughters.

"Where would you like me to start?" she asked. Maya Hogsted was a striking woman, but she looked tired and drawn, and the lines on her face spoke volumes about the hardship she had to face each day.

"We got married in 1972, just after Arleng got back from Thule." Hogsted had returned from the base with red spots covering his arms and legs. "He worked at Thule from January 1968 until April 1972," she continued. "I know he was an electrician but I'm not sure exactly what he did—he never talked about it much."

The Hogsteds' first daughter was born in 1973. Her legs were abnormally short and she had defective vision. Their next child, born four years later, had a heart attack after its first birthday which resulted in brain damage. The two youngest children, born in 1981 and 1982, also have heart problems and are physically handicapped. Arleng's own health deteriorated with each passing year, until he was experiencing severe pain in almost every part of his body.

Arleng rarely spoke of his years in Greenland, but one day he told his wife that there had been a fatal accident at the base and that the base doctor had told him it would be better not to have children. Maya did not make the connection between radiation and the illnesses of her husband and daughters until a letter arrived from his old friend, Ole. For the first time, she realized that the accident her husband had referred to had involved radioactive material.

By this time, however, her husband was already dead. "Arleng died in January 1985. He'd been on morphine for a long time by then."

Maya would probably never have had any children if she had known the full story about the accident. With help from her parents she manages to look after her handicapped daughters. Her final words to us were spoken in tones of barely suppressed anger:

"Our government should be demanding compensation from the American government through diplomatic channels. If they won't do that, then they should take steps to compensate the victims themselves."

After the plane crash in 1968, the remains of the hydrogen bombs and the aircraft were gathered up and placed in 217 large metal drums. Likewise, the contaminated ice and snow was put in sixty-seven tanks holding approximately twenty-five thousand gallons each. This enormous amount of material was taken back to the United States. In spite of this, the U.S. government is refusing to recognize any of the claims of the Danish workers at Thule, and the Danish government itself is taking a similar stance.

THE BURDEN OF NUCLEAR SUPREMACY

*H*alf a century has passed since Albert Einstein wrote to President Roosevelt in 1939 to encourage the development of an atomic bomb. Since then the United States has succeeded in developing and building up a formidable array of nuclear weapons.

Today, however, the United States faces a contamination problem for which there appears to be no immediate solution. Under increasing pressure from the public, the United States is beginning to count the cost of being at the forefront of nuclear technology.

Previous page: Containers of radioactive waste piled up at Oak Ridge nuclear weapons complex, Tennessee.

INCREASING CONCERN OVER AMERICA'S NUCLEAR POLICY

On August 6, 1989, the forty-fourth anniversary of the bombing of Hiroshima, more than a thousand people gathered outside the Oak Ridge Y12 plant to stage an antinuclear protest. The nuclear weapons complex in Oak Ridge, Tennessee was the home of the Hiroshima A-bomb, "Little Boy." Placards declaring "A 21st century without nuclear weapons" and "No more radiation!" were waved in the air, families on holiday stopped to join in, and drivers honked their horns in support. It was evident to us that people's attitudes toward nuclear weapons were undergoing a definite change.

Oak Ridge was the nerve center of America's nuclear development program, and, as is shown by its nickname "the secret city," its activities have been more closely guarded than those of any other government facility in the country. Until recently it would have been unthinkable that a thousand people would gather outside the compound yelling antinuclear slogans. The demonstration is clear evidence of an increasing uneasiness in the community concerning the safety of nuclear weapons facilities. Walking around the outside of the huge compound that houses the Y12, X10, and K25 facilities, we were horrified to see huge piles of drums containing radioactive waste—the byproducts of the weapons production process. Inside the wire fence, which seemed to stretch for miles, we could see where piles of waste drums had been buried. A sign prohibiting fishing and swimming was posted on the bank of the nearby river. Stephen Smith of the Oak Ridge Environmental Peace Alliance spoke to us about the waste:

"Just by looking at all these drums you can see how much effort the government has been putting into the development of nuclear weapons. The result has been these disgusting piles of radioactive garbage, and we've got no guarantee that this stuff won't contaminate the air or the water. It frightens me to think that one day it could make its way into the human body," said Smith, shaking his head.

No data is available to back up claims of illness caused by exposure to radiation from the Oak Ridge plant. However, Paul White, who had worked at Oak Ridge for thirty-six years, assured us that if the factory records were opened up to public scrutiny a lot more suffering would probably come to light. White himself suffers from a brain tumor, while his brother and a large number of his former colleagues are also troubled with deteriorating health. According to him, details of accidents at the plant have been kept a tightly guarded secret. On one occasion, 1,500 pounds of enriched uranium were mysteriously lost from the plant; large quantities of mercury have also been discharged into the environment. The task of uncovering the sordid history of the "secret city" is only just beginning.

Nuclear weapons–related facilities administered by the DOE are spread across thirteen states. Oak Ridge in Tennessee, Hanford in Washington, and Los Alamos in New Mexico are the three original facilities built for the development of the atomic bomb under the Manhattan Project. The Cold War saw the construction of facilities at Rocky Flats in Colorado; Savannah River in South Carolina; Fernald in Ohio, and elsewhere, completing a network of nuclear weapons factories across the United States. According to Robert Alvarez of the Washington-based Environmental Policy Institute, there are at present twenty nuclear facilities in the United States incorporating a total of 250 factories and employing 110,000 workers. Their annual budget is over $9 billion.

Most of these facilities are known to be linked with radioactive contamination and health problems. For example, in an incident that occurred in 1988 at the Rocky Flats plant, three employees entered a highly contaminated room and were exposed to radiation. When this became known the factory was temporarily closed down. This particular plant has a history of accidents involving plutonium, a state of affairs that eventually lead to an FBI investigation in June 1989. The Savannah River facility has also been a source of acute embarrassment to the White House. This plant, which manufactures plutonium and tritium for use in atomic warheads, has had a total of thirty accidents in twenty-eight years, none of which the president of the United States or the chairman of the DOE were informed about.

Originally built in the interests of national security, a number of these nuclear facilities were closed down after details became known of a number of accidents involving dangerous radioactive substances. Every one of the plants supplying enriched uranium, plutonium, and tritium for use in warheads has been forced to halt operations. The closure of the plants is likely to bring about fundamental changes in U.S. nuclear policy: because of the short half-life of tritium, a halt in the supply of tritium will mean that an increasing number of warheads will become useless in the near future.

THE CRIPPLING LEGACY OF THE ARMS RACE

If America is the democracy it claims to be, it is difficult to understand why the truth about accidents and contamination at its nuclear weapons facilities has been kept from the public for so long. According to Alvarez, the practice of shielding details of military nuclear facilities from the public eye began with the Manhattan Project during the Second World War and has been upheld ever since, enabling the operation of nuclear facilities with no interference from the public. The fact that not even Congress is able to intervene in matters of nuclear policy shows a blatant disregard for democratic principles, making the general public increasingly suspicious of the government's handling of domestic nuclear issues.

Most of America's atomic-weapons factories are now over thirty years old and showing marked deterioration. Some sources have estimated that the upgrading of these facilities and the disposal of the enormous quantities of radioactive waste that have accumulated over the years would cost at least $100 billion. The U.S. government, already straining under the yoke of a huge deficit, will before long be forced to count the cost of all those years of nuclear expansionism.

The crippling legacy of the arms race will not be confined merely to the treatment of waste and the cleaning up of a contaminated environment. The most serious matter for the government's consideration is the health of its people. The number of Americans suffering from the effects of exposure to radiation are unknown; very few surveys have been carried out by government organizations, so there is little reliable information available. The only data in existence is that put out by the National Association of Radiation Survivors (NARS), based in California, which estimates the number of radiation victims to be around 886,000. According to the NARS survey, there are an estimated 15,000 victims suffering from diseases related to uranium mining, while 250,000 have been exposed to radiation from nuclear arms–manufacturing facilities and research institutes. In addition, approximately 250,000 workers at the Nevada bomb-testing site, 120,000 residents living downwind of the test area, and

250,000 ex–service personnel mobilized for testing in the Marshall Islands and elsewhere are also likely to have been exposed to huge amounts of radiation. As Fred Allingham of NARS told us, "From uranium mining to weapons manufacture, through to the disposal of nuclear waste, radiation has caused suffering at every stage of the development of nuclear arms. It would not be exaggerating to say that there are victims of radiation in almost every part of the United States."

Virtually no steps have been taken by the authorities to help people suffering from radiation-linked diseases. Public demands for an effective program of assistance have been voiced since around 1977. Although laws were passed in 1988 providing support for ex–service personnel exposed to radiation during bomb tests and now suffering from cancer, no such steps have been taken to help civilians. At present it looks like being a long time before the residents of Hanford and their compatriots in Nevada and elsewhere obtain what they see as rightful compensation. If the federal government were to recognize the existence of victims of radiation, it would have to be prepared to pay out vast sums for medical treatment and compensation for years of suffering. Not only that, but the manufacture of nuclear weapons would be rendered impossible. Allingham sees these fears as the main obstacle in the way of government provision of assistance for victims of radiation.

However, perhaps the picture is not all one of gloom and despondency. In August 1989, the DOE admitted that groups other than ex-service personnel were at risk from exposure to radiation when it acknowledged that a high rate of cancer had been detected among civilian employees at nuclear weapons facilities. One by one these plants have also been made to promise that they will release environmental data to the public.

Fred Allingham left us with these words: "For a nation to say it is acting in the best interests of the security of its citizens without taking their general health and well-being into consideration is a contradiction in terms. The legacies of the Cold War must be accounted for in a manner befitting a democratic country."

THE SOVIET UNION

THE LARGEST NUCLEAR
TEST SITE IN THE SOVIET UNION

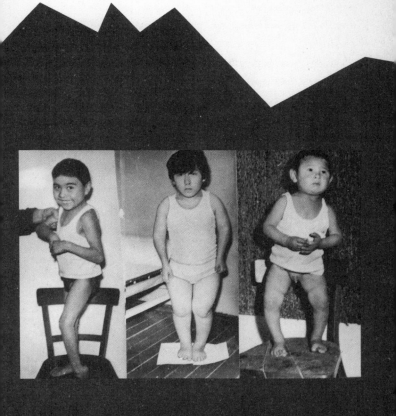

*O*n August 29, 1949, an atomic bomb was exploded on the vast plains of Kazakhstan in the southern part of the Soviet Union. Since then, at least 320 atomic and hydrogen bomb tests have been carried out in the area around the provincial capital of Semipalatinsk, making it the largest nuclear test site in the Soviet Union.

Until recently, details of atomic and hydrogen bomb testing in the Soviet Union have been shrouded in secrecy and the voices of victims of radiation have largely gone unheard. After lengthy negotiations we were given permission to enter the area, although we were bound by certain conditions. The following account of our meetings constitutes only a small part of the story of the victims of radiation, many of whom still fear the consequences of speaking out, in spite of the introduction of the open policy of glasnost.

Previous page: Children from the area around the nuclear testing site in Semipalatinsk, Kazakhstan.

THE SEEDS OF PROTEST

Arriving in Semipalatinsk, which lies three and a half hours southeast of Moscow by air, we found both the city and the vast barren plains surrounding it still frozen solid, even though it was already the middle of March. The air temperature ranged between five and fifteen degrees Fahrenheit and we were greeted by a tireless westerly wind that blew powdery snow in our faces.

We traveled to Bylirtysh Collective Farm, approximately eighteen miles west of Semipalatinsk. Bylirtysh is a poultry farm, which also keeps horses providing meat and *kumys*, the mildly alcoholic drink made from fermented mare's milk. It is also twenty-five miles from the area requisitioned by the military forty years ago for use as a nuclear testing zone and around seventy-five miles from the actual explosion site.

"Each test resulted in a tremor of between four and five on the Richter scale. They were mainly in the morning, and lasted about a minute," said an elderly lady we met in the waiting room of the farm's clinic. The young female doctor informed us that the crack in the wall of the director's office was caused by a test which had taken place in October of the previous year. The earthquakes caused by the tests became such a fact of life for the citizens of Semipalatinsk and the villages dotted around it, that after a while they stopped worrying about them. The military continued to tell them that there was "no problem," so the people had no cause to worry about the possible effects of radiation. After all, a few earthquakes did not seem that much to endure.

This relatively harmonious state of affairs continued in the Semipalatinsk region until 1989, when a candidate's speech during the elections to the Soviet People's Congress brought about a radical change in the residents' attitude.

On February 26, 1989, the first secretary of the Kazakhstan Writers' Union, Olzhas Suleymenov, stood in front of the television cameras, put away his prepared notes, and began to make an impromptu appeal to his listeners.

"As a result of two bomb tests this month, dangerous toxic substances have been released into the atmosphere. This is merely a continuation of what has been happening for the past forty years."

Suleymenov then proposed that a public meeting be held to discuss the matter two days later. This was the first time in Semipalatinsk—in fact the first time in the Soviet Union—that the issue of damage caused by nuclear testing had been raised in public. In answer to his appeal, five thousand people gathered in front of the headquarters of the Writers' Union. This was the beginning of the Nevada-Semipalatinsk movement calling for aid for radiation sufferers and the closing of the test area.

This wave of protest brought to light the horrifying facts about the testing and revealed the appalling lengths to which the authorities had gone to in order to deceive the local people.

"Everyone is beginning to worry about the effects of the testing," remarked our guide around Bylirtysh Farm, Marat Urazalin, head of the Department of Microbiology at Semipalatinsk Medical School. True enough, the atmosphere was strangely quiet, almost to the point of oppressiveness. The residents, confirming the truth of Urazalin's statement, told us about a number of incidents—the sudden death of thirty-three horses in one day in a nearby village and thirty the following day in the one next to that, a couple with two severely handicapped children—that had left them with grave fears for their own safety. The army's standard answer that there was no need to worry had done nothing to calm the growing distrust of the military among the people.

THE HYDROGEN-BOMB TESTS

We were restricted in our movements to within the area around Semipalatinsk, and thus being unable to get close to the test site itself, had to be content with using the few days we had to interview those willing to talk to us about the testing. Among those we interviewed was Toryuval Ichenov, a former government official now retired and sharing an apartment with his son's family.

In June 1949, before the first atomic test scheduled to take place that August, Ichenov was ordered to close and evacuate farms near the test site. He traveled from village to village over the next five years, getting busier as the frequency of the tests increased. In 1953, while visiting a small farm thirty-five miles east of the test site, he witnessed an unforgettable sight: the explosion of the Soviet Union's first hydrogen bomb.

"It was August 12, at a village called Krasnoyulta. Just before eleven there was a flash, then I saw a huge mass forming on the horizon, black at first, then changing to the color of red earth. After about three minutes there was a roar, and a gigantic cloud of dust blew over. I covered my mouth and threw myself on the ground. When I eventually got up I found that the blast of wind had damaged some of the nearby buildings —I was so stunned."

Throughout our discussion Ichenov glanced frequently at Urazalin, who had accompanied us, for reassurance that it was safe to discuss such matters. Urazalin encouraged him to say whatever he liked, reiterating to him that this was the era of *glasnost*, but it looked as if even Urazalin was shocked at the gravity of Ichenov's revelations.

Leonid Leznikov, a journalist for the *Kazakhstan Pravda*, was also a witness to the first hydrogen-bomb test. He was eight years old when he watched the mushroom cloud from his home in Semipalatinsk, 110 miles to the east of the test site.

"It was like a painting in black and red, and seemed less like a cloud than a strange creature with a life of its own," he told us. "Almost all the windows facing west were blown in by the blast, and radio broadcasts advised people to leave their houses."

Ichenov's job became much simpler after the hydrogen bomb test, as the farmers were too frightened to resist evacuation. The number of farms evacuated rose to eight, including some situated at the foot of Mt. Degelin, which was within the testing site. Most of the farms evacuated were located to the south of the site.

"The army told us they would only carry out tests when the wind was blowing from north to south, which makes me think now that they were aware of the danger of radiation," he remarked, gesturing toward his map. However, the army did not take the wind into consideration every time they carried out a test. A super hydrogen bomb was exploded in November 1955 when the wind was blowing from west to east—in other words toward Semipalatinsk.

The day of the blast is indelibly etched on the memories of the people of the city. Over thirty years later they are still talking about all the windows shattered by the blast, being temporarily deafened by wind pressure, fireplaces fanned into ferocious blazes, people badly injured by glass falling from high-rise buildings, the dirty rain that fell afterward, and the collapse of old wooden homes. The shock waves from the explosion wreaked havoc as far away as the city of Ust-Kamenogorsk, three hundred miles to the east, shattering all the windows that lay in its path.

The citizens of Semipalatinsk were able to speak at length about the material destruction wrought by the tests; however, when questioned about changes in the radiation level or their health directly after the blast, they made almost no comment. Little wonder that this should be the case; there was not a single instrument for measuring radiation in this city of 360,000, and nobody knew anything about the effects of exposure to radiation. Not only that, witnesses to the blast were forbidden to tell anyone that they had even seen it, let alone the extent of the destruction. To preserve secrecy, a KGB security net was thrown up around the city. The people had no choice but to keep quiet.

LIVING IN THE PATH OF THE 'ASHES OF DEATH'

Situated a hundred miles south of the testing site, the village of Karaaul, with a population of just under ten thousand, has been the scene of tragedy for the past forty years. If we are to believe the military's statement that tests were purposely carried out while a north wind was blowing, then there is no doubt that Karaaul was placed directly in the path of the wind and the "ashes of death" which it carried and deposited on the hills to the west of the town.

Although the army's claims that the wind was stronger than predicted may well be valid, there is no doubt that even if the wind had died down, the entire town still would have been exposed to high levels of radioactive contamination. Madina Makanova, aged twenty-four, works in the main headquarters of the antinuclear organization Nevada-Semipalatinsk. Her grandparents and six uncles had all lived in Karaaul, and had all died of cancer. Her grandparents passed away in the late sixties, while her uncles, each in his thirties, died one by one in the seventies. She related how her youngest uncle, a shepherd, had blamed their deaths on "that poisonous explosion" and had moved to the capital, Alma-Ata. However, in the end, he, too, was unable to escape the same fate as his brothers. Madina's father, the only one to survive, regrets that he will never be able to go back to his place of birth.

"When the rally against testing was held last summer, I just cried all the way through it," Madina said, blinking away tears at the memory.

For Toryuval Ichenov, the former government employee in charge of the requisition of land for the test site and the evacuation of residents, there remain a number of puzzling aspects concerning the evacuation he was ordered to carry out. The farms around the test site were closed at intervals of six months to a year, rather than all at once.

"The army should have evacuated everyone at once if they knew of the danger of radioactivity, but instead we were ordered to divide the area up and carry out the evacuation in stages."

This means that those forced to wait their turn were literally living among radioactive fallout. Ichenov suspects that they were deliberately used as guinea pigs for studying the effects of the tests. Unbeknown to him, we had heard a story at the headquarters of Nevada-Semipalatinsk which showed these suspicions to be correct.

In preparation for the first hydrogen-bomb test in 1953, the town of Karaaul, to which the farmers living around the site had been moved, was included in the evacuation area. However, an order was issued specifying that forty adult males should remain in the area. Those who stayed were witnesses to the huge mushroom cloud that rose up a hundred miles to the north in a collage of eerily changing colors. According to an investigation carried out by Tursonov Yelmenko, editor of Nevada-Semipalatinsk's paper, *Izbilache*, only five of these forty men are still alive.

Clenching his fists, he said, "Their deaths can only be thought of as part of a calculated experiment."

Saim Balmkhanov of the Kasav Academy of Science and head of the medical section of Nevada-Semipalatinsk states that at the time of the atmospheric testing, the level of radiation 185 miles downwind from the center of the blast would definitely have been over 200 rads. This estimate runs contrary to the army report recently released which put the level of radiation at 37 rads. Thus, there can be no doubt that for forty years the town of Karaaul was the repository of large amounts of fallout and that its citizens were used as unwitting experimental subjects. The scientific documentation which would officially confirm this has yet to come to light, but when it does it is probable that the extent of the tragedy in Karaaul and the neighboring villages of Sarzhan and Kaynar will be found to be far greater than previously thought.

THE ATOMIC LAKES

During our investigations in Semipalatinsk, we often heard the curious phrase "atomic lakes." At first our attempts to unravel the mystery met with no success; we were told that the lakes were nothing but a rumor. Then we met Ilyas Iskhakov, who has been engaged in mineral exploration in the area since 1955.

"The atomic lakes? Well, I've seen them a few times, but it's not the kind of place you want to go if you can help it."

Iskhakov travels the plains around Semipalatinsk in search of minerals, in particular gold. His work frequently takes him into the test area. "I haven't counted the smaller ones, but there are two large lakes. One is about a quarter of a mile across and just over half a mile long. It was formed in January 1965 when the ground collapsed after underground testing. They told us it had a force of 125 kilotons; that's the equivalent of ten Hiroshimas," he continued. On his trips around the plains, Iskhakov carries equipment for measuring radioactivity. This proved to be insufficient during the period that atmospheric testing was being carried out, and also later when tests were carried out underground.

"The equipment I had measured up to 1,250 microroentgens per hour, but when I turned it on, the needle just went right off the scale." In May 1965, five months after the larger of the lakes was formed, Iskhakov flicked the switch three miles from the lake shore. His ears were assaulted by an incredible screech through the headphones. This, however, ceased after a short time—the radiation level was so high that it had broken the instrument. Terrified, he abandoned his equipment and beat a hasty retreat.

"The other lake is very big," he continued. "About a third of a mile across at its widest point and three miles or so long. Originally there were lots of small lakes in the area, until they tested a 140-kiloton bomb. That made the ground collapse and one huge lake was formed."

As one who has spent many years engaged in geological surveys, Iskhakov laments the destruction of the environment that the testing has caused. "We took so much trouble to find veins of gold and seams of coal and now we find that we can't even work in the test area," he grumbled, poring over the map in front of him. "The level of radioactivity is appalling and the ground is unstable, too.

DOUBLE EXPOSURE

Another major cause for concern is the health of the nomadic peoples, whose livelihoods depend on the horses and sheep that have now been found to be contaminated. A section of the old back road that used to lead to farms within the test area has been blocked off with barbed wire, but in most areas there are only warning signs.

"Stock will wander wherever there is grass, and the radioactive substances they are exposed to end up threatening the lives of those who depend upon them most. Just the thought of it makes me shudder."

Iskhakov's fears are well founded. According to a secret document recently obtained by the Nevada-Semipalatinsk movement, the amount of radiation accumulated in the bodies of sheep in the area is, on average, twenty-two times higher than in other regions. At one location, the concentration was as much as 350 times the normal reading. Other data reported that milk had a concentration twenty-five times the average, and animal bones registered a level from four to thirty times the average. There is no record of any limits being put on the consumption of meat or milk during the years that the tests were carried out. The residents were therefore subjected to double radiation exposure: directly from nuclear fallout and indirectly from the food they ate.

Iskhakov told us about a type of freshwater fish, similar to carp, known as *sazan*, which was released into the atomic lakes for research purposes.

"There are signs by the lakes saying 'Fishing not allowed, do not eat fish bones.' As if anyone is going to fish in a place like that, let alone eat the bones."

The military has told the people nothing about the contamination of their soil, water, and livestock, and yet they put up futile warning signs in places the residents do not even go. It is this blatant lack of honesty that annoys Iskhakov the most.

A HIGH INCIDENCE OF DEFORMITIES

It is extremely likely that the fallout from over forty years of nuclear testing in the Semipalatinsk area has caused serious genetic defects. Gricia Gadikbyeva, a pediatrician who works in Semipalatinsk, showed us a long strip of photos.

"This child is seven years old. Her left leg has been twisted since she was born, and she is a bit of a slow learner.

"This girl is actually thirteen, but her weight is only that of a seven- or eight-year-old.

"This three-year-old boy's legs, as well as his toes, are bent.

"A nineteen-year-old youth in bed with terrible cramps in his legs.

"This boy has abnormally short toes . . ."

The list went on.

"All these children have one thing in common," Dr. Gadikbyeva said. "Their parents either used to live near the test site or still live there now. So far we have noted this high incidence of deformities around the test site, extending as far as forty-five miles to the east in Znaminka, ninety miles to the southwest in Kaynar, and directly downwind from the site in the village of Karaaul. But we suspect that areas further away have been affected as well."

After the Second World War, the nomadic Kazakh people were gathered into collective farms in accordance with the agricultural policy of the time.

"No doubt the tests were a real shock to them. But because the army kept telling them that there was nothing to worry about, they didn't. As far as they were concerned a nuclear test meant the same as an earthquake."

It was not only the Kazakh people who were left in the dark about the harmful effects of the tests. Dr. Gadikbyeva admitted herself that it was a long time before she knew herself what they could do to unborn children. She first became interested in radiation about ten years ago after talking with the parents of one of the handicapped children.

"I went to the head of the provincial health department to get some detailed information about radiation and genetics, but he told me it was better not to go into that subject too deeply. I'm pretty sure he knew what was going on, but he must have been under pressure from Moscow," she said, lowering her eyes.

Such a tight net of security is kept around the test site that even Soviet citizens are not allowed to enter the city of Semipalatinsk. The advice not to go into the subject of radiation-related diseases too deeply was as good as an order.

Owing to the popular movement to close the Semipalatinsk test site, which began in February 1989, Dr. Gadikbyeva is now able to contact other clinics near the test site and exchange information. The fact that she could show us the photographs freely was most certainly the result of relaxation of regulations and the improvement in communications.

"I can't say for certain that all these children's deformities were caused by their parents being exposed to radiation," she said. "But there is a very strong possibility. I just wish we could get our hands on past data."

Dr. Gadikbyeva and other pediatricians like her continue to pursue the truth about these children's deformities, though their task is not made any easier by the almost complete lack of information. One result of their work has been the discovery that the incidence of stillbirths in Semipalatinsk had actually doubled over a twenty-year period: from 6.1 per thousand in 1960 to 12.5 in 1982.

"Surveys carried out purely for the residents' benefit have only just begun. So far you probably couldn't call it a proper survey, but looking at the figures for stillbirths and deformities you can't help but come to the conclusion that radiation has something to do with them."

Forty-one years after the first test, the effects are being felt by a third generation. We asked Dr. Gadikbyeva if this web of radioactive contamination and secrecy could ever be untangled. Her determined reply was, "It's going to be difficult, but we have to do it."

SECRET RESEARCH CARRIED OUT BY THE MILITARY

During the forty-year period in which over three hundred nuclear tests were carried out on the plains of Kazakhstan, the military never deviated from its standard line of "Don't worry, there's no problem." In actual fact, though, it was quietly conducting its own investigations into the effects of radiation.

This secret research was carried out in a corner of a run-down wooden building housing the Semipalatinsk Provincial Health Department. The research laboratories were known as Section Four: a sign on the door indicated a department specifically for the study of a certain sheep disease that plagues farms in the area. The rooms, however, have not once been used for studying sheep diseases.

Only doctors and scientists directly related to the military were allowed to enter. Radiation measurements and health investigations were carried out here, right under the citizens' noses, but they were told nothing.

The deception was uncovered in October 1989 by members of the movement to close the test site; the sign on the door now reads "Radiation Medicine." Despite the abrupt change of image, though, the locals still call it Section Four in defiance of the bureaucrats who lied to them for so long.

The research secretly carried out in Section Four began in 1961, twelve years after the first test. The code name Semipalatinsk Forty was given to the work, which was conducted in collusion with the Department of Health in Moscow and the local military commander. A total of 125 staff were employed, including twenty-five doctors.

To this day, no results of any research carried out by the staff of Section Four have been used for the benefit of the local residents, either before or after its true activities were disclosed.

We interviewed Dr. Boris Guchev, who has been involved in the research at Section Four for many years and is widely believed to hold the key to the mysteries of the work carried out there.

Reporter: Why was it necessary to put up a fake sign to trick the residents?

Guchev: We were just following orders.

R: What were you studying?

G: We made regular checks on the level of radiation around the site and investigated the health of ten thousand of the residents there.

R: Did people know why the checks were being carried out?

G: The military had told them that there were no harmful effects from the tests, so we couldn't very well tell them what we were checking for.

R: What were the results of these checks?

G: We found slightly higher rates of cancer and leukemia than usual. But I can't say for certain whether these were brought on by radiation. In the early stages our survey techniques were somewhat primitive, so it's difficult to make comparisons.

R: Did you find any genetic defects?

G: I can't say.

R: Could you tell us about the results of your surveys in a little more detail?

G: I don't have the authority. I'm afraid I can't disclose anything right now.

R: Did problems caused by high doses of radiation decrease when testing moved underground?

G: The situation did improve. But I have heard that there were instances of radiation leaking up through the ground—as the military say happened in February 1989.

R: Don't you think all the material you gathered should be released as soon as possible for the sake of the residents?

G: I can't reveal anything without the proper authorization.

Interviewing Guchev was like getting blood out of a stone, and at times there were some very long pauses. The head of the provincial health department, who was present at the interview, stayed silent the whole way through. His deputy, who sat looking annoyed during most of the interview, finally told us, "Look, there are 840,000 people in this province, so the sample of 10,000 people used by Section Four is just too small. We need to expand the sample to at least 100,000 and conduct some joint research." On this note, our interview was concluded.

Glasnost as promoted by Mikhail Gorbachev has given the people of Kazakhstan the confidence to question the past and the present, as is shown by the growth of the Nevada-Semipalatinsk movement. Unfortunately, as far as the problem of nuclear testing is concerned, there is still much room for improvement. That was one thing we did learn from our interview with Dr. Guchev.

NEVADA-SEMIPALATINSK

After leaving Semipalatinsk, we returned to Moscow via Alma-Ata, capital of Kazakhstan. Olzhas Suleymenov, chairman of Nevada-Semipalatinsk, who had gone to a great deal of effort to help us in our investigations, was also in the capital to attend a meeting of the People's Assembly to be inaugurated by Mikhail Gorbachev.

"Last year (1989), eleven of the eighteen underground tests scheduled were canceled," he told us. "For almost six months, since October, there have been no tests carried out at all. But if we let down our guard, the nuclear war against the people of Kazakhstan will start again." Suleymenov did not have to spell out his willingness to do all in his power to close the test site; his confident tones and determined look said enough.

Suleymenov was born and raised in Kazakhstan. In March 1989 he was elected to the People's Assembly, and he is also a member of the Supreme Soviet. We asked him about his speech on television in February of the previous year, which brought the anti-test movement into existence.

"It was a phone call from a soldier that made up my mind to give that speech, believe or not," he said. The caller informed him that radiation leaked during the tests on February 12 and February 17 had found its way to the military base at Kurchatov, over a hundred miles to the north.

"The fact that someone from the army itself was obviously worried about radiation—that's what convinced me."

The protest meeting on February 28, which led to the establishment of a movement to stop the testing, resulted in demands being voiced for assistance to radiation sufferers, the holding of a meeting in Karaaul on August 6, and speeches at the General Assembly demanding a halt to testing. The movement continues to grow rapidly as people begin to vent forty years of suppressed anxiety about nuclear tests.

The democratization of Eastern Europe is also providing great encouragement for Suleymenov and his colleagues in Kazakhstan, but they are only too aware that they cannot afford to relax their vigilance.

"The military would start testing again tomorrow if they could," he remarked grimly. "It's like a sword hanging over our heads."

An activist we spoke to in Semipalatinsk on March 11, 1990, told us gloomily: "Yesterday, the Americans conducted a nuclear test in Nevada. It'll probably give the hawks here an excuse to start testing again."

As the name of their anti-test movement suggests, the Soviet people know that until testing stops in Nevada, the sites in their own country will never be closed.

"That's why all the radiation sufferers of the world have to unite!" said Suleymenov excitedly. "Now that the barriers between East and West are coming down, we must show our solidarity and give the militarists of the world our message of peace."

Suleymenov's biggest worry is the unknown depths of the effects of radioactive contamination from the Semipalatinsk testing area. None of the information gathered in the year after the movement began gives any cause for optimism. Quite the reverse. Cancer at a level 3.4 times that of other districts; strontium concentrations on nearby farms 360 to 2,900 times the national average; stillbirths; infant mortality; deformities; leukemia; the depressing list goes on.

"You probably couldn't call it very scientific at the moment, but we have to decide quickly who needs to be helped. And we have to make an informed judgment about which areas are dangerous. We're determined to pursue the truth, whatever the cost. There are no national borders when it comes to suffering from radiation."

CHERNOBYL THREE YEARS AFTER

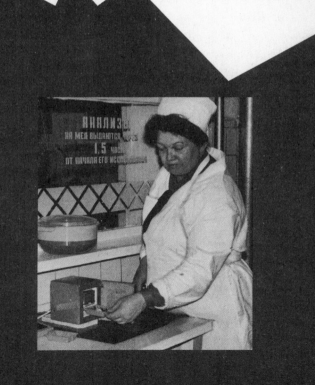

*T*he 1986 explosion at Chernobyl in the Soviet Union is widely known as the worst accident ever to occur at a nuclear power plant. The effects of the release of radioactivity have already surpassed the optimistic estimates made at the time of the accident, and the true extent of the damage is becoming clearer year by year.

The disaster has put a virtual halt to the building of new nuclear power facilities, and the name Chernobyl has become a metaphor for radioactive contamination on a hitherto unknown scale. Three years after the accident, against a background of growing uneasiness and distrust of the government on the part of the Soviet people, we traveled to Chernobyl to survey firsthand the aftermath of the disaster. A major consideration was to see how radiation victims were being treated and to discover what steps had been taken to prevent further accidents.

Previous page: Food samples being checked for radioactive contamination at a Kiev market.

VICTIMS OF CHERNOBYL

At the edge of a beech forest eighteen miles to the north of Moscow, we joined the elderly couples and families carrying flowers destined for their loved ones and passed silently through the gates of Mitinskoe Municipal Cemetery. Clustered together halfway up a hill lie a group of graves, still white and obviously new. The names and dates carved into the marble shine dully under the leaden sky:

Vladimir Shashenok
April 21, 1951 — April 26, 1986

On April 26, 1986, at around one o'clock in the morning, Shashenok, an electrician, was working in the No. 4 reactor at the Chernobyl nuclear power plant. At 1:23 A.M. there was an explosion which shook the ground and caused the roof to cave in.

Shashenok was taken to hospital, having been exposed to a radiation level of over 1,000 rems. At dawn, clutching his wife Luda, he breathed his last. Only five days before he had celebrated his thirty-fifth birthday.

Another victim of radiation was Victor Lopachuk, who had been married for exactly a year when he died. After the explosion, he went around the plant for three hours taking whatever measures he could to prevent any further damage. Lopachuk became stricken with acute radiation sickness. Thirteen days later he died with the words "I've got to turn off the switches . . ." still on his lips. He was twenty-five years old. Two weeks later his first child, Yurya, a girl, was born.

Lying unobtrusively to the right of the two neat rows of graves are two slightly different from the rest. Laid to rest here are First Lieutenant Vladimir Plavik, platoon commander of the plant's fire brigade, and First Lieutenant Victor Kivenok, commander of the 6th Fire Brigade Unit of the town of Pripyat, where the workers of Chernobyl resided. Both men were twenty-three years old at the time of the disaster. The gold stars decorating the gravestones indicate to visitors that these men are heroes of the Soviet Union.

Plavik's group was the first on the scene, arriving five minutes after the explosion. Kivenok's unit was next, arriving eleven minutes later. Both men were involved in putting out the fire in the reactor and preventing the blaze from spreading to the No. 3 reactor nearby. Before long, Plavik and Kivenok were experiencing fierce headaches and nausea together with an odd metallic taste in their mouths. From months of training, they knew only too well the meaning of that metallic taste, but the knowledge that they were exposing their bodies to huge doses of radiation did not stop them from climbing onto the roof, which was in danger of collapsing at any minute, in order to get into the machine room to extinguish the fire. Forty minutes later they lost consciousness while receiving emergency treatment from Dr. Ivan Orlov who, as a physician, was fully aware of the consequences of exposure to radiation.

A day later, Plavik and Kivenok woke up to find themselves in bed, five hundred miles away at Moscow's No. 6 Hospital. They spent fifteen days fighting the unseen enemy that had invaded their young bodies, before giving up the struggle on May 11. Dr. Orlov, who had attended Plavik and Kivenok, followed them to the grave soon after. He was forty-one.

Of the thirty-one victims of Chernobyl officially recognized by the government, twenty-seven are buried in Mitinskoe Cemetery. The fact that these twenty-seven were victims of radiation, however, is not told here at Mitinskoe. Whether in accordance with the wishes of their families or the desire of the government to play down the enormity of the disaster, there is no mention here at all of Chernobyl.

Brimming with questions, we left the cemetery and took the night train to Kiev, from where our investigations of the Chernobyl disaster would begin in earnest.

SURVIVORS OF CHERNOBYL

Many of those who were mobilized to deal with the accident were lucky to survive the high doses of radiation. However, even after three years they are still living in a state of uncertainty about their future.

At the All-Union Scientific Center of Radiation Medicine in Kiev, those exposed to radiation at the time of the Chernobyl accident are subjected regularly to exhaustive tests. Pedaling furiously on a machine designed to test the strength in one's limbs, Sergeant Vasilii Davibienko of the Kiev Fire Brigade kept an anxious eye on the wires attached to his arms and legs. When the attendant gave the word, he stopped pedaling. "How does it look?" he asked, glancing anxiously at the digital display.

"Well, it's hard to say really," came the noncommittal reply.

At this point the doctor who was acting as our guide interrupted them to reassure Davibienko that there was absolutely nothing to be worried about.

At the time of the Chernobyl explosion, Davibienko, a fireman in the Pripyat Fire Brigade, was off duty and relaxing at his home in Pripyat just over two miles away. When the emergency call came, he dressed quietly so as not to wake his two children, and hurried to the unit's headquarters. It was a little after 2 A.M. when he arrived at Chernobyl, some forty minutes after the explosion, to find that the plant looked like something out of a nightmare. Chaos reigned supreme. Technicians, limp and unconscious in the arms of firemen, were being carried out of the buildings. One of his colleagues came running out from beside the No. 4 reactor screaming like a madman. The tall chimneys of the reactor, lit up by the flames rising up from a corner of the shattered roof, loomed in an eerie glow. Davibienko stayed at the scene for approximately three hours.

For two days afterward he wore protective clothing and traveled to and from the site, until he came down with a mild case of diarrhea and was taken to a hospital in Moscow. According to Davibienko himself, his problems were not serious. "The diarrhea stopped pretty soon. We were taught about radiation sickness in training, but I didn't have any other symptoms. Lots of my workmates lost hair, but I didn't even have that problem."

His words did not quite ring true to us, though, and he sounded as if he was trying to reassure himself, more than anybody else.

The half-yearly checkups began six months after the accident, in the autumn of 1986. While in hospital for his third checkup, Davibienko discovered for the first time that he had been exposed to a radiation level of 100 rems. According to the Soviet system of using four levels to describe the gravity of radiation sickness, this dosage is classed in the lowest ranking, i.e. Level 1, which indicates a dosage of from 80 to 210 rems of radiation.

No doubt the immediate effects on Davibienko's body were not serious. In three years he has experienced no problems with his health. He goes to a clinic every three or four weeks, but the doctors assure him that there is nothing to worry about. He still cannot get the scenes of the accident and the hospital in Moscow out of his head, however.

"On May 10, while I was in hospital, my best friend, Nikolai Tichenok, died. Although he was a year younger than me—he was just twenty-three—we could talk about anything." Davibienko was just starting to recover from the shock of his friend's death when, one after the other, his other colleagues began to fall victim to radiation. In one week alone, six died, all of them men in their twenties like himself.

Some time has passed since then, enough for him to begin to breathe a little easier. However, each time he goes back for a checkup, the specter of that hellish night comes back to haunt him.

He fired anxious questions at us.

"What's it like in Hiroshima? Is the soil radioactive? Is there a lot of cancer? Has it affected the children?"

It was clear that Davibienko was frustrated with the platitudes of the doctors. When he goes home, his wife asks him the same questions that he asks the doctors. Then it is his turn to be reassuring, he told us, while deep down he is still afraid of what that 100 rems might be doing to his body.

VISITING THE SITE OF THE ACCIDENT

As we drew closer to the plant at Chernobyl, the needle on the radiation detector recorded increasingly larger amounts of radioactivity. Even though we had anticipated this, it was difficult to remain calm. At Kiev, about eighty miles from the site of the accident, the instrument had registered 0.01 to 0.02 milliroentgens. When we reached the eighteen-mile checkpoint, the reading was 0.06 to 0.08 milliroentgens and at the six-mile checkpoint, 0.20 to 0.25. Inside the control rooms for reactors No. 1 and 2, we recorded 1.00 to 1.50 and then, 210 yards from the site of the explosion, the needle jumped to 3.00 and 5.00 milliroentgens.

Radiation cannot be detected by any of our five senses. We can only be aware of its presence and potential danger through the use of special detection equipment. It is often said that radiation shows no mercy; medical experts agree that even relatively minor doses of radiation can have a harmful effect on the body.

However, the Soviet government took a different view. Although reactor No. 4 was destroyed, the government decided that if reactors Nos. 1, 2, and 3 could be cleared of contamination, they could be used again. By the end of 1986, eight months after the accident, reactor No. 4 had been sealed up and reactors Nos. 1, 2, and 3 had been brought back into operation.

Our guide in the control room for reactors Nos. 1 and 2, Mikhail Umanets, who took over the job of plant manager after the accident, assured us that the lessons of the tragedy had been learned. According to him, the control rods were now better positioned, there was now increased stability at low output levels, and the emergency shutdown facilities had been improved. All these changes concerned technical problems; we wondered if the same care had been taken regarding the health of employees exposed to radiation.

We were able to observe new safety measures in force at the city of Slavtiti, thirty miles to the east of Chernobyl. Slavtiti, which now has a population of twelve thousand, was built to replace Pripyat, the town abandoned after the accident. Its sole connection with the plant is by four railway lines, two each going to and from the site. There is no other method of commuting to the site, the idea being to provide a means of sealing off the new town in case of the threat of radioactive contamination.

The deputy mayor of Slavtiti, Sergei Bitulin, who was himself exposed to radiation at the time of the accident, explained the procedure that the workers must follow each day on their way to and from the plant.

Each morning on arrival at Slavtiti Station, the workers change into special clothing for commuting and board the train. When they are within eighteen miles of the site they stop at a midway station, change once again, and then get on a special train which runs only in the vicinity of the plant. At Chernobyl Station they change into yet another set of clothes and enter the grounds of the plant. Altogether the employees must make six changes of clothing going to and from the plant and they are checked for radiation at each stage.

The measures taken to protect employees are not confined to these changes of clothing. Staff work on a shift basis—two weeks on and then two weeks off. Government regulations have been introduced which in theory limit lifetime exposure to radiation to 35 rems. However, whether this is effective in practice or not is another matter.

The government has put three of the reactors back into operation even though it is aware of the possible adverse effects on the employees' health, and large sums of money have been spent on the cleanup operation and building of the new town. This would seem to indicate that there has been no change in the Soviet Union's atomic energy policy, yet at the end of 1988, and in April 1989, the Soviet government halted construction of a total of ten new reactors, including Chernobyl Nos. 5 and 6, which were already eighty-five percent complete. The government's insistence that there has been no change in atomic energy policy would appear then to be far from the truth.

Chernobyl was under very tight security. After being checked for radiation, the security guard led us into the brightly lit control room, keeping a watchful eye on us all the while. We had asked the manager if we could meet someone who was working in the plant at the time of the accident, and Vladimir Tyugliv, foreman at the No. 2 reactor, was sent to greet us. Umanets, the plant manager, appeared at his side and said, "Here's your man, ask him anything you like."

A man of solid build with penetrating eyes, Tyugliv is one of the longest-serving employees at the plant, having been there since 1975, two years before reactor No. 1 had reached critical temperature and gone into operation. He was a graduate of Gorki University, majoring in nuclear physics, and was every inch the technician in his manner. On his navy blue work clothes he wore a film badge to detect radiation, though he did not appear to be very concerned about any danger.

"There's no point in being frightened of radiation. We can't see or feel it, but we don't let that worry us—no way. It's our job to find the best ways to coexist with it."

The plant manager nodded in agreement.

When we brought up the subject of the disaster, however, the foreman evaded our questions, insisting instead that No. 4 was safely sealed in its concrete "coffin," and that Nos. 1 to 3 were in perfect working order.

When the explosion occurred, Tyugliv was at his home in Pripyat. He rushed to the plant and assisted in the attempts to cool down the No. 3 reactor, which backs onto No. 4. At dawn he returned home and, after resting for a short while, helped in the evacuation of the forty-five thousand residents of Pripyat. Returning the next day to the accident site, he investigated the damage to No. 4. Tyugliv remembers having a slight headache and feeling nauseous at the time. Later he was hospitalized and found to have been exposed to a radiation level of 490 rems—Level 3 in intensity on the government scale. The tone of his voice as he told us this gave no indication that he was worried about the huge dosage he had received.

Of the twenty-two workers diagnosed as having been exposed to a radiation dosage of Level 4 intensity (600 to 1,600 rems), only one is still alive. Of the twenty-three diagnosed as Level 3 cases like Tyugliv, seven have already died. One of these men was Anatoli Citinikov, who was forty-five years old at the time. He had worked alongside Tyugliv for many years.

"He was a marvelous technician," commented Tyugliv. "Unfortunately he was inclined to be sickly . . . I was in a terrible way myself, what with losing all my hair. But in August it started to grow back, and by autumn it was back to normal.

"Can you believe that there wasn't a strand on my head after the accident?" he said, running sturdy fingers through his chestnut-colored hair to show how thick it was.

Tyugliv seemed very calm and spoke without any great emotion. The manager, who was standing beside him, seemed satisfied with what he was saying.

"At the time of the accident, there were four thousand people working at Chernobyl. Of these, eleven hundred have returned here to work, including ten who were hospitalized. Tyugliv here was one of those—he's indispensable for the operation of the plant." According to Umanets, Tyugliv came to him six months after the accident and asked if he could start work again. Leaving his wife and son in Kiev, he rented a house twenty-five miles away and returned to his post. In December 1986, two months after Tyugliv started back at the plant, reactor No. 3, which backed onto the concrete-encased No. 4, was brought back into operation.

Umanets proceeded to give us a long and detailed explanation of the plant's operations after the accident. He himself was brought in to replace Bulkhanov, the manager at the time of the accident. Bulkhanov was dismissed from his post and sentenced to ten years' loss of freedom.

Following this rather frustrating session in the manager's office, we met with Mr. Ilyin, vice president of the Soviet Academy of Medical Sciences in Moscow. In our discussions he stated quite clearly that under the laws enacted since the accident, a person exposed to more than the lifetime limit of 35 rems of radiation was forbidden to work at a nuclear power plant. If this was the case, then Tyugliv's presence at Chernobyl was clearly illegal. The glaring differences between government regulations and what is really happening in the areas concerned could not have been made more blatantly obvious and illustrate well the general state of affairs in the Soviet Union three years after the accident at Chernobyl.

RADIOPHOBIA

Among the Soviet people, it is said with more than a touch of irony that there are two "truths" about the events at Chernobyl. One is the "scientific data" released by the government. The other consists of the rumors that circulate among the people by word of mouth. The scientific data is a form of deception which seems credible enough to be true, while the rumors are stories which seem too incredible to be true.

The rumors seem to have quietened down compared with the period just after the accident. However, whenever the authorities release more scientific data, they begin to circulate anew. It is hardly surprising that this should be the case. The Soviet people had been led to believe by their government that there was "nothing safer than nuclear power," but any faith they had in these assurances was destroyed the moment that Chernobyl's reactor No. 4 exploded in 1986. Not only those directly exposed to the radiation, but the Soviet people in general have been infected with a mistrust of nuclear power ever since. Since the accident, each official announcement has brought with it a new wave of speculation about the facts.

To describe this state of mind whereby a person becomes paranoid about radiation and its effects, the Soviet media often uses the word *radiophobia*. It expresses the feelings of the Soviet public, who are torn between the truth as told to them by the government, and the rumors they hear through unofficial channels.

We experienced this radiophobia firsthand while visiting Logena collective farm in the Gomel region of Belorussiya. There we spoke to Aleksandr Obrichenko, a truck driver who had moved to the farm from his home village of Dabradi, about ten miles from Chernobyl. On hearing where we were from, he bombarded us with questions about Hiroshima. The focus of Obrichenko's worry was his children, aged nine and four.

For twelve days after the accident no information was given out regarding contamination. On May 8, the family was evacuated to the village of Galloutiti. When it became known that this village was also contaminated, they moved to Logena Farm five months later.

Since that time he has had medical checkups twice a year, which include blood tests and a throat examination. The doctors consistently give him a clean bill of health, but he is still worried about his throat because he once heard that a swollen throat can turn cancerous. He asked us if this was true. A doctor who had joined our discussions with the group of evacuees began to explain to them about iodine-131 and its effects on the thyroid gland, but he was soon shouted down by the others who insisted that they were more interested in hearing about Hiroshima.

It is hardly surprising that the residents of Logena Farm had little time for the doctor's words. Figures released for the first time by the Soviet meteorological service just before the third anniversary of Chernobyl show that a far wider area of land than previously acknowledged had been subject to high levels of radioactive contamination. The affected area extended well over the eighteen-mile-radius evacuation zone. This put the farm, which for most of the residents was their second refuge, within the danger zone. One of the evacuees, Maria Petrenko, expressed the feelings of the group in her outburst of frustration condemning the authorities.

"What are we supposed to do? I have a weak heart, my husband coughs constantly. If this place is contaminated too, we might as well have stayed where we were to get cancer!"

The director of health for Gomel, Anton Aromanovsky, who had been showing us around, stayed silent. He had no answer for her.

Around the time that this new information was released the Soviet government announced a further series of evacuations covering a total of twenty-five villages in the Ukraine and in Belorussiya. Aromanovsky was given the thankless task of evacuating eight of these villages—with a total population of two thousand. He not only had the evacuation to contend with, but also the ominous spread of radiophobia beyond these eight villages to the rest of the area under his jurisdiction. It is difficult to see how this new disease born out of the Chernobyl disaster can ever be cured when nothing is done to allay fears and prevent the virus of suspicion from flourishing among the Soviet public.

REPORTING ABOUT CHERNOBYL

After our hurried trip to the northern Ukraine and the south of Belorussiya, we returned to Kiev to meet Vladimir Kolinko of the Ukraine office of the Novosti News Agency. He was introduced to us by our young Russian interpreter as the first journalist to go into Chernobyl after the accident.

Kolinko first heard about the accident on April 28—two days after it had occurred—via a Reuters dispatch from Stockholm which stated that there had been an accident at a nuclear power station in the Soviet Union. He had trouble getting permission to enter the affected area, so by the time he was able to make it to the scene, it was April 29. When his report finally made it onto the newsstands on May 4, eight days had passed since the explosion.

Using the nearby village of Kopati as a base, Kolinko spent two days covering the efforts of scientists and soldiers to seal in the radiation, and watching the rapid transformation of the city of Pripyat into a ghost town. During the course of his investigations, he himself was exposed to a radiation level of 100 rems, but fortunately he did not suffer from radiation sickness.

The day we visited Kolinko in his Kiev office, he had just completed an intensive four-week medical checkup. Although he was ashamed to admit it, he confessed to us that he had known virtually nothing about nuclear power or the effects of radiation until he did the articles on Chernobyl.

Of course, he was not the only journalist exposed to high doses of radiation. Journalists and cameramen from newspapers, news agencies, and television stations all exposed themselves to danger. There was Igor Kostin, a photographer and colleague of Kolinko's, who won a number of international awards for his photos of Chernobyl. And Leonid Muduk of Ukraine Television, who wrote the scripts for a series of four documentaries about the disaster. All of them had believed, as did the general public, that nuclear power was safe, and all had spent some part of their working lives helping to reassure others that it was. However, while they were writing articles on the victims of radiation, the sealing of reactor No. 4 in its concrete coffin, and all the other aspects of the disaster, they were able to experience firsthand the destructive power of radiation.

Since they themselves had also been exposed to radiation, they could not help but change their views. Their accurate reporting of the Chernobyl disaster was made possible in part as a result of Mikhail Gorbachev's policy of *glasnost*.

Since the accident, journalists in Kiev have continued to keep a close watch on Chernobyl and have followed up their reports with investigations into the health of the residents in the contaminated areas and the safety of their food and water supplies.

An article by Kolinko, published in February 1989, reported an increase in the number of cancer patients as well as deformities in livestock born since Chernobyl. His methods, however, were branded unscientific by Moscow's medical community and he was criticized by the party newspaper, *Pravda*, for lacking in objectivity.

Kolinko has refused to give up the fight to expose the dangers of radiation. "Both the academics in Moscow and the reporters at *Pravda* are attacking me without even seeing for themselves the situation at Chernobyl. All I did was talk to the doctors and vets who are facing these facts every day. When I told them what I'd heard, they responded by questioning the competence of those doctors. It would seem that it's not me that's being unscientific, but my critics."

The material for the article in question was gathered in the Narodichi district of the Zhitomir region, between thirty and fifty-five miles from the accident site. Kolinko had been shocked to find animals with severe birth defects, such as pigs born without eyes. The article was written to draw attention to these occurrences, with the aim of prompting an investigation which would determine whether the defects were caused by radiation. In actual fact, soon after the article was published the government did carry out a hurried survey of the residents' health, as well as checks on soil and foodstuffs. The investigations resulted in an immediate evacuation order. There is no doubt that if Kolinko had not written the article, the residents would still be living in the same district, the unwitting victims of radioactive contamination.

"Academics and bureaucrats are far too optimistic about the effects of radiation. Unless we can get them to consider the people's health more, things are only going to get worse," he said, a note of impatience clearly discernible in his voice.

THE CONTAMINATION OF FOODSTUFFS

The gravest cause of concern for health authorities in the Ukraine and Belorussiya is the absorption of large amounts of iodine-131 and cesium-137 into the body. Although iodine-131 has a short half-life of eight days, it accumulates in the thyroid gland, generating hypothyroidism and causing cancer. It is particularly dangerous for children. Cesium-137 has a half-life of thirty years and, when absorbed into the muscles, can cause cancer. Both iodine-131 and cesium-137 may be readily absorbed into the body through the small intestine from contaminated food. The radiation released into the atmosphere may gradually decrease over time, but absorbed by plants from the soil and water, then by animals and finally humans, radiation leaves its legacy in the food chain, and thus in the bodies of human beings.

In Kiev we decided to visit a marketplace to see if the accident at Chernobyl had had any effect on the supply of foodstuffs.

Zuitoni market is one of the many which supply the kitchens of this city of 2.4 million. When we arrived there was a line of shoppers spilling out onto the pavement. Making our way through the crowd, we walked round to the back entrance and entered a room marked "Testing Room," to find a woman in a laboratory coat absorbed in testing food samples. This was Rjabov Kulbrik, head of hygiene inspection at Zuitoni market. Pointing to the vegetables and dairy products on the table, she told us that all foodstuffs had to be checked and then stamped with an "edible" mark before they could be sold at the market.

Before the accident at Chernobyl, her main tasks were to check the processing dates on dairy products, to ascertain the purity of honey, and to screen out any poisonous mushrooms. However, since the radioactive plumes emitted from Chernobyl had passed over the grain-growing area of the Ukraine, the nature of the work done by the testing section has changed completely. On top of the shiny new table was a small lead box approximately eight inches square. This box, used for measuring radiation, has become an indispensable piece of equipment.

Since the accident at Chernobyl, it has become compulsory to test samples of all vegetables, mushrooms, fruit, meat, eggs, and dairy products. In the first year after the accident, radiation levels above those acceptable were often found, and a large quantity of foodstuffs had to be destroyed. Recently, in many areas, testing is being carried out at the point of production in order to defray the cost of transportation, so the amount of unsuitable produce appearing at the market has decreased. This has meant that city-dwellers are doubly certain of being protected from harmful substances. We wondered if the same could be said for the producers themselves.

After the accident at Chernobyl, the government bought up foodstuffs produced in the affected areas and gave out an allowance of one ruble per day per person. At first glance, this would seem a satisfactory method of preventing the consumption of contaminated produce. In reality, however, the villagers knew that this policy would not solve the problem completely, because of the overall shortage of "safe" produce. For this reason the health authorities in Kiev acknowledge the possibility of radiation accumulating in the bodies of those living in rural areas. Of particular concern is the produce grown on private plots by villagers for their own consumption. Gregorii Ahalamienko, deputy head of the Belorussiyan Health Department, admitted that the problem was a difficult one to solve.

"Private plots are not under the same supervision as *sovkhozy* (state farms) and *kolkhozy* (collective farms), so all we can do is warn people."

In an article on Belorussiya, "The Continuing Aftereffects of Chernobyl," published by the Tokyo office of the Novosti Press Agency in its APN Press News issue of April 28, 1989, mention was made that warnings about contamination had been pasted up on notice boards in several hundred villages. The article concluded with the following words:

"People soon become accustomed to warnings. As long as this is the case, the danger posed by radiation will not diminish."

LEARNING FROM HIROSHIMA AND NAGASAKI

While gathering material about Chernobyl and the surrounding areas affected by radioactive contamination, we were continually frustrated at the difficulty involved in obtaining a total picture of the damage. Our investigations showed that the scale of the damage was increasing year by year, and there was no indication that the situation would stabilize in the near future. We could not help thinking that part of the reason why it was such a daunting task to grasp the overall picture was that the Soviet government itself had little idea of the true extent of the damage done to the environment after the accident at Chernobyl.

Soviet doctors concerned with the effects of radiation from Chernobyl are using studies and surveys undertaken in Hiroshima and Nagasaki as reference materials in their own investigations. This was borne out in our meeting with Angelina Guskova, director of hematology at Moscow's Hospital No. 6 and the leading authority in the field of radiation sickness in the Soviet Union. Directly after the accident she had worked twenty-four hours a day overseeing the treatment of casualties. During our interview, she expressed a desire to study in Hiroshima and asked us if it would be possible. It was clear that she felt a visit to the place with the most experience in treating victims of radiation was extremely important for her research.

With the aim of providing a center for observing the condition of victims of radiation over a long period, the All-Union Scientific Center of Radiation Medicine was established in Kiev in October 1986, six months after the accident. The structure of the organization and its methods of data collection are modeled on those of the joint Japanese-American Radiation Effects Research Foundation (RERF), which has been conducting surveys in Hiroshima and Nagasaki for over forty years. The data obtained from follow-up surveys of victims of radiation in Hiroshima and Nagasaki constitutes the world's only real reference book dealing with the effects of radiation.

For example, a survey carried out by RERF covering a sample of 100,000 people who had been exposed to radiation, which took note of life span, cause of death, progression of illness, and genetic effects, was used as a model by the Kiev center. Like the RERF survey, the center's observations covered three main fields of medicine: clinical, epidemiological, and radiobiological. The survey covered 600,000 people including 209 patients suffering from acute radiation sickness, 116,000 evacuees from an area within an eighteen-mile radius of the plant, 230,000 residents from the contaminated area outside the eighteen-mile-zone, and 160,000 people who had worked at Chernobyl and/or were involved in the cleanup operation, as well as the children of those exposed to radiation. In addition, children born within the designated areas after the accident—as of 1989 there were 3,200 births—were also investigated. The Chernobyl research differs from that conducted in Hiroshima and

Nagasaki in the scale of the survey: 600,000 people were observed as opposed to 100,000 in Japan. Also, victims of the Chernobyl accident were not affected by heat or a bomb blast as occurred in Japan.

Most of the data concerning radiation-related illnesses, as well as international standards for safe levels of radiation, are based on studies done in Japan. There is no doubt that the information drawn from research in Hiroshima and Nagasaki, ranging from overall figures to detailed technical know-how, is of major interest to the Soviet Union, which is learning to deal with the consequences of the worst nuclear accident in history.

In March 1989, the deputy director of the Kiev center, Oleg Pyatak, visited Hiroshima. Close ties were further established when the chairman of RERF, Shigematsu Itsuzo, and the director of the Hiroshima University Research Institute for Nuclear Medicine and Biology, Kuramoto Atsushi, visited the Soviet Union at the invitation of the Soviet government.

Results obtained in Hiroshima and Nagasaki show that leukemia begins to appear three years after exposure to radiation, and thyroid dysfunction and lung cancer from between five and thirty years afterward.

While visiting the research institute at Hiroshima University, Pyatak, commenting on the surveys that have been carried out over the previous two and a half years, remarked, "At this stage we have had no cases of leukemia or cancer, and there appears to have been no ill effects on children aged fifteen and under. However, we expect that problems will start to appear in the near future."

Although it remains to be seen whether the Soviet data will produce the same results as those of Hiroshima, it is clear that the real problems are only just beginning for those who received high doses during and after the accident at Chernobyl. The Soviet medical community continues to use research done in Japan as reference, while the attention of the world's doctors is in turn focused on Chernobyl.

THE CONTINUING EFFECTS OF RADIOACTIVE CONTAMINATION

The April 1986 explosion at Chernobyl in the Soviet Union was the worst accident at a nuclear power plant in history. The name Chernobyl became synonymous with global contamination, throwing not only the Soviet Union and the countries of Europe but the whole world into a state of panic about the dangers of radiation.

In April 1990, four years after the disaster, the Soviet government announced its plan for a new series of evacuations involving between 180,000 and 200,000 people. This was, in effect, an admission of the government's failure to take adequate countermeasures to deal with the accident.

When we visited Belorussiya in March 1989 we reported that areas to which the evacuees had been moved after the accident were in fact themselves contaminated by high levels of radiation. In spite of this, it took over a year for the government to announce plans to evacuate these areas. During that time people were needlessly exposed to larger doses of radiation than they had been already.

Belorussiya is the area which has been worst affected by the Chernobyl disaster. In March 1990 an appeal for foreign aid for Belorussiya was announced at the headquarters of the IAEA (International Atomic Energy Agency) in Vienna. According to the same announcement, approximately twenty percent of Belorussiya's population, some 2.2 million people, are living within the contaminated area, and twenty percent of farmland in the state was contaminated after the accident. New areas of concentrated contamination known as hot spots are still being discovered, and in the worst-affected area 170,000 people including 37,000 children are receiving regular medical examinations and treatment. Of the total number of people living in contaminated areas, over 118,000 should be evacuated to unaffected areas immediately.

Directly after this appeal for aid, Oleg Zadero, professor of radiobiology at the University of Belorussiya, reported on conditions in Belorussiya to an academic conference in Poland:

"Belorussiya is in the midst of a 'nuclear plague.' People are living on contaminated land and eating contaminated crops—several thousands of people are still in danger."

This report demonstrates how the people of Belorussiya are suffering even more than residents of the Ukraine, where the Chernobyl disaster actually occurred, because measures were not taken to minimize the threat of contamination there until much later.

On the fourth anniversary of the Chernobyl accident, *Pravda* reported that six provinces in the Ukraine are contaminated, and that, apart from the 92,000 people evacuated from within the thirty-kilometer (nineteen miles) zone directly after the accident, 60,000 people are still living in restricted areas. In 1990 plans were made to evacuate only 14,000 of these. The number of people suffering from leukemia, thyroid conditions, and other radiation-related diseases is increasing rapidly in the contaminated areas. Of these patients approximately five hundred have been sent to Israel, Cuba, India, and the Netherlands as adequate treatment is unavailable in the Soviet Union. The helicopter pilot who flew over the accident site at Chernobyl was given a bone marrow transplant at a Seattle hospital on April 27, 1990, in an attempt to halt the progress of leukemia. He died on July 3 the same year. Due to the fragmented nature of information coming out of the Soviet Union, even four years after the disaster little is known about the present health of those exposed to radiation.

The Kiev center has registered 600,000 people and is carrying out medical examinations and treatment along the lines of similar programs in Hiroshima and Nagasaki, but the practical details of this operation and the results obtained have so far not been made public. Soviet scientists and physicians who travel overseas are only able to give information about their own hospitals or regions, and even then the accuracy of their data is often questionable.

From the experiences of Hiroshima and Nagasaki it was established that radiation-related illnesses such as cancer, leukemia, and thyroid conditions begin to appear in significant numbers from between three and five years after exposure. Chernobyl and the surrounding areas have now entered this phase, and a shortage of medical equipment combined with the growing mistrust of the government among the Soviet people is certain to make the situation even worse than it is now.

THE SPREAD OF NUCLEAR CONTAMINATION OVER SWEDEN

The fallout from Chernobyl not only caused widespread con-
tamination of the Soviet Union, but, carried by the wind, it
also affected vast areas of Europe. Across the Baltic Sea in Sweden,
radiation has brought destruction on a huge scale to the home of
the nomadic Lapps, who live by following the herds of reindeer
which roam the plains of Lappland, and has seriously affected
dairy-farming regions in the center of the country.

Previous page: A Lapp examines a reindeer contaminated with cesium after the accident at Chernobyl.

RADIATION: A THREAT TO A WAY OF LIFE

The aftereffects of being in the path of the fallout were still painfully in evidence when we visited Sweden three years after the Chernobyl disaster. We met Per Anders Blind and his wife Anna, resting from a long and arduous journey, at their summer home in the village of Klimpfjäll in the highlands near the Norwegian border. They had followed the reindeer herds for 125 miles across the plains of Swedish Lappland, which were just beginning to thaw after the winter.

"Of the eight hundred head or so of reindeer that we managed to process last year, only sixteen were approved for human consumption. All the others had to be either used for mink feed or disposed of completely." She shrugged resignedly. It was the middle of May; the village was still covered in a layer of sparkling snow, the lake frozen over. "It's hard to believe that somewhere as beautiful as this could be contaminated by radiation," she said.

Reindeer breed in fall and calves are born in May and June, during which time they are left on their own in the mountains. In July, the reindeer are tagged according to owner, and in August and September they are herded into one area and the required number are slaughtered and processed for meat. At the start of winter the remainder are herded into the forests on the plains. This pattern has not changed over the years; the Lapps have coexisted with nature for centuries. However, their native Lappland has now become contaminated by radioactive substances that fell with the rain two days after the accident at Chernobyl. The soil around Klimpfjäll, one of the worst-affected regions in Sweden, was contaminated with cesium-137 at a level of 60,000 to 80,000 becquerels per square meter.

In the year following the accident, a total of 95,000 reindeer were processed for meat. Of these, 75,000 were found to contain levels of cesium-137 far above the safe level, which was defined at the time as 300 becquerels per kilogram of meat. The government disposed of these carcasses and handed out compensation to the owners.

The Swedish government, finding itself faced with a crippling financial burden, decided to ease the restrictions on a number of food items such as wild strawberries, mushrooms, reindeer and moose meat, and freshwater fish. The safe level of cesium-137 was raised to 1,500 becquerels. However, since 1986, reindeer meat, and fish caught in lakes in Lappland continue to show levels of up to 50,000 becquerels, and moose meat consistently registers levels of 5,000 becquerels per kilogram. The half-life of cesium-137 is relatively long: thirty years. Consequently, the effects on the animals of grazing on contaminated grass and moss may be expected to continue for some time yet.

The Blinds seem resigned to living with the effects of radiation: "Even if we're affected by contamination for the next ten or twenty years, it is too late to change our life-style," Per Anders told us. While the Blinds had decided that they would try and maintain the nomadic life-style they had followed all their lives, the younger generation were aware that it would not be so easy.

"We'd all have nervous breakdowns if we did nothing but think about the radiation all the time," said Åsa Baer, whom we met at the Blinds' house. Åsa and the Blinds' eldest son, Per Bjorn, were living close to the Blinds and carrying on the traditional Lapp life-style of herding reindeer. "Two years ago," she continued, "I had a test for cesium, and they found I had a level of ten thousand. But I haven't bothered since then."

Åsa told us that they are trying to forget about the contamination. However, when the killing season of August and September comes around, they cannot help but be reminded of it; in 1988 they again had to dispose of most of their reindeer meat because it did not meet the safe level, which by this time had been raised to 1,500 becquerels per kilogram. "We get compensation from the government for the contaminated meat, so there's no worry on that score," she continued, "but it seems such a waste to throw it out, it makes us wonder what we're bothering to work for."

Åsa is, however, adamant about her choice to lead the same life as her ancestors before her. "I'm not afraid of something that I can't detect with any of my senses. I love Lappland, it is the place where I was born and raised, and it's so beautiful, how could I leave it?"

Even though the number of young people who can speak the Lapp language is decreasing year by year, Åsa and Per Bjorn, as well as his brother Yon-Olov, are as fluent in Lapp as they are in Swedish, and they also have a good command of English. Thanks to modern technology, the Lapps are able to keep up with the news in the outside world, and they are well aware of the destruction of the earth's environment.

Life is much easier for Lapp youth than when their parents herded reindeer over one hundred miles with only skis and their legs to carry them—nowadays Japanese snowmobiles and motorbikes are used. Even so, the number of young Lapps making a living by herding reindeer is gradually decreasing, and the accident at Chernobyl has accelerated this trend. Summing up the feelings of the Lapps of his generation, Yon-Olov said, "When you realize that the cesium contamination is going to continue for the next twenty or thirty years, you can understand why young people find it difficult to commit themselves wholeheartedly to the traditional way of life. Plus there's no guarantee that the same type of accident won't occur again." The Chernobyl disaster has made Lapp youth uncertain about the future of the traditional life-style in a way that would have been unthinkable five years ago. If their way of life is destroyed, the consequences for Lapp culture will be disastrous. The young people hold the key to the future, but at the moment they are wary about committing themselves to the Lapp life-style.

Baer's concern about the future of Lapp tradition is combined with uncertainty about the effects on her health of the radiation which has built up in her body. Both she and Per Bjorn would like children, but the thought of the possible effects of exposure to a high dose of radiation is always at the back of their minds.

TRADITIONAL LAPP FOODSTUFFS CONTAMINATED

Curious to find out more about the effects of radioactive contamination in the area, we left the Blinds' and traveled to the next village, Saxnas. "Have a taste of this," said Gustav Fjællstrom, offering us some smoked reindeer meat. Fjællstrom, a geography teacher at the local high school, had learned the technique of smoking reindeer meat from his father, and he was obviously proud of his skill at preparing this traditional Lapp food.

The meat had a delicate flavor, which became more apparent the more we chewed. Fjællstrom noted our appreciation and nodded. "However," he said, his expression becoming more serious, "there's something I should tell you about this meat."

"When I had it checked at the laboratory, they told me that it contained a cesium level of 5,000 becquerels. I was cautioned not to eat more than one hundred grams (4 oz.) per month. I still find this hard to believe, so I was wondering if you could take some back to Hiroshima and test it for me?" The Lapps' main source of protein is reindeer meat, and adults eat up to five hundred grams (18 oz.) per day. This adds up to 180 kilograms per year, or four head of reindeer. Setting a limit of one hundred grams per month is virtually the same as telling the Lapps not to eat their meat at all.

Since the Chernobyl disaster, Lapps living in the worst-affected areas have had no choice but to buy meat from the relatively unaffected northern part of Lappland. There are still those who take the risk of eating their own reindeer meat, however. Nearly as important as reindeer meat in the Lapp diet is freshwater fish, such as trout and char, but the lakes from which these fish are caught have also become contaminated with cesium.

The only way to avoid accumulating cesium in the body is to avoid all contaminated foodstuffs. But for the largely self-sufficient Lapps, this is not a realistic alternative. It is ironic that these people, who live in a land devoid of exhaust fumes and agricultural chemicals and who have enjoyed for generations the bounty of nature in the form of fish and reindeer, now show the highest levels of radiation in the whole of Sweden. At Umeå University on the edge of Lappland, a group of thirty Lapps (eleven females and nineteen males) has been tested for cesium contamination every six months since the accident at Chernobyl. Professor Göran Wickman, who has been engaged in this work, discussed some of the results with us while showing us around the campus.

"The highest levels we have recorded so far have been 193,000 becquerels for males and 84,000 for females. The average reading for the beginning of this year was 26,000 for males and 11,000 for females."

These levels are 360 to 860 times higher than the average level recorded in Japan. "The figures may seem high, but we are not worried about health problems, as they are still below the internationally accepted level of exposure, which is 0.1 rem," he continued.

Not all the experts are so optimistic, though. Professor Lars Engstedt of the Karolinska Research Institute, which is known for its work on cancer, is one who disagrees.

"It cannot be said with absolute certainty that there are no effects at that level. There are still too many things we don't know about radiation and its internal effects."

We took the reindeer meat that Gustav Fjællstrom had given us back to Hiroshima and had it tested at the Department of Applied Nuclear Physics at Hiroshima University. As expected, the reading was 5,000 becquerels, thirteen times the legal limit of 370 becquerels imposed on imports into Japan. The result was no surprise to Fjællstrom, but he still sounded subdued when we passed on the results to him over the phone.

STRUGGLING FOR SURVIVAL

What will become of the traditional nomadic way of life of the Lapps, now that they are being so severely affected by cesium contamination? We visited the office of the Lapp Association of Sweden, in Umeå, and spoke to the secretary, a tall, striking man by the name of Bror Saitton, about the Lapps' future prospects. He showed us a map of the contaminated areas and explained the current situation. "We've been trying to do whatever we can to protect the traditional way of life of the Lapp people, but Chernobyl has thrown all our work into chaos," he told us.

The total number of Lapps, spread over the wide area known as Lapland, which encompasses parts of Sweden, Norway, Finland, and the Soviet Union, is estimated to be fifty-eight thousand. However, not all of these people are engaged in the traditional pursuits of fishing and herding reindeer. For example, in Sweden, of a total Lapp population of seventeen thousand, only eight hundred households or approximately twenty-five hundred people are leading a nomadic life. The Lapps who live the way their ancestors did are in fact a minority within a minority, as the majority leave Lappland and go to live in the cities. Saitton is emphatic that everything possible must be done to prevent the old ways from dying out. Since Chernobyl, Saitton and the other five staff have been working ceaselessly on the problems faced by that minority of eight hundred households.

First of all, they visited the Lapps and surveyed the damage done to them and their livestock by cesium contamination. The results of this survey were then used to negotiate for compensation from the government. Logically, the association ought to have applied to the Soviet government for compensation, but, according to Saitton, they could see no practical means of doing so, and so in the end the Lapps had no choice but to take their claims to their own government. Their demands for compensation covered not only the loss of income from reindeer meat, but also the cost of buying feed for the reindeer from safe areas to reduce the chances of contamination. Saitton knows, however, having spent ten years living the nomadic life-style himself, that this is in reality only a stopgap measure. As he explains:

"Lapps live a nomadic existence and so depend totally on the natural environment for sustenance. The grass and moss the reindeer graze on, the water; these are what matter the most. All of these have been affected by cesium contamination and they will continue to be for the next twenty or thirty years. This destruction of the environment could well lead to the destruction of Lapp culture."

When Saitton left his Lappland home to go and work as a public servant in the city, his father advised him never to lose sight of his Lapp background. These words were later to convince him to take on the task of helping his people. In the three years since the accident at Chernobyl, he has come to feel that things will never be the same for the Lapps. For Saitton, a major problem caused by the contamination is how to continue teaching the Lapp culture. Until recently there were seven boarding schools in Lappland specifically for Lapps. These schools have a history going back ninety years and include many of the items that form the basis of the Lapp culture, such as language, customs, and reindeer husbandry in their curricula. They are now facing the worst crisis since their establishment. One of the schools was forced to close in 1988 due to a falling roll; the six remaining schools have a total roll of 133 pupils, only half that of ten years ago.

"The rolls were gradually dropping before the accident at Chernobyl, but now many parents are so uncertain about the future of the traditional Lapp life-style that they are thinking twice about sending their children to Lapp schools. If only Chernobyl had never happened . . ." Saitton said with a sigh. The prospect of fighting against cesium-137 for the next twenty or thirty years has, naturally, very little appeal.

DAIRY FARMERS FIGHT CESIUM CONTAMINATION

The radioactive contamination of Sweden was not confined to Lappland. Rain containing a cesium concentration of 100,000 becquerels per square meter fell on the city of Gävle and the surrounding area, one hundred miles north of Stockholm. This level is actually higher than that recorded in Lappland, and in one area stretching sixty miles south from Gävle to the city of Uppsala, levels of between 30,000 and 60,000 becquerels were recorded. Directly after the accident at Chernobyl, the *Arbetarbladet*, the Gävle newspaper, reported almost every day on the damaging effects of the cesium with headlines like "100,000 liters of nuclear milk dumped daily" and "15,000 becquerels—the contamination of grass continues." Lars Erik Hillbom, who keeps eighty head of beef cattle on the outskirts of Gävle, recalled events immediately after the accident was announced.

"We were told to throw away all of our hay and manure, and not to sell any stock. It was terrible."

One elderly couple on a dairy farm just outside Uppsala was unfortunate enough to be living on the worst-affected piece of land in the area. Even in August 1986, four months after the accident, the milk their cows were producing still had a cesium level of over 300 becquerels per liter. With no improvement in sight in the near future, the couple sold out and gave up farming. The farm was bought by Sören Farmgren and his wife Ingela. They began to operate it again as a dairy farm in January 1987. It was an opportunity for them to farm independently, rather than as tenants as they had been until then.

"Naturally we were worried about the contamination. But we figured that eventually the problem would work itself out, so we decided to buy the place," Sören said in his unhurried manner. "The first year was really tough," he added.

Their first task was to obtain feed from low contamination areas, but even by doing this, they were unable to get the cesium level lower than 100 becquerels per liter.

In Sweden, annual per capita milk consumption is two hundred liters (approx. fifty-three gallons). Fearful of an increase in the amount of cesium absorbed into the body from drinking contaminated milk, the government directed farmers to get the cesium level of their milk down to 30 becquerels, a tenth of the highest level at which milk can legally be put on the market. The milk processors have managed to bring this down further, and consumers are now drinking milk which has a level of around 10 becquerels. This policy stands in stark contrast to that applied to the minority Lapps, for whom the regulations concerning levels of cesium in meat were relaxed considerably to ease the financial burden on the government.

Meanwhile, the Farmgrens were still left with the problem of how to reduce the 100-bequerel level. Sören plowed all his land, digging down to a depth of between twelve and twenty inches, burying the topsoil and exposing the uncontaminated soil underneath. He then added potassium to decrease the amount of cesium absorbed by the grass.

As a result of his efforts, the couple has succeeded in bringing the cesium concentration in their milk down to the acceptable level.

"I've been looking after the cows these two years, poor Sören has had his work cut out for him with the soil," Ingela remarked jovially. However, when we interviewed them their task was still not complete, as over half of the eighty-five–hectare farm had still to be turned over and treated with potassium. In 1989, the Farmgrens had thirty-eight dairy cows, including thirteen calves. Daily milk production was around four hundred liters, and they have plans to increase the number of stock. In order to do this, they must first bring the remainder of their land into production. It is a time-consuming and frustrating task, but one that is necessary to reduce the levels of cesium contamination.

SCIENTISTS BATTLE AGAINST RADIOACTIVE CONTAMINATION

Sweden's scientific community is also putting a great deal of energy into the fight against radioactive contamination. We joined one of the researchers as he went on a survey of pastures, one of many studies being carried out with the aim of bringing contaminated land back into production.

Klas Rösen, a researcher in the Department of Radioecology at the Swedish University of Agricultural Sciences, drove us out twenty-five miles east of Uppsala.

"Look over there!" he exclaimed, pointing to a field. "The length of the grass changes every five meters, according to the amount of potassium added to the soil."

Rösen started experimenting with potassium a year after the accident at Chernobyl. Cesium and potassium are similar in composition, but, as plants absorb potassium first, a large amount of potassium in the soil reduces the amount of cesium absorbed by the stock which graze on the grass.

The first results were encouraging, so the practice of mixing contaminated soil with potassium has become widespread. Naturally, one of the reasons for the technique's unusually rapid adoption on farms has been the government's desire to reduce the cesium concentration in humans to as low a level as possible.

As befitting a country which is situated on the doorstep of one of the nuclear superpowers, Sweden has, since 1950, had a system in place to monitor and give warning of radioactive contamination and has also carefully worked out what countermeasures should be taken in the event of a nuclear war. The monitoring system has successfully detected evidence of Soviet nuclear testing several times, and in 1986, its reliability was once again demonstrated: Sweden was the first foreign country to detect that there had been an accident at Chernobyl.

Sweden's decision to dismantle all nuclear power stations in the country by the year 2010 may be seen as the culmination of these policies. Based on a referendum conducted in 1980, the year after the accident at Three Mile Island, the Swedish government resolved to phase out all twelve reactors currently in operation within the next thirty years.

"The Chernobyl disaster confirmed the wisdom of this decision," Rösen said. "But," he added, "it also showed us that we hadn't taken enough precautions to prevent our country from becoming contaminated by radioactive fallout."

The cesium contamination caused by Chernobyl was between ten and forty times greater than that caused by the atmospheric testing carried out at the beginning of the 1960s by the United States and the Soviet Union. The effect on agricultural produce, livestock, and wild animals was, therefore, much greater than the Swedish government had ever bargained for.

"In short," Rösen said with a note of irritation in his voice, "we just don't have the technology to cope."

The Department of Radioecology, where Rösen works, hurriedly increased the number of staff from fifteen to thirty after the accident, and concentrated their energies on finding practical methods of combating the contamination. One result of their research has been the discovery that cesium in grass tends to concentrate near the roots; consequently, they have advised farmers not to cut their grass right down. The discovery of the potassium treatment was another of the department's successes.

Rösen, who is responsible for a major proportion of the research, is proud of the department's success in conducting research that has received worldwide recognition. However, he realizes that there is still a long way to go.

"Our research has been concentrated on the agricultural sector. We have been unable to do anything about the forests and lakes. And, in addition to the problem of cesium, we're faced with acid rain and the destruction of the ozone layer—problems for which we simply don't have any solutions."

UNTOLD NUCLEAR CONTAMINATION

*I*n the little-known history of Soviet atomic energy, there is an accident which predates Chernobyl by thirty years. Known as the Ural Nuclear Disaster, the accident took place in 1957 at a nuclear waste dump at the Kyshtym nuclear weapons manufacturing plant in the eastern Urals. The explosion only became known to the outside world in 1976, nineteen years after the event, when the dissident biologist Zhores Medvedev wrote an article about it for the British scientific journal New Scientist. It took another thirteen years before the accident was officially acknowledged by the Soviet authorities, in June 1989.

Previous page: Huge fissures in the earth caused by nuclear testing.

THE TRUTH ABOUT THE URAL NUCLEAR DISASTER

The accident known as the Ural Nuclear Disaster occurred on the evening of September 29, 1957, at the Kyshtym nuclear weapons facility in the city of Kasli, approximately sixty miles north of Chelyabinsk, one of the Soviet Union's numerous industrial centers. A tank containing waste material produced during the processing of plutonium for nuclear weapons exploded, and of the twenty million curies of highly radioactive material released, two million were discharged into the atmosphere.

When we spoke to Medvedev in London, where he is continuing his research, he informed us that he had known about the disaster since the late fifties, but at that time had only been able to obtain fragmented information. Since his arrival in Britain he had finally managed to put together the whole picture of what had happened at Kyshtym.

According to him, the accident occurred when there was a failure in the waste cooling system, causing highly radioactive liquid waste to heat up and eventually explode. The force of the explosion caused the yard-thick concrete cover to blow off the tank, which had a capacity of over one thousand cubic feet, leaving a crater thirty-five yards wide and five yards deep. The explosion was said to be equivalent to a blast using seventy tons of dynamite.

According to the Soviet account the radiation blown three-quarters of a mile into the air was carried off by a southwesterly wind, and radioactivity continued to fall for almost half a day. Contamination by strontium-90 amounted to 0.1 curie per square kilometer and was spread over fifteen thousand square kilometers, an area home to 270,000 people. The worst-affected region was a strip almost a kilometer wide and 105 kilometers (66 miles) in length for which the reading was over 2 curies per square kilometer. The 10,700 residents of thirteen villages living in this area were evacuated, starting with those in the three villages nearest the site. Within ten days, approximately one thousand people had left their homes. The radiation levels within their bodies averaged between 50 and 52 rems, with the highest recorded being 72 rems.

The remaining residents were evacuated within a year. Of the first batch of evacuees, six hundred of those with the highest absorption levels were hospitalized for checkups. Tests showed that their white blood cell counts were down to sixty percent of the level immediately after the accident, and within eighteen months normal levels had been recovered. According to the Biophysics Research Section, which has conducted follow-up surveys on those exposed to the radiation for the past thirty-three years, there has been no increase in cancer, infant mortality, genetic defects, or any of the other problems generally associated with high doses of radiation. Signs have been put up in the 167-square-kilometer area worst affected by nuclear fallout advising against hunting, and the region is still strictly off limits to former residents. The area is still contaminated, and in some parts gamma rays of 50 microroentgens per hour have been detected, five times the level of natural background radiation.

The topsoil of farmland outside the restricted area was dug up and buried deep under the ground. As a result of this measure, farming has begun once again in some parts. According to the researchers, produce grown in this area complies with Soviet standards for safe levels of radioactivity.

The intelligence services of Britain and the United States knew about the Ural nuclear disaster not long after its occurrence. Medvedev claims in his book *Nuclear Disaster in the Urals* that the CIA was aware of the accident by 1958. The question is, why was the American public not informed?

Medvedev believes there were two reasons for withholding information of an accident involving radiation. Firstly, at around the same time as the Ural disaster, an accident occurred at the Enrico Fermi reactor near Detroit which had received extensive coverage from the media. Secondly, there was a fire in a plutonium pile at the Windscale (now known as Sellafield) nuclear complex in Britain. Consequently, the fear of exposure to radiation from nuclear power plants was already growing among the citizens of both powers, without being fanned by reports of disaster in the Urals. As Medvedev commented, "The publicizing of the Soviet accident could only do harm to the nuclear policies of the Western nations, so it was deliberately kept a secret from the people."

The year after the Ural disaster, in 1958, the premier at the time, Nikita Khrushchev, suddenly announced the suspension of all nuclear testing. Medvedev's view is that this move was motivated not by any antinuclear ideals on the part of Khrushchev, but rather by the accident, which had put an abrupt halt to weapons production at Kyshtym.

As the arms race gathered momentum, there was a corresponding escalation of tension between the United States and the Soviet Union. At that time the Kyshtym plant was known among the Soviet authorities by the code name "Chelyabinsk Forty," and it was the subject of increasing attention from the CIA. A well-known incident occurred in May 1960, three years after the accident, when an American U2 spy plane was shot down over Soviet territory. The plane had in fact been flying over Chelyabinsk.

According to Medvedev's account, the town of Kasli where the accident took place is still veiled in secrecy, and the river Techa, which flows through it, is still heavily polluted, making the water unsuitable for household use.

"The government has repeatedly stated that there were no damaging effects on the health of the residents, but a look at the reports submitted to the International Atomic Energy Agency shows that the rate of infant mortality is abnormally high, as is the incidence of leukemia in adults. Problems have also been observed in the health of prisoners and soldiers who helped in the cleanup operation."

Medvedev's view of the aftereffects of the accident is much more pessimistic than the official stance. For Medvedev the dangers of withholding information from the public are well illustrated by the long list of accidents. If the government had informed the public earlier of the accident in the Urals, instead of thirty-two years later, Medvedev believes the knowledge gained could probably have prevented the tragic accident at Chernobyl.

ADDITIONAL ACCIDENTS BROUGHT TO LIGHT

In August 1989, the Soviet government revealed that there had in fact been another accident involving nuclear waste at Kyshtym, previous to the Ural Nuclear Disaster of 1957. According to this disclosure, before the tank which exploded in 1957 was built, over 100 million curies of radioactive waste were released into nearby Lake Karachay. This amount of radioactive contamination is on a totally different scale than that of the Ural disaster (2 million curies) and Chernobyl disaster (50 million curies). The government has said it will take around 60 million rubles and a period of three to four years to clean up the contaminated lake.

There has been no word, however, on the health of local residents or the damage done to the environment, even though the local water supply is under threat.

In 1989, it was also announced that during the fifties the army had exploded an atomic bomb in the southern Urals, while practicing military maneuvers to be carried out in the event of a nuclear war. It was revealed also that the aftereffects of this explosion are still being felt by the soldiers who participated in the maneuvers.

According to an article in the Soviet Defense Department's paper *Red Star*, some tanks were hurled across the training ground by the blast on September 14, 1954, while others were melted by the intense heat. The *Red Star* stated that there were no casualties, but this was disputed by *Izvestia* in a later article. A former soldier testified that a number of soldiers had been killed or wounded, and that those who did survive were still suffering from the aftereffects of exposure to large doses of radiation.

Apart from tests carried out in Semipalatinsk, little is known about the damage caused by other nuclear tests in the Soviet Union. According to the *Moscow News*, atmospheric testing carried out in the Chukchi Autonomous Area in the far east of the Soviet Union during the fifties and sixties has brought cancer, shorter life spans, and a higher rate of infant mortality to the residents there.

The article, based on a report presented to the People's Congress, states that the minority Chukchi people were exposed to a level of radiation roughly equivalent to that experienced by the residents of the areas around Chernobyl. Moreover, among the section of the Chukchi which depend on reindeers for meat and milk, the level of cesium-137 contamination is one hundred times higher than that of the maritime Chukchi who live by hunting Arctic Sea mammals. As a result, deaths from cancer of the esophagus are higher than normal, the occurrence of cancer of the liver is ten times the national average, and the incidence of lung cancer and leukemia has doubled. Most of the inhabitants of the area have contracted tuberculosis due to a lowering of their immuno-responsive systems, and the average life expectancy is said to be a mere forty-five years.

The extent of the damage caused by the discharge of radioactive substances from nuclear bomb testing and the generation of nuclear power in the Soviet Union is only now slowly being revealed after long years of silence on the part of the authorities. The recent revelations are largely due to the Chernobyl disaster and efforts of the popular movement in Semipalatinsk to close down the testing area. However, the information received so far is only a fragment of the total picture; a large part of the story still remains a closely guarded secret.

The Soviet Union has carried out over six hundred nuclear tests in the past forty years, affecting most regions of the country. The government controls all the information concerning these tests, and the residents of the regions in which they were carried out have been given very little information regarding radiation and its possible effects. In the case of Chernobyl, the government's ability to cope with a disaster was found to be inadequate, and even now the effects of exposure to high doses of radiation are continuing to be felt. Vast resources have been allocated to the development of nuclear power, but there has been a conspicuous lack of research on radioactive contamination and possible methods of preventing destruction to the environment and loss of human life.

There seems no doubt that, as a more complete picture of the history of nuclear development in the Soviet Union comes to light, a great number of its people will begin to face growing uncertainty about the state of their health.

PART 3

THE SOUTH PACIFIC AND AUSTRALIA

THE NUCLEAR REFUGEES OF
THE MARSHALL ISLANDS

*O*ne year after the cities of Hiroshima and Nagasaki were destroyed by atomic bombs, the fourth nuclear explosion in history took place at Bikini, an atoll in the western chain of the Marshall Islands in the central Pacific Ocean.

In the thirteen years that followed, the United States carried out a total of sixty-six nuclear tests on the two atolls of Bikini and Eniwetok. It is just over thirty years since the last test was conducted, but on our visit to the neighboring islands, we found that the fallout from years of testing was still having a profound influence on the daily lives of the people there. Time, it appears, does not necessarily heal the wounds caused by nuclear testing.

Previous page: Refugees of the Marshall Islands still have no place they can call home.

ESCAPING THE 'POISON'

In May 1985, the three hundred inhabitants of the island of Rongelap, 120 miles east of Bikini, regretfully turned their backs on their island home and boarded a ship belonging to the international environmental organization Greenpeace. With them they carried all their worldly goods, from kitchen utensils to livestock. Their destination was the uninhabited island of Mejato, 120 miles to the south.

Their new home was a small island on the northern edge of Kwajalein Atoll, and the islanders had no illusions that it would be any kind of promised land. Despite this the people had had no choice but to leave their homes on Rongelap, if they were to escape once and for all from what they had come to know as "the poison."

This poison is more commonly called radioactive contamination. The history of the poison which eventually drove the Rongelap islanders from their home goes back thirty years to the mid-1950s. At dawn on March 1, 1954, America's first hydrogen bomb, "Bravo," was exploded at Bikini Atoll, the infamous test which caused the twenty-three crew members of the Japanese fishing boat *Daigo Fukuryu Maru* to be exposed to high doses of radiation. Radioactive fragments of coral and ashes, carried by the westerly wind, fell like snow east of Bikini, seriously contaminating the island of Rongelap.

The islanders were overcome by all the symptoms of acute radiation sickness: severe bouts of vomiting, inflammation of the skin, and hair loss. Taken off this island by the U.S. Navy, the islanders were forced to spend three years drifting from place to place living off food supplies from the United States. In 1957, they were informed that it was safe to go home, so they returned to Rongelap.

Nelson Anjain, who served as our interpreter during the visit, spoke to us about the islanders' return home:

"Nothing at all seemed to have changed in the three years we had been away. But when we tried to eat the coconuts and the roots of plants growing on the island, we all came down with diarrhea. We soon realized that this wasn't the same place that we had left."

About ten years after their return, illnesses previously unknown on Rongelap, such as cancer of the thyroid and leukemia, began to afflict the islanders. Medical teams came from the United States once every two years and took those in need of treatment back to hospitals in Hawaii and on the mainland. Every year, with chilling regularity, someone would die of one of these illnesses. Many of those who fell ill were children. People began to blame the poison, and wanted to flee the island.

"I felt that I was really too old to move," a former Rongelap resident told us. "But when I thought of what the poison might do to my children and grandchildren, I knew we had no choice but to leave."

We traveled by motorboat for ten hours to the island of Mejato to speak with the Rongelap islanders. Ajji Kun, a father of three, told us wistfully that, in comparison to their old home, the island was not blessed with coconuts or breadfruit in great quantities, nor was the fishing very good.

The islanders were in a state of chronic undernourishment, having to rely mainly on erratic food aid from the United States. They had been living this way for four years, barely managing to keep their heads above water, when they began to realize that their lives were once again in danger. Even though they had escaped from the fallout of Rongelap, they could not escape from the radioactive substances that had been absorbed into their bodies.

CHILDREN SUFFERING FROM PREVIOUSLY UNKNOWN DISEASES

Profoundly disturbing—the photographs we were shown could not be described in any other way. The child in the picture had some features that were recognizable as eyes, nose, and a mouth. But its arms, legs, and torso were completely undeveloped.

Willy Mwekto of the Rongelap Liaison Office in Majuro, the seat of the U.S. government in the Marshall Islands, showed us this photo of a stillborn child when we visited him. It was dated January 9, 1989. The baby's parents, who had been brought up on Rongelap, had fled their home along with the other islanders four years previously.

Mwekto's hand shook with anger as he held up the photo. "Does this look like a human baby to you?" he demanded. "Can you think of anything else that could have done this but radioactive fallout?"

We returned to the Rongelap islanders' new home on the island of Mejato. There we visited one of the simple tin-roofed huts of the villagers, where eleven-year-old Kimo Jorju lay bedridden in a dimly lit room about five yards square. He was unable to talk or stand. Staring beyond us, he groaned with pain every now and then. Kimo's grandmother, Tanira, was looking after him as his parents had been in hospital in Hawaii for quite some time.

"This poor little boy," she said, "he's been like this since just before his first birthday. The poison got his grandfather as well, you know. That's the only thing it can be—we've never had so many people sick in our family before."

The former Rongelap islanders are given medical examinations twice a year by doctors from the Brookhaven National Laboratory in New York, who are sent out by the Department of Energy. Kimo, who lived on Rongelap until he was seven, is one of those who receives a checkup. Tanira always makes a point of asking the doctors if they think her grandson's illness was caused by the poison, but invariably her questions remain unanswered.

The islanders know two things for certain: ever since radioactive material rained down on them in March 1954, they have fallen victim to a host of previously unknown diseases; and secondly, the majority of casualties have been small children.

The Brookhaven National Laboratory published a report in 1981 which recognized the statistical relationship between the radiation and the incidence of diseases in children. It noted that of the twenty-two islanders who were children under the age of ten at the time of the Bravo test, seventeen have thyroid conditions.

The radioactive material iodine-131, which was released into the atmosphere at the time of the test and which later fell on the island, was absorbed into the thyroid glands of the children, where it destroyed the ability of that gland to excrete the growth hormone. Not only were children affected, but also 9.1 percent of adults have been found to be suffering from thyroid problems. The relationship between the high incidence of thyroid conditions and exposure to huge doses of radiation cannot be denied.

There is no doctor on Mejato—just one man with nursing qualifications, the minister, John Pearson. He informed us that miscarriages, stillbirths, and babies born with deformities became common occurrences among the Rongelap islanders after the tests. According to

Pearson, fourteen islanders had died since moving to Mejato four years previously, and of these, seven were children under ten.

"No doubt malnourishment plays a part as well, but the effect of exposure to large doses of radiation cannot be ignored."

The village headman of Rongelap at the time of the 1954 hydrogen bomb test was John Anjain, who is now aged sixty-seven. At present he is living on Ebeye, in the Kwajalein Atoll group. When we visited him at his home there, he showed us an old, tattered notebook.

Anjain began his record, *Rongelap Exposed*, in 1963, nine years after the test, when thyroid problems first began to appear among the islanders. This is the only such record kept by anyone exposed to the radiation.

The notebook contained a list of eighty-six names: the sixty-three people living on Rongelap, nineteen living on the nearby atoll of Ailinginae at the time of the test, and four babies born after the tests. In the margin were two types of mark: black stars and white stars. The black stars indicated that the person had already died and the white stars that they had had a thyroid operation. Altogether there were twenty-six black stars and thirty-six white stars. Only twenty-four of the eighty-six had no mark by their names. In other words, sixty-two of the islanders had died or had suffered lasting effects from exposure to radiation.

Among the names with a black star was Lekoj Anjain, the headman's son who died in 1972 of leukemia at the age of nineteen. In a broken voice Anjain recalled his son toddling around as a little boy, chuckling gleefully while the ashes fell.

Anjain told us of the tragic case of one woman for whom an operation had come too late. Her swollen throat burst and she vomited blood and a bluish substance before dying in great pain.

Year after year, he has kept this heartbreaking record of the deaths of his people. Of the thirty-six who have had operations on their thyroid glands, at least five were found to have cancer. Operations alone, however, cannot save the people from the legacy of radioactive fallout.

Believing the assurances of the U.S. government, the islanders returned home three years after the testing. When Anjain began to keep his record in 1963, American medical teams still insisted that there was nothing to worry about, despite the appearance of previously unknown diseases among the islanders.

"The Americans knew exactly what was going on. We were the ones who didn't realize that we were being used as part of a human experiment—we were nothing but guinea pigs," said Anjain. Ebeye, where he lives, is a small island one mile long and a little over two hundred yards wide. Nine thousand people are crammed onto this tiny area of land. From Ebeye can be seen the main island of Kwajalein, which, with its radar dishes and antennae, is an important site of U.S. nuclear warfare operations. It is used as a landing site for missiles fired from the mainland United States and is an integral part of the SDI (Strategic Defense Initiative) program. The basis of Ebeye's economy has become the $9 million rent paid each year by the American government, and the employment provided by the base. Even if the residents do not like the idea of having missiles exploding on their doorstep, their fortunes are too tied to those of the base to complain about it.

When we visited Anjain, he and a number of other islanders were preparing to go to the United States to plead for food supplies to be sent to the Rongelap islanders now living on Mejato. They planned to hold talks at the United Nations in New York as well as in Congress. It would be their seventeenth journey to the country whose policies had caused them so much pain.

However, not one word of anger, resentment, or frustration was included in the draft of their request for aid.

"We can only do the same as we always have," said Anjain, holding the yellowing notebook in his hand. "Just try as hard as we can, and pray for the best."

LOW DOSES OF RADIATION ALSO POSE THREAT

The devastation caused by radioactive fallout was not confined to Rongelap. We witnessed proof of this when we visited Majuro, an island in the Marshall group southeast of Bikini.

Risen Mikel had just returned from the United States when we interviewed him. He had been there for his second operation to have a tumor removed from his thyroid gland. The base of his throat was marked by a painful-looking crescent-shaped scar.

Utirik Island, where he was born and raised, lies 325 miles to the east of the Bikini test site. He was eighteen years old at the time of the

Bravo test. "I heard that Rongelap was covered in one or two inches of ashes after the test. On my island it was more like mist than snow," he said.

According to the findings of the Atomic Energy Commission (AEC), forerunner to the Department of Energy, the average radiation dosage of the Utirik islanders was 14 rads. This figure was not even a tenth of that of the Rongelap islanders, so the AEC came to the conclusion that the environment and the health of the islanders would not be affected by the explosion. On the basis of this data, 157 former residents of Utirik, including Mikel, were permitted to return home barely three months after the test. Despite reassurances from the U.S. government that the island was safe, the effects of the ashes began slowly but surely to make themselves felt. Whereas the Rongelap islanders had begun to feel the effects of the testing during the 1960s, it was not until ten years later that the residents of Utirik began to comprehend fully the consequences of that day in 1954 when their island had been bathed in a mist of ashes.

The medical survey teams which visit Utirik once every two years had always assured the islanders that there was nothing for them to worry about. Hearing this the people were relieved that they had escaped any ill effects of the test. This state of affairs continued until around 1970, when a lump appeared in Mikel's throat. After several examinations, the doctors acknowledged that the lump was in fact caused by exposure to radiation. In 1980 he went to the United States for his first operation.

Another of the Utirik islanders now living in Majuro, Carl Joel, aged seventy-three, counted the number of his fellow islanders who had been operated on for thyroid conditions.

"There are at least forty people," he said, "including, strangely enough, some who weren't even living on the island at the time of the tests." One of these is Mote Brian, who arrived in Utirik to take up his duties as a minister in August 1954, five months after the test. He spent nine years there before returning to Majuro. Brian also began to have problems with his throat in the early 1970s, resulting in the eventual removal of a tumor in 1980. Despite the relatively low radiation dosage of 14 rads, the people of Utirik have not escaped the effects of the 1954 test, nor have some of those whose exposure was only secondary. The case of the Utirik islanders seems to defy the conventional wisdom of the world of radiation medicine.

One of the most popular foods among the people of the Marshall Islands is the coconut crab. This large crustacean, which is so named because coconuts are its main source of food, has a curious habit; it eats the shell which it sheds every year. Unfortunately, its diet of coconuts and the habit of eating its own shell have caused an unusually large amount of radioactive substances to accumulate in its body.

The AEC was aware of the danger of eating this highly contaminated crab, so its consumption was banned on Rongelap. However, no such warning was given to the people of Utirik. As Brian remarked wistfully, "We used to catch and eat those crabs all the time. If only they had told us, we would never have touched the meat."

Mikel, Brian, and the others who have had throat operations all carry bottles of small pink pills. These are thyroid hormones prescribed by the doctor each time they go for a checkup, with the warning: "Every day you forget a pill takes a year off your life." Coping with the aftereffects of those 14 rads has become a lifelong struggle for the Utirik islanders.

THE FUTURE OF BIKINI

A recent issue of the weekly *Marshall Islands Journal* carried an article entitled "A Brief Glimpse of Their Homeland for the Women of Bikini." It detailed how sixty young women born after the war and presently living on the island of Kili had traveled to Bikini for a look at the homeland they have never known. The women wept as they took their first steps on the land of their forefathers, and later left with memories they would hold precious for the rest of their lives.

Bikini was commandeered by the U.S. government for its nuclear testing program in 1946; the inhabitants were forced off the island with no explanation apart from that they should move for the good of humanity. Almost fifty years have passed since their forced emigration to the isolated island of Kili, more than six hundred miles to the south, but the islanders, who now number over five hundred, have never given up hope of one day returning to their homeland.

In 1973 the growing number of demands to return to Bikini from the former islanders prompted the U.S. government to clean up the remaining contaminated areas. Palm trees were planted and houses built, and finally a small number of islanders were allowed to move back.

They discovered, however, that it takes more than replacement of the topsoil to combat the contamination accumulated after twenty-three nuclear explosions. Five years later, those islanders who had returned were found once again to have high levels of radioactive substances in their bodies, and they were sent back to their exile on Kili. The disappointment of these islanders, forced to give up long-cherished dreams of their home-land, and the tears of the young women upon viewing it for the first and possibly only time, are just two more episodes in the tragic history of the displaced people of Bikini Atoll.

The nuclear debate in the Marshall Islands has recently entered a new phase, due to a proposal supported by President Amata Kabua to build a nuclear waste dump. According to the plan, dangerous contaminated ma-terials would be shipped to an island in the northern part of the Rongelap Atoll from nations currently making use of nuclear power generation, such as Japan and the United States. Naturally enough, the former resi-dents of Rongelap, now residing on Mejato, are protesting vigorously against the plan, so for the time being it has been put on hold. When we visited the president in his prefab White House we could see that he was determined that the construction of the waste dump would go ahead in spite of the residents' protests.

President Kabua, the supreme authority in the Marshall Islands, ex-plained to us the reasoning behind his support for the radioactive waste dump. "The northern part of the Rongelap group is already contami-nated. If Japan and America build strong, fail-safe storage facilities, I can see no reason why the people can't return to the southern part of the atoll. The scientists have assured me that it is safe. Besides," he added in Japanese learned during the occupation, "the Marshalls need the money."

The facilities the president had in mind were no doubt similar to the concrete dome located on Runit Island in the northern part of the Eniwetok Atoll.

Eniwetok was used as a nuclear test site in the same way as Bikini; be-tween 1948 and 1958 a total of forty-three bomb tests were carried out. In 1977, in order to return the island to its former inhabitants, all the contaminated material was bulldozed into a large crater formed by the explosions, then covered with a concrete dome. With the encouragement of the U.S. government the exiled islanders have now returned to the southern part of Eniwetok. The northern part where the dome is located is strictly off limits. The apparent safety of this arrangement is what has given President Kabua the confidence to make similar plans for Rongelap.

"I've heard the word 'safe' used so many times before, and I refuse to accept the president's proposal." These were the indignant words of Edmil Edmond, one of those we interviewed on Mejato. Playing the devil's advocate, we suggested that perhaps the plan wasn't such a bad idea, considering that his homeland was already contaminated, and that the islanders could probably make some money out of the proposal.

He was ready with a reply: "If the concrete breaks or the dome is destroyed by a tidal wave, the effects sure as hell won't be confined to the Marshall Islands."

When we visited the exiled Rongelap islanders in their new home on Mejato, a DOE patrol boat, which was used to transport the medical team on its regular visit to Mejato, was anchored offshore. We went over for a closer look at the vessel.

Three containers on the deck had been converted into rooms for the examination of patients. In the urine analysis room, where the islanders would be checked for the presence of strontium, some boys were watching a video while waiting their turn. In another of the rooms, a middle-aged woman was having the level of radiation in her body measured by a cylindrical device positioned over her stomach.

When we took some photos over the head of the technician, the leader of the team, Dr. Casper Sun of the Brookhaven National Laboratory, called out to us: "We've never found any plutonium or cesium present in the islanders' systems, you know. The only thing that ever shows up is K-40 (potassium), and we all have that in our bodies." In short, the doctor wanted to reassure us that there was nothing to make a fuss about.

When we returned to the island and passed on his words to our interpreter, Nelson Anjain, he did not seem at all surprised.

"They always lie like that," he said, shaking his head. It is hardly surprising that the islanders do not trust the U.S. government. In 1987, they decided to get a second opinion, and called in Canadian and West German specialists to do an independent evaluation of the level of radioactivity on Rongelap. The resulting report, which was completed in April 1988, cast serious doubts on the U.S. assurances of safety.

Using the DOE data as a base, the report concluded that plutonium and americium, supposedly not present in the islanders' bodies, had in fact been detected in small quantities in the urine of some of those tested. Regarding the levels of radiation in the islanders, which the U.S. team had insisted were "safe," it was recommended that everything possible should be done to reduce the amount of radiation, and that any move to return to Rongelap should be given very careful consideration.

Not long before the release of this independent report, the doctors of the DOE medical team had told the residents of Mejato that the rate of thyroid dysfunction in the Marshalls has already passed its peak. This statement only served to further arouse the suspicion and anger of the islanders, who found it very difficult to take at face value.

During our investigations in the Marshall Islands, we were often asked about the fate of the twenty-three crew members of the *Daigo Fukuryu Maru*, the Japanese fishing boat caught in radioactive fallout only twenty miles from Rongelap during the Bravo test in 1954. We explained that eight of the crew had since passed away, including one killed in a car accident, and that the remainder were checked every year by doctors of the National Institute of Radiological Sciences, who so far said that they had found no abnormalities. At this, the islanders expressed the opinion that the men were lucky to be receiving what seemed to be proper medical advice. The quiet words of the islander Jabwe Jorju, whom we had met in the capital of Majuro, have stayed with us ever since:

"I heard that in Japan there are a lot of doctors who specialize in treating people affected by the poison. I don't suppose it would be possible to have an examination there, would it?"

Even now, more than thirty-five years after they were forced out of their homes, the victims of nuclear testing in the Marshall Islands are still not provided with medical care that they can trust. Jorju's words echoed the feelings of all the islanders, who despair of ever being told the truth.

CAUGHT IN THE FALLOUT—
DAIGO FUKURYU MARU

*T*he hydrogen bomb exploded by the United States at Bikini Atoll on March 1, 1954, unleashed a new wave of fear throughout the world. The twenty-three crew members of the Japanese tuna trawler Daigo Fukuryu Maru, *which was drifting downwind of the explosion, experienced this fear firsthand. Thirty-six years have passed since that day, during which time eight of the crew have died, while many of the survivors live with health problems that they claim were caused by exposure to radiation in 1954.*

Previous page: A survivor of the fallout at the *Daigo Fukuryu Maru* exhibition in Tokyo.

THE 'ASHES OF DEATH'

We spoke to Oishi Matashichi, one of the former crew members, at his home in Tokyo. Oishi had worked in the freezing section of the *Fukuryu Maru*. He was able to relate the events of that day in 1954 to us as clearly as if it were yesterday. "A column of fire shot up into the air, and for a second the sky and sea were bathed in a yellowish glow. It was terrifying." It was 6:45 A.M. local time, one hundred miles east of Bikini, and the crew were engaged in the final trawling operation of their trip. "Seven or eight minutes after the flash of light there was a terrific roar that seemed to shake the sea bed, and the ship was tossed about like a toy," Oishi continued. "Misaki, who was in charge of the fishing side of operations, told us to take up the nets, so we worked frantically to bring in the longline."

The mushroom cloud stretched away above their heads to the east. The sea became rough, and about two hours later white ashes rained down on the vessel. The men could not open their eyes, and it was impossible to breathe outside. It was a six-hour struggle to bring in the net, and during that period all the crew members were exposed to the radioactive fallout. Soon after, they were overwhelmed with nausea, then diarrhea. Suffering from burns and hair loss, they continued their fifty-two–day voyage, limping into their home port on March 14.

The faces of the crew were burned almost black. A local doctor, after hearing their story, diagnosed their condition as acute radiation sickness. Two of the men, who had particularly severe burns, were sent straight to hospitals in Tokyo. The others, including Oishi, followed two weeks later on March 28.

The white blood cell count of the patients decreased day by day. Oishi remembers having diarrhea and a temperature until July. The doctors treated him every day with blood transfusions, vitamin injections, and antibiotics, and slowly his white blood cell count began to recover. No sooner had he begun to improve, however, when his liver failed and he started to show symptoms of jaundice.

In September of the same year, the Bikini test claimed its first victim among the crew, wireless operator Kuboyama Aikichi. He was forty years old. "All the crew were really worried when he died," said Oishi. "We all started to wonder whether we'd be the next to go." Fortunately, all the men were deemed fit enough to be discharged from hospital in May the following year.

Oishi is the eldest of six and had worked on trawlers since the age of thirteen when his father died in the final year of the Second World War. After the incident at Bikini, however, he never felt strong enough to return to fishing. "I stayed at home for a year, then came out to Tokyo and helped my brother with his dry-cleaning business. Of course, I couldn't impose on him forever, so I started off on my own." He now manages a dry-cleaning business with his wife, Nobuko.

"Believe me, I've had more than my fair share of bad luck since getting that dose of radiation. I seem to spend most of my time physically and mentally exhausted. And no matter how hard I try, I just can't forget that day." Sometimes when he has time he goes to see the *Fukuryu Maru*, which is on display at Yumenoshima in Tokyo, and talks to the mothers and children gathered there. His latest project is an autobiography. "I just wish my body could keep up with all the things I want to do," he told us with a laugh. But on one matter he is extremely serious: "As far as I'm concerned," he told us, "there is no justification whatsoever for nuclear weapons or nuclear testing."

"That experience has meant that I have had to take twice as much care of my health as anyone else. Naturally I'd rather not think about it, but I know I'll never be rid of the radiation." The deaths one by one of his fellow crew members over the last few years have convinced him of this. Not only that, but most of his former workmates died of liver complaints, many similar to the chronic hepatitis which plagued him for years. It is little wonder that Oishi still harbors fears about his own ability to escape the final effect of the huge dose of radiation.

ADDITIONAL FISHERMEN UNDER THREAT

The crew of the *Daigo Fukuryu Maru* were not the only fishermen to feel the effects of the hydrogen bomb test at Bikini—there were hundreds of other boats working in the Marshall Islands area at the time. A team led by Professor Yoshitomi Keiichiro of Kochi University has succeeded in uncovering evidence of radiation-linked illnesses among the crews of other boats. Of the 241 fishermen so far surveyed, sixty-one have already died, mainly of leukemia, cancer, or cirrhosis of the liver.

We visited one of the surviving fishermen at his home in Muroto, Kochi Prefecture. "I remember when we used to pull in tuna weighing over 370 kilograms," Yamashita Shoichi told us proudly, while fingering one of the longlines he had used in his younger days.

At the time of the Bikini test, Yamashita was a wireless operator on the *Daini Kosei Maru*, which was owned by his father. They left the port of Uraga in Kanagawa Prefecture a month after the *Fukuryu Maru*, on February 24, and headed for a stretch of water 560 miles east of the Marshall Islands. After completing operations they returned to Tsukiji in Tokyo on April 15. The period during which they were in the vicinity of the Marshall Islands coincided with tests carried out at Bikini on March 1, March 27, and April 7.

"I can't remember being exposed to any radiation myself," Yamashita told us. "But when we returned to Tsukiji we were advised to have a check with a geiger counter. It was quite a shock when a reading of 250 was given for my hair." The other twenty-four crew members had similar experiences, and the boat and all of its equipment were found to be contaminated as well. "I don't think any ashes fell," he continued. "The radioactive material must have been mixed in with rain." When it rained it was usual for the men to go up on deck and rinse the salt off their bodies. This must have been when they were exposed. "At the time, we were more worried about not being able to sell the tuna . . ."

Yamashita, who had owned a boat himself at the height of his career, gave up tuna fishing in 1974 when the industry was in a state of depression. He turned his hand to processing, and retired from the fishing industry altogether at the end of 1989. Apart from an operation for a stomach ulcer, he has had no major health problems. He was amazed to hear that of the twenty-five men who had sailed on the *Kosei Maru* on that voyage in 1954, twelve had died of cancer or cirrhosis of the liver.

"The most incredible thing is that most of them were younger than me," he said sadly. "I don't like to think their deaths were caused by the radiation, not after all this time. But to have this many pass away . . ."

AN UNUSUALLY HIGH INCIDENCE OF LIVER AILMENTS

Returning to the case of the *Fukuryu Maru*, we found that eight of the original twenty-three crew members had died. Discounting one who died in a car accident, four died of cancer of the liver and the others of various other liver ailments.

Dr. Kumatori Toshiyuki was the physician in charge of the crew's treatment in Tokyo directly after their return in 1954, and he continued to be involved with them as director general of the National Institute of Radiological Sciences until 1986. He examined the men regularly over this thirty-year period. We asked him to explain why so many of the crew had died of liver ailments.

"Over a fourteen-day period the men were exposed to doses of radiation of between 170 and 600 rads. Their blood corpuscle count declined, and in some cases sperm production was halted for two years. However, I can't say with complete certainty that their liver damage was caused by exposure to radiation—it may have been a virus they were infected with via the blood transfusions." Aoki Yoshiro, director of the Division of Radiation Health at the institute, has been continuing Dr. Kumatori's work. Dr. Aoki told us that his examinations of nine of the crew in February 1990 revealed five with some type of liver complaint. He was reluctant to make any connection with radiation, but he did acknowledge that this figure is abnormally high. Professor Miyoshi Kazuo, another doctor who treated the crew of the *Fukuryu Maru* soon after their arrival back in Japan, is deeply concerned about this unusually high incidence of liver damage.

"The crew of the *Fukuryu Maru* are more likely than the survivors of Hiroshima and Nagasaki to have absorbed radiation through inhalation or food," he commented. "Therefore, it's the liver that is most likely to be affected, as its function is to filter out harmful substances." When asked whether the crew's liver conditions could have been caused by a virus, he told us that radiation is known to lower the body's resistance. In other words, either directly or indirectly, he believes that their illnesses were probably caused by exposure to radiation from the Bikini test in 1954.

THE FRENCH COVER-UP IN POLYNESIA

The islands of Polynesia are known as the jewels of the South Pacific and have often been described as the last paradise on earth. Since the government of Charles de Gaulle turned the area into a nuclear testing site in 1966, over 150 hydrogen and atomic bomb tests have been carried out, and testing still continues in the South Pacific to this day. We traveled there to find out what was really going on behind the idyllic tropical facade of those islands forced to coexist with the bomb.

Previous page: A resident of Polynesia displays pictures of airships used for transporting atomic bombs.

PARADISE LOST

Stepping out into the bright sunlight at Faa'a Airport, gateway to French Polynesia, we felt the rush of a light sea breeze. To the accompaniment of guitar and ukulele music smiling young women in traditional Tahitian costume handed out bright red flowers. It was truly the kind of welcome one would expect when arriving in a tropical paradise. Unfortunately, this is only one face of Polynesia. James, a resident of the islands whom we chanced to meet near the airport, took two yellowing photographs out of a crumpled paper bag and showed them to us, taking care first to ensure that nobody was watching. "Take a look at these," James said. "I took them secretly in July 1973, when I was working at Mururoa." The photos showed a black object hanging from the undercarriage of an airship.

"It's an atomic bomb, that's what it is." So saying he lowered his voice and began to tell his story.

During the period from 1965, a year before testing began, until 1980, James had gone to Mururoa many times to work on the wharf there.

"Not long after the tests began, a lot of the other guys came down with this mysterious illness. After that the navy started to tell us not to eat the fish or drink the coconut juice."

Convinced that the bombs were the cause, James defied regulations and took the two photos as evidence. Afraid of repercussions from the navy, he has kept them well hidden.

"This is the first time I've shown them to anybody," he said. "I figured that you'll believe me because you're from Hiroshima."

During our stay in Tahiti, we spoke once more with James. It was in front of the statue of Pouvanaa'a Oopa, on the occasion of the annual May memorial service for the Polynesian hero.

"Oopa was the leader of the Polynesian independence movement, as well as the antinuclear movement. He was the man who stood up to de Gaulle. The French did all they could to silence him—they even threw him in a French jail for eleven years," James said. The atmosphere at the service was solemn, but there was no mistaking the determination on the faces of those who stood in front of the statue.

"It takes courage to talk about Mururoa here," James said in a low voice. "If the French authorities find out, you lose your job pretty damn fast."

Some of the people standing around us nodded in agreement. These are the islands where Gauguin spent the latter part of his life and where the romantic scenes of the musical *South Pacific* were set. But if you open your eyes and ears you can see the gloom and hear the stifled anguish of a people born in a tropical paradise but living within the shadow of the atomic bomb. Slowly but surely, the islanders and their way of life are falling victim to French nuclear autonomy. Soon after our return to Japan, a report came from New Zealand that the fourth underground test for that year (1989) had been carried out at Fagataufa Atoll, bringing the total number of tests to 107. We got in touch with our acquaintances in Tahiti, only to find that nobody knew about the test. There are 160,000 Polynesians living on more than 310 islands scattered over this vast stretch of ocean large enough to contain the whole continent of Europe. The knowledge of what nuclear testing can do to the environment is, however, still confined to a small minority of these people.

It was clear that the fastest way to find out about the effects of the tests on the local people was to investigate for ourselves by traveling to the islands surrounding Mururoa. However, it is difficult to get into Polynesia itself for any reason other than sightseeing, let alone obtain permission from the French government to enter the test area. We had no choice, therefore, but to stay in Tahiti and speak to those who had seen the site. One such person was Edward, who was the only Polynesian to have been involved in the checking of radiation levels at the Mururoa test site. He worked at Mururoa for twelve years, from the time of the first tests. Believing the French assurances that there was no danger, he worked in the radioactive contamination survey unit, and, on approximately thirty occasions over the next seven years, walked around the atoll directly after bomb tests.

The surveys were always carried out the day after a test. From a warship waiting outside the area designated as dangerous, the four members of the survey team would travel by helicopter to the contaminated area. There they would don protective clothing and gas masks, and walk around the site using a geiger counter to measure the level of radioactivity.

"When we flicked the switch on the counter it would just let out a continuous high-pitched scream. It was particularly bad in the northern part of the group where tests had been carried out many times. The worst areas we had to fence off and put up No Entry signs. At times half of the thirty-mile length of the atoll was designated as off-limits."

We couldn't help but shiver, recalling the glistening white beaches of the atolls that we had admired from the plane.

"There were some workers whose hair suddenly fell out, then they died soon after. Others ate shellfish and died in terrible pain, driven mad by the itching. Their families were sworn to silence, and their coworkers are too afraid to say anything for fear of losing their jobs," Edward continued. One cannot say with absolute certainty that these people were killed by radiation, but there is a strong possibility that exposure to high levels of radiation was the cause of their deaths.

Edward also informed us that radioactive contamination had spread beyond Mururoa to the island of Mangareva, which lies 225 miles east of the test site and has a population of five hundred. When he traveled with the survey team to the area, Edward found that the levels of contamination in migratory fish were particularly high. It does not take a great deal of imagination to link this fact to the secondary radiation exposure of the islanders. The French government expanded its investigations to encompass a wider area, at the same time consistently denying to the rest of the world that the tests had any negative effects.

This complete suppression of all information regarding the tests left the local people with nothing but rumors to rely on. However, it has also led other nations on the Pacific Rim to launch their own investigations in the interests of national security. In Western Samoa, more than two thousand miles west of Mururoa, a New Zealand government observation post recorded that the level of radioactivity in rainwater there was found to be 13,500 picocuries per liter after the detonation of a bomb at Mururoa in the presence of President de Gaulle on September 11, 1966. The bomb was equivalent to eight Hiroshimas.

The same high levels of radiation were detected in the Cook Islands and Fiji, also a long way from Mururoa, so it may be concluded that an even greater quantity of radioactive fallout must have contaminated French Polynesia.

Surveys by neighboring countries showed that the level of contamination in the atmosphere was the same in 1971 as in 1963, the year in which plutonium-producing nations were hurrying to conduct as many tests as they could before the signing of a treaty which would bring about a partial reduction in nuclear testing.

France, which for many years had ignored the treaty, was finally forced to give in to international pressure in 1975, and in that year switched from atmospheric to underground testing.

RADIATION LEAKAGE FROM CRACKS IN THE CORAL

The end of atmospheric testing did not mean, unfortunately, that Polynesia was no longer threatened by radiation. In 1988, the issue of radioactive contamination came once again to the fore, when allegations were made that radioactive material was leaking out from cracks in the atoll resulting from underground explosions.

The problems caused by underground testing were brought to the attention of the government by a document known as the Cousteau Report. In 1987, the French government had commissioned the famous marine biologist Jacques Cousteau to investigate the geological stability of Mururoa Atoll's coral base. Cousteau and his crew stayed in the Mururoa area for five days, witnessing a test and then diving down to a depth of over six hundred feet in a submarine to investigate the condition of the coral. The result of these investigations was the discovery of a series of cracks running through the wall of the atoll.

The report indicated that there was danger of radiation leakage from these fissures, and recommended that the three-thousand-foot hole bored for use in the tests be filled with concrete.

We spoke to Fillippe Siu, a marine biologist, about the report. Siu holds the title of technical adviser to the minister of health and environment of the Territorial Assembly, and is also the leader of Tahiti's antinuclear party, Power To The People. He told us excitedly: "It was common knowledge here that marine life was in danger of becoming contaminated by radioactive material leaking from cracks in the coral, but the Cousteau Report was a landmark, the first official proof of what we had known for years."

The coral reef, which makes up the structure of the atoll, is constructed of limestone and consequently is not very resistant to the shock of a nuclear explosion. The actual point of the explosion is three thousand feet underground in a layer of basalt, which is also fragile, making the atoll a geologically unsuitable site for nuclear testing.

The problem lies not only with the geology of the area. The islands are only six to ten feet above sea level at the most, and do not have a very large area. A number of accidents are known to have occurred which may be blamed, at least partly, on these topographical limitations.

In July 1979, six workmen were injured in a tidal wave caused by an underground test carried out at a shallower point than usual. Radiation leakage was also suspected.

In August 1979, according to French workmen, plutonium leaked from the laboratory into the reef. The area was covered in asphalt.

In March 1981, a cyclone caused a stack of radioactive waste to be washed away; over forty pounds of plutonium were scattered in the sea.

Plutonium is an extremely radioactive material. Yet there was no explanation as to why no action was taken to minimize its dispersal into the sea. There are also reports of subsidence caused by testing. The Polynesian council has requested on a number of occasions in the past that independent doctors and scientists be permitted to investigate contamination and land stability in the area. The French government, however, has persisted in covering up the truth by whatever means available.

For example, in 1982, seismologists chosen by the French authorities were sent to investigate the situation at Mururoa. However, they spent only two days on the atoll, and the nuclear test which they witnessed was on a much smaller scale than usual: one kiloton rather than the usual amount of between ten and seventy kilotons was detonated. In October 1983, a party of New Zealand scientists was reluctantly allowed into the test area, but they were refused information regarding radiation leakage and were forced to collect samples under French supervision. Needless to say, neither of these investigations was able to uncover any problems caused by the testing.

The Cousteau Report was different, however. The French government was forced to admit that the foundations of the atoll were damaged and that the danger of radiation leakage existed. There is no doubt that the cracks found by Cousteau in the coral of Mururoa have served to strengthen the argument for a complete ban on testing.

THE TRAGEDY OF CARELESS PLANNING

As we talked to the people of the islands it gradually became clear that the French had gone to considerable lengths to deceive the locals in their drive to carry out nuclear testing.

In May 1966, two months before the first test, the French authorities issued a statement to all residents and shipping to the effect that a wedge-shaped area around Mururoa Atoll, extending 460 miles to the east, had been designated a danger zone and that all entry was forbidden. However, the order neglected to take note of the fact that seven inhabited islands were located within this danger zone. When one of the anti-test activists pointed this out, the zone was shrunk to an area 139 miles around Mururoa. Even then there was still one island left within the forbidden area.

This was the island of Tureia, seventy-five miles north of Mururoa. Its fifty inhabitants lived quiet lives and were totally self-sufficient. The French government, wishing to continue its testing program with no more interference, finally announced that there would be no tests carried out when a northerly wind was blowing. The Polynesian islands, however, are located in the trade wind zone, with predominantly northerly winds, so no matter what excuses the French government might give, the chances were that Tureia would be on the receiving end of nuclear fallout.

Then, in July 1968, just prior to the first hydrogen bomb test, the inhabitants of Tureia seemed to evaporate into thin air. It soon became clear what had happened to them—they had been picked up by a French naval vessel and taken back to Tahiti, where they were put in quarantine at a navy camp.

The navy denied having any knowledge of the incident until the truth became widely known; and then they insisted that the islanders had asked to be taken to Tahiti of their own free will. The navy also insisted that the incident had nothing to do with the impending hydrogen bomb test, and even went so far as to have the Tureia islanders express their gratitude to the navy on television. The normally easygoing people of Polynesia were by this time getting extremely concerned about what they saw as French duplicity—the careless way in which the danger zone had been determined; the lame excuses about only carrying out tests when the wind was blowing a certain way; the enforced evacuation of the Tureia islanders.

The people of Polynesia began to resist. On one occasion a group of local politicians decided to hold a television debate, inviting scientists and a number of different groups, including those sympathetic to France, to participate in the program. The proposal was completely ignored by the high commissioner.

Tureia Island, of course, remained in the danger zone, but we wondered what had become of those islands which had suddenly become safe enough to be left out when the restricted zone was revised. One such island was Mangareva, a member of the Gambier group, located 225 miles to the east of Mururoa. It had a population of five hundred.

"After the tests, a lot of the Mangareva islanders got sick from eating fish," said William, a former policeman who lived on Mangareva from 1963 to 1968. According to William, a shelter was built on the island just before the first hydrogen bomb test, in preparation for the fallout from Mururoa. After the tests the French naval vessels would sail into the lagoon to be washed down with sea water. The islanders' source of water is rainwater, and as their diet consists mainly of coconuts and seafood, there is a very strong possibility that radioactive substances would have been absorbed into their bodies. "The French would visit the island at regular intervals to give the islanders medical checkups," continued Willliam, "but we never heard any of the results."

On neither Tureia nor Mangareva is the present state of the people's health known. There are no doctors, and the Tahitian nurse living there was transferred and replaced by a French nurse just before testing began. "That is typical of the French way of doing things," William said regretfully. From time to time word reaches Tahiti of cancer or of children being ill on these islands, but it is extremely difficult to find out exactly what is going on. Tourists, let alone journalists, are strictly forbidden to visit them.

FRENCH DECEPTION

France has shown that it is willing to employ any means necessary to ensure the continuation of its nuclear testing in Polynesia, despite the opposition of the whole of the South Pacific. The French government has knowingly withheld information regarding the tests, deceived the local people, and even resorted to force against one of its allies in the region.

When Philip, a former worker at Mururoa, went to see a French doctor about a problem that was bothering him, he was told that his illness had nothing to do with radiation. But the same doctor's parting words were, "Now don't tell anybody about it, will you?"

Philip's strong brown arms were covered in patches of mottled pink. The same marks could be seen all over his stomach and back.

"This is what happened when I went swimming at Mururoa," he told us. "This horrible rash broke out all over my body." He looked down at his arms. Six years ago when Philip was working as a laborer in Papeete, his father told him that the money was better at the test site, so he got a job on Mururoa. His work there consisted of carrying water to the explosion site to clean contaminated equipment. Heeding the warnings he and his fellow workers were given by the French, he made sure not to eat any fish caught near the site.

As he got used to working on the site, however, he let down his guard a little. One afternoon when it was particularly hot, he decided it wouldn't do any harm to go for a quick dip in the sea, although it was forbidden to do so.

In no time at all he realized the folly of his actions. That same evening, a red rash broke out all over his body, and he was almost driven mad by the itching.

Admittedly, it is not absolutely certain that Philip's skin condition was brought on by sea water contaminated by nuclear testing, as it is extremely difficult to prove any definite relationship between radiation and disease. However, whenever any Polynesian, concerned about the effects of radiation, consults a French doctor, he or she is invariably told that there is nothing to worry about.

The most frustrating thing for the islanders is the lack of advanced medical care in Polynesia. On the one hand the French authorities say that nuclear testing poses no particular health threats, yet the French send all cancer and leukemia patients to Paris for treatment, and do not reveal any details about their illnesses.

Starting in 1966 when the first test was carried out, France has engaged in a blatant cover-up of health statistics in Polynesia. Since that year no data has been revealed on the number or causes of deaths in the colony. Nor has any information been released regarding nuclear fallout from the tests. The reports filed at the request of the United Nations are said to be next to useless, being obvious substitutes for the real thing. There has been no improvement in this state of affairs, despite severe criticism from the International Labor Organization and the World Health Organization.

"If only we had doctors we could trust."

Philip's plea was echoed by all the islanders we spoke to. Excluding dentists, the overwhelming majority of medical practitioners in French Polynesia are French. For one of the local people to become a doctor, they would first of all have to master the French language, then go to France to study. The cost of this is far beyond the means of a Polynesian family.

By silencing the residents, neglecting to reveal vital data, and making use of a French monopoly on doctors, the French would appear to have found a watertight system for covering their tracks in Polynesia.

POISONOUS FISH

After the sun has colored the ocean a brilliant red and begun to sink beyond the horizon, the fishing boats of Papeete drift one by one into port for the night. Their catches are unloaded and taken to the nearby market, where eager buyers are waiting. The most popular delicacy is yellowfin tuna, and those over eighteen inches in length are sold out within half an hour.

Fish is the main source of protein for Polynesians, featuring prominently on the menu of every restaurant in Tahiti. However, for an increasing number of people in recent years, the enjoyment of eating fish has been marred by nausea, diarrhea, and itching which may continue for days or, in the worst cases, years.

Dr. Tilman Ruff of Melbourne's Monash University told us that the symptoms indicated a type of fish poisoning known as ciguatera. Ruff, a lecturer in social and preventive medicine, has been interested in fish poisoning ever since a friend in the antinuclear movement told him about the effects of bomb testing in Polynesia three years ago.

Eating fish containing this poison generally causes nausea and other acute symptoms, including miscarriages or stillbirths in pregnant women. If the itching persists for an extended period the nervous system may be affected, resulting in death.

Ruff sees radiation from nuclear testing as an important factor in the recent prevalence of this illness, and showed us a paper he had written supporting his theory which was published in the January 1989 edition of a British medical journal. According to the statistics he had gathered, there were a hundred known cases of ciguatera poisoning in 1960. The number began to increase toward the end of that decade, coinciding with the start of French atmospheric testing in the South Pacific, and peaked in 1973 when fourteen hundred cases were recorded. From 1974 onward there was a slight decrease, and at present the number of cases is steady with approximately one thousand annually.

When a further analysis of the data is carried out according to region, the results are even more startling. The Gambier Islands, downwind from the test site, show the highest incidence of fish poisoning, the rate of which is 45.4 times the level of the Society Islands, which include Tahiti. The Tuamotu Islands, which include Mururoa, have a rate 3.4 times that of Tahiti, but Ruff attributes this relatively low figure to French warnings not to eat fish caught in this area. Ruff has suggested that radioactive fallout and waste material leaking into the ocean somehow cause a change in the ecosystem of coral which in turn causes a complex series of factors to combine to change the structure of some of the plankton, making it poisonous. Fish eat this plankton; the poison accumulates in their bodies and finally the fish is eaten by a human who then becomes ill with food poisoning.

"If we can just pin down the poison that is the culprit and work out how it gets into the fish's system, I'm pretty sure that the connection with radioactive contamination will become clear," he told us confidently. "If France were to disclose detailed information about radiation leakage and the rate of fish poisoning, I'm sure we'd find that the situation is even worse than we'd imagined."

CAMPAIGNING FOR INDEPENDENCE AND AN END TO TESTING

Information about French activities at Mururoa has been tightly controlled since the first test was carried out in 1966. In spite of this, the Polynesians have been actively resisting French attempts to continue their nuclear testing program in the Pacific.

On the main road linking Papeete to the international airport, the sign *Faa'a Oire Patoi Atomi Manava* (Welcome to the Nuclear-free City of Faa'a) broadcasts the antinuclear feeling of Faa'a's citizens to all who visit. Faa'a is the largest city in French Polynesia, with a population of twenty-four thousand. In 1985 it declared itself a nuclear-free zone, and the sign was erected.

We visited the mayor of Faa'a, Oscar Temaru, at his small, single-story city offices. The mayor is also the leader of the Polynesian Liberation Front formed in 1976, which is campaigning for independence from France and an end to the underground tests. He witnessed tests at Mururoa during his time working as a customs official. "Before the tests began," he told us, "nobody in Polynesia, including myself, of course, knew what radiation was or how destructive it could be. The French told us nothing." His tone was even but his anger apparent.

Damage wrought by the tests on the natural surroundings strengthened Temaru's determination to campaign against the French. Temaru was elected for his first term as mayor of Faa'a in 1983. In 1986 he was chosen as a member of the Territorial Assembly, which has a total of forty-one members, and he drew sixty percent of the vote in the 1989 mayoral elections to win another term. Although Temaru carries the weight of public opinion behind him in his fight against the French, there are many obstacles in his way. He has had to deal with the secrecy of the French government, harassment of the anti-testing movement, the shortage of Polynesian scientists and doctors, and a dearth of information regarding radiation and nuclear weapons. His biggest problem is the scattered nature of the islands themselves, which makes it difficult to organize resistance among victims of radiation. The media also is largely controlled by French interests; there are only two newspapers in Tahiti, both are written in French, and the contents tend to be pro-French as well.

The Liberation Front holds three main events during the year for the public—the antinuclear meetings on Bikini Day in March and on Hiroshima Day in August, and the memorial service for Oopa, father of the independence movement, held on May Day. According to Temaru, none of these events has ever been reported by the local French media.

The group has invited doctors and other specialists from Australia and Japan to the islands in attempts to uncover some facts about radioactive contamination, and has sent representatives to antinuclear conferences in Hiroshima. With help from Faa'a city they have also started an antinuclear radio station which broadcasts information on nuclear issues. All the group's actions are monitored by the French authorities, who clamp down on them from time to time when they feel that they have gone too far out of line. The bombing of the Greenpeace vessel *Rainbow Warrior* in Auckland harbor in New Zealand on the night of July 10, 1985, is a classic example of attempts to obstruct antinuclear activities. The ship was destroyed just prior to setting out on a protest voyage to Mururoa, and one person was killed. It was discovered that this crime had been perpetrated by two members of the French secret service, who were arrested soon after. In spite of international criticism over the *Rainbow Warrior* affair, as it later became known, France chose to continue the tests.

Since testing began, the French answer to Polynesian doubts about radiation has been restricted to two worn-out phrases: "it's safe" and "there is nothing to worry about." The question which not only the Liberation Front but the whole of Polynesia has been asking the French government is, "If it's so safe, why don't you do it in France?" Temaru believes that there will only be an end to atomic bomb testing in the Pacific when Polynesia succeeds in becoming independent from France. To him, opposition to the testing and Polynesian independence are inextricably linked.

APPEALING TO THE WORLD ON BEHALF OF THE ISLANDS

Several times during our investigations in French Polynesia mention was made of a couple who have been working for years to bring the crimes of French nuclear testing to the attention of the world. Hearing that they were in Australia on a lecture tour, we stopped off in Sydney on our way back to Japan.

We met anthropologists Bengt and Marie Therese Danielsson at the University of New South Wales in Sydney, where they were due to speak to a group of about ten students and local citizens about the remaining colonial outposts in the Pacific.

The lecture lasted approximately two hours and covered a number of topics, including the history of French Polynesia and the environmental damage wrought by the tests. At the end of the session one student raised her hand. She introduced herself as a French exchange student, and went on to admit tearfully that, to her shame, she had had no idea of the tragic situation her country was causing in the South Pacific.

Danielsson later remarked, "It's not just that student who doesn't know; the French government has not told anybody anything about this. That's why we believe our task is to inform people about the situation. If only one person goes away today with some knowledge about what's going on in French Polynesia, we feel that we've done some good."

The pair have traveled all over the world appealing to the public in the hope that their actions will help to force the French to give up underground testing.

Danielsson is Swedish. In 1947 he took part in the famous Kon-tiki expedition, and traveled over five thousand miles across the Pacific by raft from Peru in an effort to unravel the mystery of the origins of the Polynesians. Since 1949 he has lived with his French wife, Marie Therese, in Papeete. While continuing his anthropological fieldwork, he observed the tests and became a thorn in the side of the French authorities.

The couple's belief that nuclear testing is destroying the land they love and the health and way of life of its people, has become the basis for all their actions. The period from 1972 to 1974, when public opinion forced the French to take their testing underground, is particularly memorable for the Danielssons. With their help, the nations of Oceania brought an action against France in the International Court of Law, protest ships sailed to Mururoa, and there were boycotts of French goods as far away as South America and Southeast Asia. "If that enthusiasm could be generated again, we could stop the underground testing as well," said Marie Therese. Her husband agreed. "It would be marvellous to have that level of support again," he remarked wistfuly, stroking his beard.

The Danielssons' dream may well be realized in the not-too-distant future. Since Jacques Cousteau reported that there were fissures in the coral at Mururoa and Fangataufa, the French Department of Atomic Energy has begun to search for a new test site, and time is running out. One candidate for the new test site is the Marquesas Islands, situated approximately 930 miles to the north of Mururoa and about 930 miles northeast of Tahiti, with a population of seven thousand.

The couple are determined to ensure that the Marquesas do not become the third island to be destroyed by French nuclear testing, and consequently they have been traveling widely through Oceania, Western Europe, and South America, speaking to people in a renewed effort to heighten public awareness. With the people's support, they are hoping to force France to give up underground testing before it decides upon the new site, with the aim of halting the further increase in radiation-linked diseases in the South Pacific.

BRITAIN'S FORGOTTEN LEGACY

On October 3, 1952, an atomic bomb was set off at Monte Bello Island in the northwest of Australia, heralding the arrival of Britain as the third nuclear power after the United States and the Soviet Union. Unbeknown to many people, tests continued to be carried out in the Australian desert and on Pacific islands by the British until 1958. During those six years, a number of Australian Aborigines as well as Australian and New Zealand servicemen were exposed to radiation, but it was many years later before the tests were finally acknowledged by the British government.

Previous page: Aborigines, whose homeland was used as a nuclear test site by the British, discuss their experiences of the explosions.

DISPLACED ABORIGINES

Aboriginal settlements can be found dotted all over the vast expanses of red earth and eucalyptus trees that make up Southern Australia's Great Victoria Desert. This is the home of Australia's original inhabitants, the Aborigines. We took a small plane to visit the Aboriginal settlement of Oak Valley, 560 miles from Adelaide.

The residents of Oak Valley were evicted in the fifties when the British decided to conduct nuclear tests at Maralinga, sixty miles southeast of their village. Forced to move 120 miles south to Yalata, the people of Oak Valley and other local Aborigines were only permitted to return to their land thirty years later, in late 1984. The villagers, numbering thirty in all, decided to return to their homeland.

When we touched down on the runway, only distinguishable as such by its lone windsock, one of the local men drove up to check us out. When we told him that we wanted to talk about Maralinga, he took us into the village. There we met several people who had witnessed a bomb test.

One of the men, by the name of Pepa, began to tell their story: "While we were moving south, a huge mushroom-shaped cloud rose up into the sky and drifted over our heads."

"The earth shook, frightening the dogs that were walking with us," another said. "Our dog started to howl when he heard the noise—it was like thunder."

"It was the strangest cloud we'd ever seen," Pepa added.

We asked them when and where they had seen the cloud, opening up a map. The map, however, was of little use—the only thing they knew was that it had happened while they were moving south. As to why they were moving south, they had no idea except that one of the whites had come and ordered them to go, with no explanation whatsoever. Reluctantly they had packed up and started to walk.

After witnessing the explosion they traveled south for several days, hunting as they went. Unable to catch any kangaroo, their favorite delicacy, or even wild rabbits or lizards, they had to be content with insects from the roots of trees.

On their arrival in Yalata, they found a number of groups that had been ordered south in the same way as themselves. They were too afraid to mention the mushroom cloud, they said. A compound was built, and the displaced Aborigines began a new life, still with no explanation of why they were there or when they could go home.

Was anyone sick? Did you have any examinations? For a people with no knowledge of radiation or medical care, these were meaningless questions. All they did was shrug their shoulders.

ABORIGINES FREE TO ROAM THE MARALINGA TEST SITE

The area of land around the Maralinga test site that was returned to the Aborigines in 1984 is approximately 130 miles square. Responsible for the administration of the land as well as assisting returnees is the Maralinga Tjarutja Land Holding Body, located in the town of Ceduna, South Australia, 150 miles southwest of Maralinga. We visited their offices and spoke to the chief administrator, Archie Barton.

"We really have no idea how many Aborigines were living in the area at the time of the testing, let alone how many were exposed to radiation," he said with a touch of resignation.

Barton showed us a black-and-white photo of two elderly Aborigines whom he suspected may have wandered into the test area by mistake, although he had no conclusive evidence. He explained to us the difficulty of getting such evidence.

"The residents of this area didn't even know what a nuclear test was, so hardly any of them remember where they were or what they were doing at the time. The government put up warning signs, but not all the people here can read. There were people living close to the site totally unaware of the danger; it's extremely hard for us to tell who was exposed to radiation."

In 1984 the Australian government set up a committee to investigate possible cases of exposure, but was only able to prove conclusively that four Aborigines had received large doses of radiation. These four were a family who had been discovered wandering lost in the test area by army personnel. Even this incident had been kept secret for a long time, according to Barton.

The family, consisting of mother, father, and two children, accompanied by two dogs, entered the Maralinga site on the night of May 13,

1957. They stumbled into one of the craters created by the testing, and were discovered the next morning. The crater was still contaminated after a test conducted five months previously.

They were taken to the base, where they were checked for radiation and made to take decontamination showers several times. The same day they were driven to the Yalata compound 120 miles to the south. Low levels of radiation had been detected in their bodies, but not enough, it was decided, to have any adverse effects on their health. However, the child that the mother was carrying at the time was stillborn.

Barton told us, "This episode shows just how easy it was to enter the test site. The government didn't take enough care to ensure the safety of Aborigines living in the desert, and they can't deny it."

The mother of the family is still alive and well. At present she is seeking compensation from the Australian government on the grounds that it approved British plans to conduct nuclear tests without taking enough care to protect the local people.

The Aborigines have been on the retreat since Europeans first settled in Australia in the latter half of the eighteenth century. Deprived of their ancestral lands, the population, estimated at five hundred thousand at the time of the Europeans' arrival, dropped drastically to a low of fifty thousand in the 1930s. Aboriginal civil rights were finally recognized in 1967, and their numbers have recovered to an estimated two hundred thousand at the present time. Even so, there is no doubt that the confiscation of their land for use as a nuclear testing site has served to hasten the decline of the Aboriginal culture. The traditional life-style based on hunting and the village community is already in ruins, according to Barton. His main task at present is providing basic foodstuffs for those returning to the area.

The government acknowledges that Aborigines of the Great Victoria Desert may have suffered from contamination, but does not seem inclined to find out precisely who has been affected. At present the committee has adopted a policy of carrying out investigations, but only if an Aborigine makes a claim first. The vast majority of Aborigines, however, are not even aware that they may have been exposed to radiation, so few claims are likely to be made.

THE FIGHT FOR COMPENSATION

"It was that black fog at the time of the test, that's what made me lose my sight."

This claim by Aboriginal rights activist Yami Lester was headline news in the May 3, 1980, edition of the *Advertiser*, an Adelaide paper.

Although it had been twenty-eight years since the British last conducted nuclear tests in Australia, this was the first time that the issue of radiation-linked diseases suffered by Aborigines had been raised in public. Lester is at present claiming compensation from the government for the loss of his sight.

Lester witnessed the black fog on October 15, 1953. At the time he was with forty other members of his tribe outside the restricted area at Wallatinna, 110 miles northeast of the Emu Test Site in the Great Victoria Desert.

"That morning we heard this great explosion, and suddenly everyone was running round in a panic. About four or five minutes later this black fog with sand mixed in it covered the camp."

Two weeks later Lester lost the use of his right eye. The vision in his left eye was also greatly impaired, and four years later he became totally blind.

"Some of my friends got sick, too. Diarrhea, nausea, sore eyes," said Lester, listing the symptoms of acute radiation sickness. "But I was only twelve at the time, so I don't really remember what happened to the others," he added.

Following the publicity given to Lester's case in the press, new evidence supporting his claims and those of other Aborigines began to come to light. White residents added their voices to the growing demands for a proper investigation; some claimed to have seen dead Aborigines in the desert, others said that they too had experienced the black fog, and yet others confirmed that people living in the areas near the site had not been warned about the tests.

Military personnel who had participated in the tests also began to seek compensation. The government found itself no longer in a position to ignore the problem, so in July 1984 a committee was established to conduct a thorough investigation into the alleged effects of the testing. A year later, the committee reported that there was a strong possibility that the Aboriginal community at Wallatinna had been exposed to radioactive fallout, and recommended that some form of compensation be given. However, the committee was not convinced that Lester's blindness had been caused by exposure to radiation. The majority of committee members believed that his condition had been brought about rather by trachoma, a severe eye inflammation caused by insanitary conditions and a poor diet.

Lester visited Hiroshima and Nagasaki in August 1989, to speak about his experiences at several public meetings, and to meet with Japanese radiation victims. He described his reason for publicizing his story as follows: "I heard a scientist saying on the radio how they had done their best to ensure that no Aborigines were within range of the radiation. This made me so angry I went to the papers with my story. We've not only lost our land, but we're also suffering from radiation-linked diseases. The government is really taking its time in handing out compensation and getting round to cleaning up the contaminated area."

The Australian government has drawn up a plan of compensation for the Aborigines which is based on the general accident compensation law. The result is that the amount of compensation offered would be the same as the unemployment allowance.

Lester disagrees strongly with this policy, claiming that it is ridiculous to place exposure to radioactive fallout on the same level as unemployment. The government has recently indicated that it is nearing a final decision on the question of compensation. In all there are fifteen Aborigines making claims, and Lester is prepared to fight in court until their demands are met.

MINOR TRIALS CAUSE MAJOR CONTAMINATION

While interviewing radiation victims in Australia, we often heard talk about a type of test known as a minor trial. This type of test is different from the tests involving powerful atomic and hydrogen bombs in that ordinary explosives are used to disperse radioactive material. The aim of such trials is to obtain information that would be useful in, for example, the storage of nuclear weapons, protection against radiation, and countermeasures to be taken in the event of an accident involving the transport or storage of radioactive material. The materials used are plutonium, uranium, beryllium, and americium. Although atmospheric testing was halted in 1958, these minor trials continued until 1963. A total of 580 such tests were carried out in Australia. Avon Hudson, who worked on minor trials at the Maralinga site from 1961 to 1963, described his work:

"They used to explode various radioactive materials on top of a metal tower one hundred feet high. Our job was to go around the next day, pick up the pieces of the tower that were scattered, and rebuild it. We were advised to wear protective clothing, but the temperature is often over forty degrees (104°F) there, and it would've been unbearable—nobody told us it was dangerous." Hudson now runs an antique shop in an Adelaide suburb and is chairman of the South Australian branch of the Australian Nuclear Veterans Association.

"Four years after I stopped working there, I got skin cancer," he said, taking off his socks and showing us the black marks that still remained on his ankles. "I'm sure radioactive material has had some effect on me."

Minor tests can still contaminate the environment in a major way; the plutonium exploded at Maralinga, for example, was dispersed over a thirteen-mile radius. The total quantity scattered during the years in which the trials were carried out is estimated to be approximately fifty pounds. When calculated in accordance with the standards set by the International Commission on Radiological Protection (ICRP), this adds up to the alarming figure of 130 billion times the recommended safe level per person per year. In 1967 Britain began a cleanup operation and buried the topsoil deep in the earth. However, according to a survey carried out in 1980 by the Australian Radiation Laboratory, the cleanup was not enough to make the area safe for human inhabitation.

When we tried to visit the test site, we found the road blocked off and two government employees patrolling the compound. An area over thirty miles square around Maralinga still remains off limits to outsiders.

The same type of small-scale trials were frequently carried out at the Emu test site, and the soil there remains contaminated. The land surrounding the Emu base was returned to the local Aborigines at the end of 1984. At the time, they were warned to stay away from the former test area, but it is doubtful whether they are fully aware of the implications of the term "radioactive contamination."

Sooner or later the test sites themselves must be returned to the native people, and in preparation for this the Australian government is investigating a variety of methods to clean up the areas. However, an official at the Department of Primary Industries and Energy told us, "If the cost of the cleanup operation is found to be excessive, there is the possibility that it may not be completed." It seems there is no way of telling when the twice-daily patrols will end and the Aborigines will be allowed to return to their homeland.

EX-SERVICEMEN FIGHTING A CRITICAL BATTLE

On December 1988, in a verdict handed down by the New South Wales Supreme Court, it was declared that compensation should be paid by the government to former army personnel who took part in nuclear tests. The plaintiff was Richard Johnston, chairman of the Australian Nuclear Veterans Association. The amount awarded was A\$867,000. It was a landmark case: the first compensation awarded to an ex-serviceman in Australia for illnesses caused by exposure to radiation. However, for Johnston, it was a hollow victory.

The verdict recognized that Johnston suffered from a radiation-linked illness, but Johnston was still not satisfied. The compensation had not been awarded for his skin cancer or high blood pressure but for his schizophrenia which had been induced by the government's lack of response to his fears about radiation exposure. While in the army, Johnston was based at Maralinga for a year, during which he witnessed four tests. "I was five miles away from the center of the explosion, but sometimes the ashes fell on my bare arms and made my skin tingle," Johnston told us. His job was to go into the test area after each explosion to collect the tanks and other vehicles that had been placed there to measure the effects of the bomb, and to take them back to base. Another task was to bring back the cages of the goats, rabbits, and pigeons placed in the area for experimental purposes.

"The heat just kills you out there at the base," he said. "I used to take off my mask, then undo the protective clothing, then when I couldn't stand it any more I'd take off my gloves."

Afterward he would be overwhelmed by nausea and diarrhea. Johnston himself thought that these were the symptoms of acute radiation sickness, but the army doctor dismissed his fears, saying that his condition was caused by nerves. Continuing to insist that exposure to radiation was the cause of his condition, Johnston was discharged from the army. When he demanded compensation from the government he was accused of lying which caused his mental health to deteriorate until he was finally diagnosed as a schizophrenic.

In 1972, Johnston's doctor saw a documentary about the tests which made him more sympathetic to the ex-serviceman's plight.

"That was when I at last got some decent treatment, but even so the government's attitude left a lot to be desired."

He was reluctant to talk about the matter any further, but it was clear that the government's attitude had motivated him to go to court again. Apart from the fact that only part of his claim had been recognized, there was another reason why Johnston was not completely satisfied with the judge's decision. Lawyers' fees for the case had come to A$630,000, and, in addition, he was forced to pay back the government A$260,000 in medical expenses.

"Well," he said, more for his own benefit than ours, "despite the monetary loss, I still beat the government. They can't take that away from me."

Seven hundred of the fifteen thousand Australian servicemen who took part in British nuclear tests formed the Nuclear Veterans Association in 1980, and since then they have continued to demand compensation from the government. The government, however, insists that it has no records of radiation sickness among servicemen, and refuses to ac-knowledge the adverse effects of nuclear testing. At the present time, fifty ex-servicemen are involved in court cases similar to Johnston's, fighting what may turn out to be the most critical battle of their lives.

VICTIMS OF CHRISTMAS ISLAND

*D*uring the 1950s Britain became the third power to develop a nuclear weapons capability after the United States and the Soviet Union. At five locations in Australia and the Christmas Island region, seventeen thousand British servicemen participated in a total of twenty-one atmospheric tests. Thirty years on, a disproportionately high incidence of cancer had been observed among these men, many of whose children were born with what are seen as genetic defects. A group of ex-servicemen formed the British Nuclear Tests Veterans Association, which has carried out surveys on radiation-linked diseases and begun procedures against the government in an effort to obtain compensation.

'ATOMIC KIWIS'

Christmas Island was chosen as a test site in 1957, following growing criticism of the atomic bomb tests carried out on the Australian mainland. The British chose this island for its relative remoteness, the same reason the United States had used the Marshall Islands and France was to use the islands of Polynesia. In 1958 and 1959 Britain carried out six tests at Christmas Island and three at Morden Island, five hundred miles to the southeast.

Totaling almost six hundred in all, the New Zealand servicemen who took part in the British nuclear tests are known as "Atomic Kiwis." Their main duties were patrolling the test areas to ensure that no shipping strayed into them, and recording various meteorological data.

In New Zealand, we visited Turi Blake at his home in Wanganui, north of Wellington. For the past thirty years, he has held firm to the belief that during the 1950s he and his fellow servicemen in the New Zealand Navy were unwittingly involved in an experiment to test the effects on man of exposure to large doses of radiation.

On April 28, 1958, the warship on which Blake was serving lay at anchor twenty-five miles off Christmas Island in the Pacific. A British Royal Navy vessel, also in the area, had pulled back a much greater distance from the island and was a mere speck on the horizon. Twelve crew members on the New Zealand Navy ship including Blake were ordered up on deck. He and two others carried geiger counters around their necks; they wore no protective clothing, not even socks or gloves.

Following the captain's orders, they turned their backs, closed their eyes and waited for the explosion of the hydrogen bomb.

"The moment the bomb exploded, we were dazzled by a flash of light even though we had our eyes closed. Our backs felt as if they'd been set on fire."

When they turned round fourteen seconds later as ordered, the bright red fireball was changing to orange, and a huge mushroom cloud was rising up into the sky. There was a loud explosion and the men felt the shock waves wash over them as the ship was lashed by a blast of dusty wind and geiger counters shrieked angrily. The cloud proceeded to cover the sky completely and the men were drenched by heavy rainfall. The captain assured them there was nothing to be concerned about, but Blake began to suspect that he and his fellow crew members had been used as guinea pigs in an experiment.

Blake's sight deteriorated rapidly soon after leaving the navy in 1961. His mental state deteriorated as well, making it difficult for him to stay in work, and he now receives welfare benefits.

Dr. Graham Gulbransen, a member of IPPNW (International Physicians for the Prevention of Nuclear War), is an enthusiastic supporter of the Atomic Kiwis. Dr. Gulbransen has for some time been researching the medical histories of the fifty servicemen who have died since they participated in the tests in the late fifties.

According to his research, most of the servicemen died of cancer. Some of the men had actually shown symptoms of acute radiation sickness while they were on duty at the test sites. Gulbransen has come to the conclusion that even low doses of radiation may have detrimental effects on the health. The doctor has also noted a tendency toward psychological instability among the Atomic Kiwis, as in the case of Turi Blake.

The claims of the New Zealanders were investigated by the Ministry of Defense in an inquiry commissioned in 1987.

"Naturally, if it was found that our illnesses were caused by being used as guinea pigs, then we would demand compensation from the government," said Blake. "But more than that, we want them to release all the details of damage caused by the tests to the general public."

HELL ON EARTH

Ken McGinley of Glasgow was one of four hundred soldiers who sat on the beach at Christmas Island on April 28, 1958 to witness his first nuclear test. "The countdown began, and we covered our eyes with our hands—when the flash came I could see the bones of my hands as if they were in an X-ray." The men on the beach at Christmas Island wore no protective clothing, not even glasses or masks. They were at the mercy of the searing heat, the deafening noise, and the terrifying mushroom cloud that accompanied the explosion of the megaton-class hydrogen bomb.

"It was like hell on earth," said McGinley.

There were soldiers who could not stop crying hysterically afterward, and those who were sent home to recover from the shock. McGinley's face, arms, and hands swelled up a few days later, and his entire body was covered in red spots. He was overwhelmed by nausea and was unable to eat anything; sleep was impossible because of the itching and the pain which racked his body. He was treated at the base hospital, but he never recovered his former health. After McGinley witnessed his second test in August of the same year, the condition of his throat deteriorated, and he was sent to an American military hospital in Hawaii. Tonsilitis was diagnosed, and his tonsils were removed. After he returned to Christmas Island he witnessed three more tests.

"Nobody told us why we were going to Christmas Island and when we left, we were ordered not to tell anybody about what we'd seen there. Even if national security is at stake, that's no reason to destroy the health of your own servicemen."

McGinley's health continued to deteriorate, and in December he was sent back home to Britain. McGinley attended a Christmas service at his local church, but halfway through he started coughing up blood and had to be rushed to hospital. He was operated on for a duodenal ulcer the following year, and was discharged from the army on health grounds, with a small disability pension. He was twenty years old.

Neither the swelling in McGinley's hands and feet, nor his occasional dizzy spells improved, and in 1976 his doctor finally admitted that exposure to a large dose of radiation was probably the cause of his inability to father any children.

"It was a real shock to me. That was when I realized just how much damage those nuclear tests had actually done to my body," said McGinley.

His condition worsened in 1982, just when the army pension was cut by ten percent. McGinley's anger at the government's attitude reached new heights when he tracked down his army medical records and found there was no mention of his ever being hospitalized. "I served my country without knowing what harm it would do to me, and this is how it repays me."

FIGHTING FOR RECOGNITION

A television documentary featuring McGinley drew a widespread response from viewers all over Britain. Letters and phone calls poured in from former soldiers in the same position, and from widows who had lost their husbands to cancer. McGinley had had no idea there were so many men suffering from radiation-linked diseases. He contacted as many of the ex-servicemen as he could, and together they formed the British Nuclear Test Veterans Association (BNTVA) in May 1983.

The BNTVA, which now has sixteen branches all over the United Kingdom and a total of two thousand members, including two hundred widows, has enlisted the help of lawyers and specialists in radiation medicine. According to McGinley, the fight to obtain recognition and compensation is really only just beginning.

In London we met one of the association's members, Rosalyn Levene, who was widowed sixteen years previously when her husband, Leon, died of leukemia.

"In 1988 the Department of Health and Social Security (DHSS) finally admitted my husband's death was directly related to his experiences on Christmas Island. I was thrown out of court six years ago for trying to prove the same thing. At least this means I can finally get the war widow's pension."

She spoke about her husband with difficulty, and it was obvious that the memory of his untimely death at the age of thirty-six was still a painful one. Prompted by the association's claims, the National Radiological Protection Board (NRPB) investigated the causes of death of servicemen who had taken part in nuclear tests. In January 1988 the NRPB came to the conclusion that there was an undeniable link between exposure to radiation from nuclear testing and the incidence of leukemia and bone marrow tumors among returned servicemen.

This judgment prompted the DHSS to provide an allowance for those affected. Mrs. Levene is one of only two women who have managed to obtain an allowance of £56 a week, which falls far short of her needs. It is her belief that, while it is only a small victory for the BNTVA, the way has been laid open for future claims.

Despite this victory, the BNTVA does not place a great deal of faith in the results of the board's investigation, which it considers to have been carried out in a slipshod manner. The board estimates that 22,347 people received doses of radiation, but of these, as many as 5,000 have never witnessed a test or taken part in decontamination work on any of the sites. In addition to these inconsistencies, there are no records available for any of the servicemen who died of cancer before 1971.

Following its success in obtaining war widow's pensions for Mrs. Levene and one other widow, the BNTVA has swung into action on the issue of government recognition of radiation-linked cancer among servicemen. Across the Atlantic, the United States government has already recognized thirteen types of cancer as being caused by exposure to large doses of radiation during nuclear testing.

GENETIC DEFECTS OBSERVED

The suffering of those still living with the effects of being exposed to radiation during the tests is one of the most pressing issues. This includes not only the men themselves but also their children, many of whom have been born with deformities.

We visited Robert Billings and his family at their home on the outskirts of the Yorkshire town of Ripon. Billings witnessed five nuclear tests at Christmas Island in 1958, and since then has suffered from ill health. He is blind in his left eye, and the right side of his body is completely paralyzed. He is prone to fits, and he also has a speech impediment.

His daughter Claire, who is currently at high school, was born with a deformed left leg: it is seven inches shorter than her right leg, without a heel, and with only three toes. She is able to walk short distances with the help of an artificial leg, but the prosthesis weighs ten pounds, making it impossible for her to travel long distances. Mrs. Billings, who has her hands full taking care of her disabled husband and daughter, believes both their conditions are radiation-linked.

"When Claire was born," she told us, "the doctor asked me whether I had been exposed to any radiation, or if I'd been taking thalidomide during my pregnancy. The connection with Robert's time in the army never occurred to me—until I heard about the BNTVA. Then I realized why my daughter is disabled."

According to the BNTVA's own survey, so far there have been seven hundred incidences of deformities in children fathered by ex-servicemen who participated in nuclear tests. This figure includes two hundred stillbirths. Claire Billings was actually one of the luckier ones; many other children suffer from brain damage, leukemia, or dysfunctions of the nervous system. There are also children with severe physical and intellectual disabilities, and those whose sex was indeterminable at birth.

"As one of those directly affected," Claire told us, "I want as many people as possible to know about the suffering caused by radiation."

When she was a child she was often teased by her classmates, which made her resent her parents. But now she is older and knows more about her father's experience and the effects of radiation, Claire has decided to study to become a counselor for the disabled. Once again we were reminded of the diverse effects exposure to radiation can have on one's life.

INDIA • MALAYSIA • KOREA

LIVING IN THE SHADOW OF INDIAN NUCLEAR DEVELOPMENT

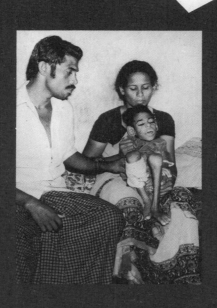

India, which shocked the world when it carried out an underground nuclear test in 1974, possesses all the facilities required for making atomic fuel, from uranium mines to fast-breeder reactors and fuel reprocessing plants. The country prides itself on being at the forefront of nuclear technology among the developing nations, but when we traveled in India we found the people living near these facilities were poor and, almost without exception, were unaware of the dangers of radioactive contamination. These are the people who have been forgotten in the eagerness of the Indian government to catch up with the big boys of nuclear development.

Previous page: A girl from Alappat, where monazite is collected and refined for use as nuclear fuel to support India's growing nuclear industry.

THE DIRTIEST NUCLEAR FACILITY IN THE WORLD

Our first destination was the village of Akarpatti, three hours north of
Bombay by road. Situated on the Arabian Sea coast, the village has a population of two thousand. Across the wide estuary, a grove of palm trees
conceals a nuclear power plant. Only one mile away from Akarpatti, the
Tarapur Nuclear Complex houses India's first two reactors, bought from
the United States and operating since 1969, and a plant for reprocessing
used nuclear fuel. Through our interpreter we explained to the villagers
our reason for coming to Akarpatti. We were the first journalists, foreign
or domestic, ever to set foot in the area, and at first the residents were
wary of speaking to us. After a while, though, they gradually began to respond to our questions, and we realized there was a lot they wanted to
tell us.

Dattatraya Patil, who could speak English, told us that the palm trees
had been wilting recently, something which had never happened before.

"Look," he said, pointing out trees as he showed us around the village, "there's one here, and some over there, too." The trees, all over
thirty feet tall, had lost their leaves and had been reduced to pathetic
shadows of their former selves.

As we were walking around the village, the group swelled until there
were perhaps thirty men following us. One of them, Shri Patil, an electrician, told us that in recent years a lot of cattle had died after wandering
across the estuary in search of feed. Nobody knew the reason, but the
people had begun to cast suspicion at the nuclear plant tucked away
inconspicuously among the palms.

The Tarapur Nuclear Complex has an unenviable reputation as the
dirtiest nuclear facility in the world, due to the frequent accidents there.
In September 1989, two of India's leading English-language dailies reported that highly radioactive iodine had been detected in seaweed
gathered in the area.

According to the scientists from the Bhabha Atomic Research Center
in Bombay who had published the results in a marine science journal, the
amount of iodine-129 found at Tarapur was 740 times the normal level.
They concluded that the main cause of this unnatural amount of iodine
was the nearby fuel reprocessing plant, but added that the discharge of

large quantities into the environment did not mean a corresponding rise in the amount of iodine absorbed by human beings.

The half-life of iodine-129 is approximately 16 million years. The amount of iodine-131 (half-life: eight days) and other radioactive substances discharged from the complex remains unknown. If iodine makes its way into the body in excessive quantities, it accumulates mainly in the thyroid gland and can cause dysfunction and cancer. None of the villagers knew this; ninety-eight percent cannot read or write. Without any explanation, their salt pans were closed and their wells put off limits. "They can't even be bothered to tell us why," Shri spat angrily.

THE UNKNOWN VICTIMS OF RADIATION

We visited Dr. Pramod Patil, whose practice is located in the town of Palghar, seven miles from Tarapur. A collection of medical equipment, including an ancient X-ray machine, was crammed into his tiny clinic. Dr. Patil told us about two patients he had treated a year previously.

"The moment I saw those two, I knew they were suffering from radiation sickness."

The men had arrived at his clinic covered in red spots and suffering from diarrhea. They were migrant laborers who had traveled to Tarapur to work for a subcontractor there.

"I tried to get some more details about their illness, but we just couldn't understand each other," the doctor continued. After examining the men, Patil asked them to return later. He never saw them again. Including sixteen official languages and a plethora of local dialects, there are over three hundred languages in everyday use in India. The workers who are most likely to be exposed to radiation are those brought up by agencies from states in the south, such as Kerala.

"Not being able to speak the local language means they can't divulge information about their experiences," Dr. Patil said with a shrug. We were told that workers are sent back home at once if they do receive a large dose of radiation, and that no official record of their ever being at Tarapur exists, let alone the fact that they were exposed to radiation.

These laborers are told nothing about radiation; most don't even know the meaning of the word. If they do succumb to radiation-related diseases in later years, neither they nor their families will ever know the cause.

Killigudi Jayaraman, nuclear physicist and science editor for the news agency Press Trust of India, estimates that at least three hundred workers at Tarapur have been exposed to levels of radiation far higher than the 5 rems per annum allowed by regulation. On March 14, 1980, for example, cooling water leaked from the No. 1 reactor, and the twenty-six workers engaged in repairs were suddenly rushed to hospital in Bombay.

Prime Minister Indira Gandhi took a dim view of the incident, and two high-ranking officials from the Department of Atomic Energy were summoned to New Delhi and reprimanded.

At first the Department of Atomic Energy refused to acknowledge the accident to the media. However, when the issue was raised in parliament, it had no choice but to admit to the accident.

"They acknowledged that there had been a pinhole in the reactor, but accused the media of blowing things out of proportion," he continued. "They're like this about everything, so there's no way anyone's going to find out how many laborers have been exposed to radiation."

In the village of Akarpatti a simple placard tells the story of one man who for eighteen years was engaged in the maintenance of the reactors at Tarapur.

> Agih Patil, aged 50. Died December 5, 1989, 9 P.M.
> Rest in Peace

His son, Parasharm, aged twenty-two, had shaved his head in accordance with Hindu funeral custom. "The cause of death was heart attack, or so they said," said Dattatraya Patil on behalf of the man's son, who sat watching us silently. "He worked in that plant with no film badge on. No matter what they say the cause of death was, how can they be so sure that radiation had nothing to do with it?"

It seemed that the villagers, who have no means of proving their suspicions, had erected this memorial in a silent gesture of defiance.

AN ATMOSPHERE OF FEAR AND DISTRUST

We left the Tarapur Nuclear Complex and headed for our next destination, the Kalpakkam complex, facing the sparkling blue Bay of Bengal forty miles south of Madras.

The Kalpakkam Nuclear Complex houses two reactors, Madras Nos. 1 and 2, which started operations in 1983 and 1986 respectively, and the

Indira Gandhi Center for Atomic Research, where work on the latest in nuclear technology is carried out using an experimental fast-breeder reactor. We had heard that in 1986 there had been a large-scale burning of fruit, vegetables, rice, and household furniture in the nearby village where the workers at Kalpakkam live. These goods had been loaded on a truck which was normally used for transporting nuclear fuel rods. When the villagers found out they panicked and burned all the goods for fear of contamination.

A.S. Panneerselvan from the newspaper, *Indian Week*, who had joined us as our interpreter, had investigated this story and exposed the authorities' negligent management of radioactive materials. It was Panneerselvan's first visit to the area and he was keen to carry out some investigations of his own. He asked a man at the side of the road the way to Kokilyamedu, the village closest to Kalpakkam. The man replied that he was from the village of Kokilyamedu itself and motioned to us to follow him to the shade of a tree, so that we would be less conspicuous. His face, burned black from the sun, made him look much older than his thirty-nine years. He told us that the authorities had warned the villagers not to talk to foreigners or any other strangers, his eyes darting around as he spoke to make sure nobody had noticed us. "We don't know anything about what goes on at the plant. But it often stops for some reason or another," he said. "You can tell from the amount of waste water and the change in the temperature of the sea; No. 2 has been closed for over a year now, you know."

At the time of writing, there are six nuclear power stations operating in India. The newest of these, Madras Nos. 1 and 2, were the first to be planned and constructed wholly in India.

The man declined to tell us anything about damage caused by the plant. He refused to have his photograph taken, or take us into the village half a mile away for fear of the consequences. He was not the only one too afraid to talk. We got the same reaction when we visited one of Panneerselvan's friends from university, a scientist who had been in charge of environmental assessment at Kalpakkam since 1983.

The scientist gave Panneerselvan a warm reception—until he heard that the journalist had company.

"Journalists from Japan? You must be joking! If it gets out that I've even met you, I'll be fired. Get out of here." He slammed the door angrily in Panneerselvan's face. "The salary's good, and if he just keeps quiet, his future is guaranteed . . ." the journalist muttered.

When construction of the nuclear facilities began twenty years previously, nine hundred people had been forced to move "for the good of India." Their new home in the village of Kokilyamedu consisted of a collection of small concrete huts, with no school or hospital, a three-mile walk from the nearest market.

At one edge of the village, a high wall with a watchtower casting an ominous shadow over the people's homes marks the boundary of the complex. The wall stopped at the beach and in its place there was a No Entry sign. We waited until the guard had disappeared for a while, then aimed our cameras over the sign in the hope of getting some shots of the grounds inside. A crowd of children gathered round calling out "Photo! Photo!" and stood in front of the sign, which none of them could read.

'WE JUST WANT TO CATCH LIVE FISH, NOT DEAD ONES'

Sadres is a quiet fishing village home to less than five hundred people located at the southern end of the Kalpakkam Nuclear Complex. Poverty reigns there just as it does in Kokilyamedu, but the atmosphere of the village is a little different. Children were studying under a roof thatched with palm leaves, and next door was a small building belonging to the Bay of Bengal Fishermen's Union.

Inside were three young men. We told them the purpose of our visit and stepped inside. Lesson plans and antinuclear posters covered the gray walls of the building. The school was in fact administered by the union.

"Why exactly are you against the nuclear facility?" we asked P., the secretary, getting straight to the point.

"We can't catch fish any more because of it, that's why," was the reply. "If you get hit by a wave while you're out fishing, you start to itch and the lower half of your body breaks out in blisters."

The boats are small, the largest being no more than a couple of tons. There was a time when crab, shrimp, shellfish, and a variety of multi-colored fish could be found in abundance near Sadres.

"The reason why our catches have declined so drastically is that plant. The warm waste water that comes out of there keeps the fish away—particularly in the area within a few miles radius of the outlet,"

P. remarked bitterly. "Lots of dead fish are floating out there," added one of his companions, a thick-set young man of about twenty. "We gather them up and make *karuvadu*."

Karuvadu is a dish made by salting and drying fish for two or three days. We often saw the women and children of Sadres preparing the fish and laying them out to dry in front of their houses. "It all goes to market. People here won't touch the stuff because they know where it's come from," the young man continued, a trifle guiltily.

The villagers take their catch of *karuvadu* to Madras and sell it there, where it provides a cheap source of protein for the poor people in the city. We asked whether it was actually safe for people to eat this fish. "Well, they're probably contaminated, but we can't catch anything else, and there's hardly any money coming in at the moment. We don't have any choice," he said gloomily.

Under normal circumstances, the temperature of the sea around Kalpakkam is about 85°F. However, according to P., when both of the reactors are in operation the temperature at the outlet shoots up to 140°F, a dangerous level. The fishermen would start itching and begin to feel tired every time they went out to sea.

In an attempt to find out exactly why these things were happening, the union recently got hold of a booklet about radiation written in easy-to-understand Bengali. Its contents include explanations about gamma and beta rays, and the Chernobyl disaster. The men have started a study group in the village using this material. P. explained to us the mood of the people concerning this issue:

"The authorities don't tell us anything except that it's safe. But it's not surprising that the people start to worry when they hear about what happened at Chernobyl."

The villagers have tried countless times to bring attention to their decreasing catches, dead fish, and illnesses. The authorities, however, will have nothing to do with their claims, accusing them of some vague ulterior motive.

The villagers' main quarrel with Kalpakkam is that it is making it extremely difficult for them to escape from the cycle of poverty in which they are trapped.

"We want to catch and sell good *live* fish, not *dead* ones!" the young man said, smiling for the first time since our interview began.

BESIEGED BY RADIATION

Traveling north along the Bay of Bengal, we arrived in Calcutta. From there we made a five-hour train trip to the steel town of Jamshedpur, in the state of Bihar. Another two hours' drive up a winding mountain road brought us to within sight of the uranium mining village of Jadugoda.

"Let's get out here and have a look at the uranium tailing pond." Our guide for this section of the trip was the Jamshedpur journalist and chairman of the Society for Environmental Consciousness, Janak Deo Pandey. We hid our cameras in our bags and walked up the steep hill for about fifty yards. When we reached the top, below us we could see the pond and the piles of tailings, dry and cracked, enveloped in an eerie silence.

When uranium ore has been refined and the uranium oxide (yellow-cake) extracted, the remaining rubble is sent down pipes to this tailing pond. The refinery, located half a mile away, reminded us of a small fortress.

Directly below us we could see another village. "That's the place besieged by radiation," Pandey commented. Dungridi is a tiny hamlet of twenty-five households, home to 125 people.

Later we walked into the courtyard of one of the houses to find Mohan Majhi, a thin young man, sitting in the sun having his lunch. Aged twenty-one, he used to work at the uranium mine. Majhi's movements were slow and deliberate and his eyes bloodshot; he was obviously not in the best of health.

"I started getting fevers after about a month at the mine," he said weakly. "I stuck it out for a while, but after two months I couldn't work any more. The doctor there told me I had blood poisoning—I don't know exactly what he meant by that." He began to cough violently. Recently, he told us, he had no energy and was beginning to lose his sight.

"I can't do anything now except hang around at home." Majhi did not even receive a medical certificate. His wages stopped as soon as he left, and he has no money to buy medicine.

"Poor Mohan lost his father two years ago, to cancer of the tongue," Shamu Majhi said sympathetically. Shamu had just come off the night shift at the mine. Mahji added, "After fifteen years at the mine, he suddenly got cancer—he was only forty-five when he died." His mother, Salke, rubbed his back as he collapsed in another fit of coughing.

"My son was healthy too before he went to work in the mine," she said. "Everyone who works there ends up with something wrong with them." There are still three young children in the family, and following her husband's death, supporting the family became Mohan's responsibility as the eldest son. Since his health deteriorated, the family has had to eke out a living from the small patch of land it owns.

"My father worked at the mine, too—for twenty years," said Shamu, who was the local youth leader. "He's been bedridden for a long time now with a fever. Another miner died of cancer here two weeks ago. The same thing is happening in the next village." Shamu himself has been working in the mine for six years. He told us that recently he had started to feel a worrying tightness in his chest. "I went for my first checkup in six years the other day. But they wouldn't tell me the results."

The men of these villages give up their lives in order to make a living for their families. However, it is not only the miners themselves who are affected. Walking around Dungridi, we realized that the contamination from the mines was spread over a wide area.

Simoti Majhi, aged eight, was standing beside one of her family's cows when we first saw her. She was wearing a torn green dress and had a towel wrapped round her head. She turned away shyly as we approached. "She's been plagued by this fever ever since she was three," her mother, Baso, told us, her brow creased with worry. "Not long after she first got it she started to lose all the feeling in her right hand. Now she can't pick anything up—she can't even lift her arm."

Simoti's shoulder blades stuck out sharply from her back. She wears the towel to cover her abnormally small head. Her eyes shifted from side to side, but she never looked straight at us. Simoti is also mute. "Simoti didn't even know her father had died," Baso sighed. Her husband, Chandrayi, had died three years previously at the age of forty-five, after three long years of illness during most of which he was bedridden. He had worked in the uranium mines for eighteen years. The doctors had said it was tuberculosis.

Near the Majhis' home lived another little girl, Jowa Soren. She was only eight months old, but when her father came out holding her, we noticed that her legs were abnormally thin. Her father, Mohan, a farmer explained that she had lost all the feeling in them when she was two months old.

"The doctor said it was polio, but she was inoculated soon after she was born, so I doubt that it can be." His wife nodded in agreement. "The air and water are poisonous around here," added Shamu Majhi, who was showing us around the village.

When the hot winds of summer blow, a material like ash is carried down into the village from the tailing pond. "When that stuff starts to blow down here, the whole village is filled with dust; it gets in our houses, on our food, it coats the crops in the fields—it's disgusting. And everyone coughs all the time," he continued.

The river water has become contaminated by the tailings pond, so the Uranium Corporation of India Limited (UCIL), which is under the direct jurisdiction of the Department of Atomic Energy, has recently installed a water pipe. Running directly above the water pipe is a three-foot-wide pipe used to transport uranium tailings; next to the water faucet we saw the women of the village washing dishes and doing their laundry. This is the only drinking water that is provided for the people of Dungridi.

At one stage during our visit to the village, a man called out to us and asked us what we were doing there. When we replied that we were investigating damage caused by radioactive contamination, he beamed and said confidently, "There's none of that here!" The man's name was Lal and he was in charge of the chemistry division at the mine. We asked him if the pond was really safe.

"Of course it is," was his reply. "All the tailings are chemically treated before they are released into the pond."

"But you must be aware that a lot of people are ill in the village?" we persisted.

"Oh, them. That lot are just ignorant . . . No matter how many times we tell them not to drink the river water or use it for washing, they never listen."

Perhaps Lal realized then that he had just contradicted his earlier assurances, because with these words he hurriedly started up his motorbike and drove away. On the edge of the village stood a small sign with the paint peeling off. With difficulty we could make out the words "Tailing Pond—Radioactive Zone. Trespassers Will Be Prosecuted."

MYSTERIOUS, PAINFUL DISEASES

The Department of Atomic Energy's Nuclear Fuel Complex (NFC) is located right next door to a densely populated area: fifteen miles northeast of Hyderabad, a city with a population of three million. All the uranium oxide mined and refined at Jadugoda is taken here.

The NFC is the department's pride and joy; the huge plant produces all of India's nuclear fuel requirements. In the opinion of the nearby residents, however, the complex is nothing but a source of mysterious, painful diseases that add to the burden of poverty that they are already saddled with.

Saritha. A girl, five years old. Her legs are twisted so badly she cannot walk but only drag herself along with her hands.

Sumalatha. A girl, three years old. Her arms and legs are very short, and she is mentally handicapped.

Sriramulu. A boy, six years old. He has been bedridden with an unidentified illness since he was three.

"If I were to give you the names of all the sick and disabled children in this village, we'd be here all day," said P. Ramulu, whom we met in Ashok Nagar, a village home to fifteen hundred people just across the road from the boundary fence of the NFC. The houses of Ashok Nagar were squat and identical, reminding us of barracks. "It's not just children," Ramulu continued. "Two men, aged thirty-one and forty, have recently died of unknown causes. Both of them worked at NFC, like I used to. Not only that," he sighed, "we've been told not to use the well water, too."

According to Professor Purushotham Reddy of Osmania University, who is also the chairman of an environmental protection group based in Hyderabad, the contamination of the underground water supply is not limited to Ashok Nagar. Eleven other villages in the vicinity of the NFC have the same problem, and the contamination is spreading day by day.

"The only possible source of the contamination is the waste storage pond, known as the lagoon, which is located in the northern part of the complex," he said. The pond works on the principle of natural evaporation from the heat of the sun. However, evaporation is impossible, as fifty thousand tons of waste water are poured into it every day.

"Whether it's radioactive material or chemical waste, they have no proper system for safely disposing of it." Reddy is particularly concerned about the possibility of the underground water supply becoming contaminated by nitrates.

Ramulu gave us two examples of the negligence of the NFC regarding safety measures. On two occasions, in 1980 and 1982, the scrap heap inside the complex burst into flames, killing children who were playing there; four in 1980 and two in 1982. "At that time there wasn't even a fence around the complex," Ramulu added. "Not even adults knew it was dangerous, let alone children." According to Professor Reddy, the waste contained highly combustible zirconium. After the first accident, all the NFC did was change the location of the dump.

"They didn't put that fence up until after the second accident—it's just criminal." The professor's amiable countenance clouded over with anger.

Although the Department of Atomic Energy has forbidden the people of Ashok Nagar to use their well—the lifeline of the village—they have not replaced it with any proper alternative. Plans for a reliable water supply are still on the drawing board, and until they are put into practice the villagers must rely on a water tanker which only delivers every other day. No matter how much care they take not to waste the precious liquid, the supply is still not sufficient and the villagers find they have no choice but to dip into the forbidden well.

"As far as the NFC is concerned, we're nothing but insects to be trodden on," muttered Ramulu.

FIGHTING FOR A NUCLEAR-FREE ZONE IN SOUTHEAST ASIA

"We demand that the new government of V.P. Singh tear back the veil of secrecy that has surrounded nuclear policy in this country for too long. The time has come for the government to acknowledge the damage done to the environment, and to conduct a survey to find out exactly how many people have been affected by radiation."

The speaker was Dhirendra Sharma, associate professor at Jawaharlal Nehru University. His audience consisted of thirty-five members of the Hyderabad Press Club. "Unfortunately neither those living close to nuclear facilities nor media people like yourselves know much about radiation. But I can assure you, the problem of contamination is extremely serious—one which includes exposure to radioactive substances from the nuclear fuel complex located not far from where we are now . . ."

Sharma's field is science policy. During the forty-two years from independence to the government of Rajiv Gandhi, no open debate on nuclear policy was permitted. In an effort to break down the wall of secrecy built up by successive governments, he formed the Committee for a Sane Nuclear Policy in 1981. Two years later, Sharma published a book, *India's Nuclear Estate*, based on the findings of a survey he had carried out himself, which was widely acclaimed as the first publication to criticize the government's atomic energy policy.

"They put a lot of pressure on me," he commented jovially. His failure to be promoted from associate professor is seen as one consequence of the publication of his book. Sharma refuses to give up the fight, though. He believes that democracy will never flourish anywhere without criticism. "Once a mistake has been made in science policy, it's almost impossible to retrieve the situation." Sharma's experiences of studying for long periods in Britain and the United States have also had a strong influence on his ideas.

The belief that atomic energy is the key to the country's development is deeply rooted among India's rulers. Political and military factors also play a part; in particular the longstanding border dispute with China and the equally longstanding conflict with Pakistan.

"Possession of nuclear technology is also seen as a kind of passport to developed-nation status," said Sharma. He showed us the latest five-year plan for the period up to 1990, which included a listing of the various areas of development allocated a percentage of the budget:

> Atomic energy development: 15%
> Space technology: 17%
> Military: 37%

These three alone capture 69% of the budget. On the other hand, social services, including education and welfare, manage only 5%, while development of rural areas merits only 0.1% of the total expenditure.

"There are over eight hundred million people in this country, eighty-five percent of whom live in rural areas. Do they really think they're going to get rid of poverty with a pathetic 0.1% of the budget? It's inexcusable."

Sharma sees the emphasis placed on nuclear development as one reason why poverty is slow to disappear in India, particularly considering that the amount invested in atomic energy is totally out of proportion with the number of facilities actually in operation. "The damage done to the environment is inexcusable as well. The chairman of the Atomic Energy Regulatory Board, which is supposedly a watchdog organization, is on record as saying 'We don't have the money, the technology, or the equipment, so we have to rely on data supplied to us by the Department of Atomic Energy.' That seems to sum up the situation in India at the moment."

Sharma and other members of the Committee for a Sane Nuclear Policy appealed to the government for a moratorium on nuclear development. Their campaign has included a photographic exhibition of environmental damage and victims of radiation, which was held in all the major cities. The group has not confined its appeal to India—the members are calling for the whole of South Asia to be made a nuclear-free zone. "Pakistan can no more afford the expense of nuclear development than we can. The ideal thing would be for both countries to put a stop to all this stupidity."

It remains to be seen which the Indian government will find more important: a way out of poverty for its people or the continued development of nuclear power.

THE RADIATION COAST

In the southern state of Kerala, facing the Arabian Sea, there is a beach known locally as "the radiation coast." The twenty-three-mile stretch of sand has a level of natural background radioactivity between five and fifty times the safe level set by the International Radiological Protection Board. This high level of radiation is caused by large deposits of monazite in the sand. At present the public corporation, Indian Rare Earths, is refining the sand to produce rare earths and thorium-232, which is used for nuclear fuel. The radioactive sand which the company collects from the area is posing a grave danger to the nearby residents.

We drove by jeep along the coast, passing small houses dotted among the palm trees, toward the village of Alappat. We were accompanied by V. T. Padmanabhan, coordinator of the Center for Industrial Safety and Environmental Concerns, a private research organization. The center has its office in Quilon City, and for the past few years it has been conducting health surveys in the area.

"Let's stop here and measure the level of radioactivity," he said. We got out of the jeep near the outskirts of Alappat and put our geiger counters to work. They began to give off a high-pitched beep. We calculated the level of radioactivity to be 1.8 rems per year, ten times the internationally recognized public exposure limit.

We traveled a little further down the expanse of glittering black sand to the village and pulled up at one of the houses there. The whole place was no more than ten or twelve yards square. As we entered, immediately in front of us we saw a small girl asleep in bed, her mouth hanging open. She was very thin, and her legs were twisted. Her name was Asha and she was seven years old. "The only thing Asha understands is when she is hungry . . ." the girl's mother, Viswhawma, said, looking sadly at her daughter. "We have to feed her on soft food like milk and bananas—rice is too hard for her to chew," her husband, Raja, added. The strain of looking after her daughter was apparent on Viswhawma's face.

The couple started to notice something odd about Asha when she was about eight months old. She had hardly grown at all, and she never made a sound. The child began to suffer from frequent bouts of fever, until she was spending all her time in bed. A terrible suspicion took hold of Raja and Viswhawma; their eldest daughter had shown exactly the same symptoms before she died in 1985 at the age of six. The local doctor told them that Asha's condition was due to a congenital disease, but was unable to pinpoint the cause. The couple could not think of anything either.

They heard the word radiation for the first time recently, but were not aware of what it could do to the human body. "Even supposing it was dangerous," said Raja, "this village is the only place for us." He looked down at his daughter and added, "I wonder how long she will be with us." His wife's eyes glittered with tears.

We left their home wishing there was something we could have said or done to comfort them, and walked around the village. There seemed to be an unusual number of disabled people in Alappat; we saw people with deformed shoulders, children with multiple disabilities, a child with Down's syndrome, three out of five children in one family had badly impaired vision. We found ourselves wondering if such a concentration of disabled children and young adults in one area was due to exposure to radiation.

Four villages, home to a total of fifty thousand people, lie within this area of high natural background levels of radiation. In 1977, the All India Institute of Medical Sciences of New Delhi conducted a comparative survey of thirteen thousand people living in a highly radioactive area and six thousand people living in areas with acceptable levels of background radiation. The results showed that while the highly radioactive area included twelve children with Down's syndrome, the other area had none. The number of severely mentally and physically handicapped children in each area was twelve and one respectively, and that of patients with unidentified illnesses, eleven and three. In short, the institute found major differences between the two areas. Furthermore, the report stated that genetic defects were far more frequent in the high-level radiation area.

Representatives from the government-sponsored Bhabha Atomic Research Center in Bombay disagree and insist that there is no greater incidence of illness or disability among residents receiving high doses of radiation in that area than anywhere else. Padmanabhan dismisses their claims as part of the myth of safety promoted by the Department of Atomic Energy, and criticizes the Bhabha Center for not carrying out a thorough enough survey. He also criticizes the survey of the Institute of Medical Sciences as not giving a clear overall picture of the situation, especially with regard to the incidence of radiation-related diseases.

In order to fill in the gaps left by these previous surveys, the Center for Industrial Safety and Environmental Concerns launched an epidemiological survey in March 1988, covering a total of ninety thousand people; all the families in the high-level radiation area, plus forty thousand people from neighboring areas with normal levels. Padmanabhan told us that he expected different results from the data obtained from research on Hiroshima and Nagasaki victims, because the people were exposed to radiation in a different manner. Victims of the A-bombs in Hiroshima and Nagasaki were bathed in a huge quantity of radiation for a second, but the people of the radiation coast are exposed to radiation throughout their entire lives. Padmanabhan also plans to invite experts from the United States and Japan to help analyze the data and assist in producing a plan of action to save the people from any further harm.

Monazite was first discovered on the coast by a German in 1909, and in 1912 a British company began extracting the mineral, continuing to do so until the end of the Second World War. At that time, this area produced half of the world's output of monazite. In 1948, a year after independence, the Indian government established the Department of Atomic Energy and banned the export of monazite, hoping to use the thorium-232 in it as nuclear fuel. In 1950, the company Indian Rare Earths was formed and two years later it began extracting thorium at a refinery in Alwaye, ninety miles away from Quilon City.

India boasts the largest deposits of monazite in the world. The company refines three thousand tons of ore per year, and is thought to have a stockpile of between three thousand and thirty-five hundred tons of thorium for use in the future as nuclear fuel. The Department of Atomic Energy had planned to bring a number of fast-breeder reactors using thorium for fuel into operation by the 1980s. However, this plan is running a long way behind schedule, and, at present, demand for thorium on the domestic market is way below their expectations. Fortunately for the Indian government, the rare earths found in monazite have recently begun to be widely used by developed nations in high-technology industries such as electronics, which has lead to an increase in demand. These rare earths have become a valuable foreign exchange earner, and thorium has dropped to the status of a byproduct.

THORIUM CONTAMINATION IN MALAYSIA

*R*ecently several Japanese companies have been criticized for their operations in Southeast Asia which take advantage of low wages and governments that, in their eagerness for industrial development, are willing to turn a blind eye to dangerous practices.

In Malaysia, a Japanese company is causing widespread environmental damage with its careless disposal of radioactive waste. In Japan, strict regulations brought a halt to the extraction of rare earths in 1972. However, in Malaysia, these substances are still being refined, although thorium-232, a byproduct of this process, is considered a danger to the environment and the health of the local people. At present, local residents are fighting the company in court in an effort to stop refining operations and obtain compensation.

Previous page: Bags of thorium-232 carelessly abandoned in Bukit Merah, Malaysia.

LIVING ON THE EDGE OF A NUCLEAR-WASTE DUMP

The area around the city of Ipoh in the northwestern state of Perak is Malaysia's largest tin-producing region. In the same ore is found the mineral monazite, the raw material from which rare earths are extracted. Located on the southern edge of Ipoh, which has a population of three hundred thousand, is the Asian Rare Earths complex (ARE), thirty-five percent of which is owned by the Tokyo-based company Mitsubishi Chemicals. ARE's refinery has two hundred employees, and is in operation twenty-four hours a day, disgorging an endless stream of white smoke from its chimneys.

ARE started its refining operation in 1982. Monazite contains seven percent thorium, a radioactive substance which ARE considers a waste byproduct of the refining process. The Malaysian government asked the company to store the thorium, with the aim of utilizing it as an atomic fuel in the future.

Hew Yoon Tat, aged forty-five, lives in the village of Bukit Merah, west of the refinery. He is a butcher by trade, and also chairman of the Perak Anti-Radioactive Action Committee.

"They only had permission from the government to conduct trial operations there, but they went straight into normal production, and at first they didn't bother building any waste storage facilities," he told us angrily.

ARE moved into full production and by the end of 1983 the company had built a waste storage facility three miles from the refinery in the village of Papan. However, there was fierce opposition from the local residents when they discovered that radioactive waste was going to be stored on their doorsteps. The government commissioned the International Atomic Energy Agency (IAEA) to carry out an investigation of the facility. After the agency reported that it was indeed dangerous, ARE was forced to suspend further plans to store the thorium.

This was the first time that the residents of Bukit Merah, a mere half-mile from the refinery complex, had heard anything about radioactive waste. "We were the closest, yet we didn't have a clue . . ." said Hew. The residents wrote to ARE, demanding to know exactly what was being manufactured and what was contained in the waste from their operations. They received no reply. When the various rare-earth metals, such as yttrium, which is used in color television cathode ray tubes, had been extracted at ARE they were exported to Japan and Europe. According to the company, the waste material was then "stored in a trench."

"Stored? Don't make me laugh," was Hew's response. "The people here know that they just dumped the stuff. We don't need Japan's unwanted waste."

IRRESPONSIBLE HANDLING OF RADIOACTIVE SUBSTANCES

It was nine in the evening when we visited the home of electrician Yoon Siew Hee. He had just come home from work. Yoon lives in the village of Menglembu, close to Bukit Merah, and is a former employee of ARE, where he worked for four years from April 1982, the month the refinery was opened. "I left ARE because I was afraid of cancer," he told us candidly. His wife sat in the room with their five children making bags to sell, occasionally throwing a glance at her husband and saying, "You shouldn't really talk about it," in worried tones. Yoon told us he had been threatened by his former bosses since testifying as a witness for the residents against the company in the High Court in Ipoh in July 1988. Since then he had not spoken to anyone about the refinery.

Yoon agreed to speak to us on hearing that we were Japanese journalists. Hesitantly, he began to tell his story:

"Three times a day I used to go round the plant and check all the electrical fittings. I didn't know anything about radiation, of course, and there were no signs up to warn us of any danger. We had no protective clothing; I used to go home in my work gear. The thorium waste scattered around the grounds was washed out of the pipes into the Serokai River next door." The first time Yoon heard talk of radiation was when a protest in Papan against the waste storage facility was reported in the papers. Even after this incident, the company still kept telling its employees that there was nothing to worry about.

"When I changed jobs my salary dropped from thirteen hundred Malaysian dollars to seven hundred a month; quite a difference, but I figured my life was more important." Yoon told us he had no regrets about leaving his job, but that he was still very worried about his health as well as that of his family.

Ng Toong Foo runs a transport company, and also has a gas station in

Menglembu. For two years starting in 1983, he worked under contract to ARE, transporting waste material.

"They told me the stuff was thorium cake, and that it could be used for fertilizer," he told us. "I used to load it on a dump truck and cart it round to an abandoned tin mine at the back of the refinery and dump it. Some of it got thrown in household refuse dumps, or in vegetable patches, even in the river."

Ng claims that he received no instructions from the company regarding where the thorium was to be dumped. "The company knew it was being disposed of in all sorts of places," he added.

Michael Wan, general manager of ARE, disagreed. According to him, specific orders were given about where the waste was to be stored. "The transport company was just dumping it where they felt like it—I'm beginning to regret not supervising them more closely . . ."

When one of Ng's employees showed signs of burns on his hands from handling the waste, and the locals started to boycott his gas station, Ng broke his contract with ARE.

One still afternoon after a short burst of rainfall, Ng took us to where his contaminated truck had been dumped. Its body was rusted and overgrown with ivy. Nearby were some houses and a car repair business.

Three years previously, an expert from Japan had checked the radioactivity of this truck and found it to be 7.8 rems, well over the limit of 5 rems per year set for workers dealing with radioactive materials.

THE PERAK ANTI-RADIOACTIVE ACTION COMMITTEE

"When we first started the movement we weren't very well organized and we didn't know what we were doing. At times we were completely lost," said Thai Siew Foong, reflecting on the last five years. She lives in Bukit Merah, and when she is not working at her regular job she is involved in the activities of the Perak Anti-Radioactive Action Committee.

The instinctive feeling that radiation posed some kind of threat had formed the basis for the group. When the committee started, though, they had no idea what level of radiation they were talking about, and no scientific backing for their movement.

The local residents, working through the Consumers' Association of Penang and environmental groups, invited Ichikawa Sadao of Saitama

University, Japan, to measure the level of radioactivity in the area. Professor Ichikawa is known for his research on low-level radiation dosage. "When I was there, ARE had put barbed wire around the waste dump in response to the demands of the local residents in 1984, but there were no signs to warn people of radiation, and you could get into the compound through the back entrance quite easily," recalled Ishikawa. At the time, 350 tons of thorium waste had already been dumped there.

The readings were taken in public over a four-day period; the highest reading around the waste dump was 4.82 rems per annum, approximately ten times the maximum level of 0.5 rems initially set by the International Commission for Radiation Protection, and forty-eight times the revised level of 0.1 rems currently in general use. "The most important point to remember is that while beta and gamma rays can be measured, short-wave alpha rays are not picked up. Quantities of nuclei such as thorium-232 and radon-220, which give off alpha rays, cannot therefore be measured," the professor explained.

The same warning had been given by Edward Radford, of Pittsburgh University, and a former visiting researcher at the Radiation Effects Research Foundation of Hiroshima, when he visited the area two months prior to Professor Ichikawa. Professor Radford also noted that if radon was given off in gaseous form, then there was a strong possibility of it being inhaled and contaminating food, and in his report he stated that "a potentially serious health problem already exists for workers within the plant itself and may exist . . . for the people nearby."

Though they confessed to being a little confused at first by all the technical terms, Thai and her fellow committee members realized that this was the scientific proof they had been waiting for. In February 1985, they brought a suit against ARE in the Ipoh High Court in the name of eight residents of Bukit Merah. Their aim was to close down the refinery. In October that year, the court came down in favor of the residents and ARE was ordered to halt operations and to take action to deal with the waste.

ARE obeyed the ruling and halted operations a month later. After the mountain of waste was packed into drums, the former dump was covered over and the company built a temporary storage facility on the site in 1986, which is currently still in use. A radiation expert formerly at the IAEA who was invited to take readings in the area confirmed that radiation was at a safe level, so the company was able to obtain permission from the Malaysian government to start production again. Operations were recommenced in February 1987.

"Safety is our Concern" boasts the sign in English and Malay on the fence of the storage area. However, this does not alter the fact that Professor Ichikawa's investigations continue to reveal unsafe levels of radiation even though they were carried out after the new storage area was built, nor that the harmful effects feared by the Anti-Radiation Action Committee are beginning to be observed in the local community.

A HIGH INCIDENCE OF LEUKEMIA IN BUKIT MERAH

Just over five hundred yards from the site of the ARE refinery, we entered a house to find ourselves in a living room lit by a 15-watt fluorescent light that allowed us to make out piles of cardboard boxes heaped haphazardly on top of one another. A child appeared from another room, calling out "Hello!" Her radiant smile and cheerful tone seemed to light up the house, and we shook hands with pleasure. Lam Lai Kuan was eleven years old, and in sixth grade. She was completely bald, and for a second we mistook her for a boy, until we spotted the necklace and anklet she was wearing. In January of that year (1989), she had been diagnosed as having acute lymphatic leukemia. She had lost all her hair as a result of the radiation therapy.

"I started getting a sore back in November last year—it got worse and worse till I couldn't walk anymore." After she had seen the doctor in Bukit Merah, the girl was sent to Ipoh General Hospital, where she was treated for three and a half months. Her condition improved, and she was able to return to school, although continuing to make frequent visits to the hospital. However, the symptoms appeared once again, and from August till October of 1989 she was hospitalized in Kuala Lumpur. "We've only just got back," called out her mother, Hiew Chao Thye, from where she was sitting bouncing her first grandchild on her knees. She looked very tired, as if worry about her daughter's health was taking its toll.

Lai Kuan herself found out she had leukemia during her second spell in hospital. "The doctors said it was a difficult disease to cure, but because they found out about it early they said it'd be alright." There was not a hint of worry in her voice. "Everyone asks me why all my hair has fallen out," she said. "Some of my friends ran away when I told them it was because of radiation." She is the youngest of three daughters. Her father died in an accident at work when she was three. "I want to become a teacher when I grow up," she told us. Her mother made no comment.

We left Lam Lai Kuan's home and walked a few yards to our next stop, the home of Koh Poo Onn, another leukemia patient.

Koh was nineteen years old, but the disease had aged him beyond his years; his body was emaciated, his complexion a sickly white. The youth had been sent to Ipoh General Hospital with jaundice in October 1988, where it was discovered that he had leukemia. He had just started work at a small shoe factory in Bukit Merah.

"It was a real shock when I found out that I had leukemia. I blamed myself, trying to think what I could have done to cause it." Koh still goes to the hospital once a week for treatment. His back gives him trouble, making it impossible for him to get a proper job because he cannot work for long periods. When he is feeling well enough he helps a friend to make shoes.

"The doctor told me that it would be better for me to move away from Bukit Merah because my resistance has been lowered by the loss of so many white blood cells . . . but I don't have the money to leave."

There was one more leukemia patient in the village, a five-year-old boy whose home was a mere hundred yards from the ARE complex. He was in the University Hospital of Kuala Lumpur when we visited Bukit Merah.

Three leukemia cases had been diagnosed within a year in this town of seven thousand. In the previous five years there had been none. Malaysia's annual rate of leukemia is three cases per one hundred thousand people, making the incidence of leukemia in Bukit Merah fourteen times higher than the national average.

Although difficult to prove, it would seem likely that the high incidence of leukemia was caused by thorium contamination from ARE.

"Getting compensation won't improve our health—what we really need is for that place to close as soon as possible," concluded Koh.

MULTIPLE BURDENS

Kasturi was just over a year old, yet she could neither sit up by herself nor crawl. Her body was covered in a rash, part of her skull was missing, she had difficulty breathing and was mentally handicapped.

"I didn't really want to have Kasturi—it would've been better that way for her too," said Pancharvanam Shauniugam, cuddling her daughter. The doctor at Bukit Merah had recommended an abortion on the grounds that she had been exposed to radiation. Unfortunately for Pancharvanam, an abortion was beyond her means.

She and her husband, Chellan Muniandy, already had two daughters aged five and six. On her husband's income of between three and four hundred Malaysian dollars a month (approx. U.S. $115–$150) they had to not only support themselves but also help Chellan's parents, who lived by themselves. The two hundred dollars a month Pancharvanam had earned at a local lumber mill had been an essential source of income for the family. That lumber mill was next door to the ARE refinery.

Pancharvanam worked at the mill for approximately four years, from 1985 until she gave birth to Kasturi in 1988. She knew her workplace had abnormally high levels of radiation, thanks to the survey carried out by Professor Ichikawa, and had already had one abortion in February 1987. Unable to afford a second, she was forced to leave work to look after her disabled daughter.

The family was squatting in an empty house left by tin miners on the banks of the Serokai River three hundred yards from the ARE refinery. Until water pipes were put in two years previously, they had relied on a well for water. A large battery was providing power for a single light bulb and a black-and-white TV, on which the two older girls were disinterestedly watching an Indian program in Tamil.

"We really want to move for the sake of our two healthy daughters, but . . ." Chellan said, without enthusiasm.

Cheah Kok Leong is another of the children of Bukit Merah with multiple disabilities. Six years old, Kok Leong is deaf and cataracts have made him blind. He also has a hole in his heart, his bones are weak, and he is unable to support himself. His mother Lai Kwan had experienced no such difficulties with any of her eleven other children, the oldest of whom is twenty-eight. "I think it was because I worked on the extension of the ARE site while I was carrying him. I can't think what else it could be." She had just got home from her job as a day laborer on a construction site and was preparing dinner as she spoke to us.

Lai worked at ARE for just over a year, from the beginning of 1982 until February 1983. She gave birth to Kok Leong in April 1983. "There was this horrible smell at the site and I often used to get bad headaches.

The supervisor was Japanese. He knew that I was pregnant but he never once warned me about radiation."

Lai's husband walked out on the family when Kok Leong was two years old. During the day the two junior high school age daughters take care of him while their mother goes out to work. Her monthly income is around two hundred Malaysian dollars (approx. U.S. $75). "With the help of the kids, we manage to make ends meet somehow."

In September 1988, Kok Leong had an operation on his left eye, enabling him to distinguish light from dark. He is also able to stand now. "If only I had enough money for a heart operation for him . . ." Lai Kwan remarked wistfully.

To these families for whom life itself is a daily struggle, the presence of a disabled child is an especially heavy burden.

DOING HIS UTMOST TO SERVE THE PEOPLE

In the center of Bukit Merah stands a converted Chinese-style house, and outside it a sign saying *Klinik Desa* (Rural Clinic). On a nearby wall are two carved wooden signs in Chinese which Dr. Thambyappa Jayabalan received from grateful residents of the village. One says "Dispensing Care with Kindness and Sympathy" and the other "Doing his Utmost to Serve the People."

"I consider it a great honor," he said, his eyes crinkling into a smile behind his glasses. An examination table, some basic medical equipment, various drugs, and a box of medical files were crammed into a space about twelve feet square.

"It's not really enough," he continued, looking round the room. "But we manage somehow."

After working at Ipoh General Hospital, Dr. Jayabalan opened his own practice in Kuala Lumpur in 1983, then moved to Bukit Merah in January 1987. He is the first resident doctor the village has ever had. His wife and two children remain in Madras for the sake of the children's education. "Why did I come here? Professional curiosity, I suppose. I wanted to know what sort of effects low doses of radiation have on the human body; it was a whole new field for me."

Dr. Jayabalan's speciality is pediatrics, and in addition to his everyday work, he made a comparison of the white blood cell counts of 260 children in Bukit Merah with those of 191 children on Carey Island, Selangor.

"I chose Carey Island because of the similarity of the environment to here; the reason I chose to investigate the single-nucleus white blood cell count was because I'd read that a decrease was noted among people exposed to radiation in the Marshall Islands. I thought there might be a similar result because exposure to radiation was common in both cases." Single-nucleus white blood cells are one of the most important elements of the body's immune system and the body becomes more susceptible to disease if they are damaged in any way.

Dr. Jayabalan was surprised at the results he received from the hematology research center in Kuala Lumpur. While the children of Carey Island showed no abnormalities, half of the children surveyed in Bukit Merah had white blood cell counts of under two hundred. The usual figure is between two hundred and eight hundred.

"All the island children showed normal counts, but five children here had very low counts. I think this result can be put down to radiation." Dr. Jayabalan also conducted a survey on miscarriages in Bukit Merah. He studied 108 women who had become pregnant between 1982 and 1987, excluding those over the age of thirty and those who had had abortions. Seven miscarriages in two hundred pregnancies were noted.

"On average there were forty pregnancies each year. In 1982 and 1986 there were two miscarriages, a rate of 5%. This is three times the national average of 1.8% and higher than the rate in other years."

The doctor felt a sense of foreboding about these figures, which was heightened by the sudden appearance of three cases of leukemia, the death of a young employee of ARE from meningitis, and the discovery of a malignant tumor in a five-year-old boy.

Dr. Jayabalan is an Indian Malaysian, but most of his patients are of Chinese origin. He treats the poor for no fee. During the day a young woman is employed part time as a receptionist; in the evenings, adults work at the clinic on a voluntary basis. Between consultations the doctor works on his own research. "It's a twenty-four–hour job here. I'm always on the verge of bankruptcy, but the locals rely on me, so I can't let them down." In cooperation with the village people the doctor has established a medical fund to help those in need of major operations. He also expressed the hope that one day he will be able to build a proper hospital, with proper equipment.

THE FUTURE OF BUKIT MERAH

"I've lived in Bukit Merah for thirty years, and I've never been more concerned about my family or the future of the village." These were the words of Chong Kim Choy, aged seventy-three, one of the plaintiffs in the suit being brought against ARE. His brow furrowed as he glanced at the photographs of his children and grandchildren. Three years ago, fifteen members of his family had lived on the same land two hundred yards from the refinery. Now only he and his wife are left. The others have gone to live in Ipoh, afraid of being exposed to radiation in Bukit Merah. They come to visit sometimes, but never stay.

The village of Bukit Merah was created by the British after the Second World War, when they regained control of the country after the Japanese defeat. Chinese immigrants were settled there in 1951 as part of a strategy to cut off support for the Communist guerrillas, who at that time were fighting for independence. Being an artificially created town, its streets run in a grid pattern, and the houses are neatly arranged in rows. These days, many of the houses are empty. "They've all left the village. Some because of work, but most for fear of radiation," Chong informed us.

In 1985 Bukit Merah had a population of eleven thousand. In four years that figure dropped to seven thousand. The number of households has also decreased, from fourteen hundred to twelve hundred. Increasingly, the remaining households are made up solely of elderly couples like the Chongs.

"I remember that before we knew anything about the radiation, I used to take the grandchildren for walks by that thorium dump," he continued. "One of them is always getting fevers and is very sickly. My daughter-in-law is not in the best of health, either. When we realized these problems were caused by that thorium, I had no choice but to tell them to go and live somewhere safer. So one by one, they've left . . ."

Chong took us to see the village of Taman Badrishah, a new residential area about half a mile from the ARE complex. Civil servants and bank workers from Ipoh started to move out here in the late 1970s. The homes are newer than those in Bukit Merah, and there are several apartment buildings. Strangely enough, though, there are more vacant homes here than in Bukit Merah. Chong explained that the people have higher incomes here, so it is easier for them to move out. Of the five hundred houses in Taman Badrishah, two hundred are vacant. The asking price for most is much lower than would be expected, but still there are few buyers. Fear of radiation has caused a steady migration from the area around the ARE complex. Most of those who leave are young, and they take with them the future of the village. Their absence is a tragedy particularly for the Chinese, who traditionally like to have three or four generations live together under one roof.

In September 1987 Chong gave the following testimony in the Ipoh High Court. "I don't care whether it was the Ministry of Health or the Ministry of Trade that gave ARE permission to operate. What I care about is the health of the people of Bukit Merah. I want ARE with its poisonous radiation to get out." Chong admitted he has had a lot of sleepless nights since the appearance of leukemia and the unusually high incidence of disabled children in the village. "Mitsubishi Chemicals says that the ARE plant is helping the people of Malaysia, but it's never brought us anything but pain," he said, turning to his wife for confirmation.

JUDGMENT DAY LOOMING FOR JAPANESE COMPANIES IN ASIA

Lawyer Meenakshi Raman is one of those representing the people of Bukit Merah in their fight against ARE. When we visited her she was snowed under with meetings and the preparation of material for the case. Her office is on the island of Penang, in a stately white building reminiscent of colonial days. For the past eight years, Raman has been legal adviser to the Penang Consumers' Association, and has been involved with the ARE case since its initial stages in 1984. She sees the case as having important consequences for the health of all the people of Malaysia. "I'll explain why ARE's operations are illegal," she began. "Firstly, ARE's actual operations are dangerous because of the radioactive gas, dust, and waste materials produced. Secondly, Mitsubishi Chemicals, which for all intents and purposes is the owner, while well aware of the danger of thorium, did not bother to construct even one storage facility."

This is the first time that radiation damage has been the subject of a court case in Malaysia. Raman herself had to study radiation from the basics. "Certainly it's a mammoth task to produce scientific proof for all our claims." Her efforts are not helped by the Malaysian government, which is pushing ARE's cause as part of its Look East policy, whereby states are encouraged to develop by learning from the examples of Japan and South Korea.

Raman and four of the citizens of Bukit Merah were arrested under the Internal Security Act, proclaimed one month after the case first appeared in court, in October 1987. To prove that radiation was responsible for the low white blood cell counts and the high incidence of miscarriages, the residents of Bukit Merah are relying on the results of the epidemiological survey. ARE manager Michael Wan, however, is confident that the decision will be in his company's favor.

"The level of natural background radiation is high in this area, although certainly not high enough to damage people's health. The locals and the academics are getting too emotional about the whole thing. I've heard," he added, "that their radiation readings were not accepted for the court records."

"If the ARE claims are correct, then the people here have very vivid imaginations," commented Raman indignantly. "Refineries like this in Japan stopped operating in 1972, so why are they allowed to carry out operations in Malaysia?"

The book *Rare Earths*, published by the Japan Society of Newer Metals, explains that refining was banned in Japan because there is a danger of contamination from thorium and uranium when rare earths are extracted from monazite. The book goes on to state that this is the main reason why monazite has not been imported into Japan since 1972. Ironically, the general manager of ARE, Shigenobu Tamio, was one of the editors of this publication.

It is not surprising that Raman should ask us how Japan can carry out such an operation in Malaysia when it is considered too dangerous to do at home. "The lives of Japanese are more valuable perhaps . . ."

Mitsubishi Chemicals is the direct culprit in the case of Bukit Merah, but the real issue is a much wider one. It is not just one company that is being judged in the thorium contamination case. It is time for all Japanese businesses that operate in the international environment, the Japanese government, and ultimately the Japanese consumers, who enjoy the benefits of these operations, to face up to their responsibilities.

SOUTH KOREA'S
POISONOUS EMISSIONS

The people of South Korea often speak of the miracle of the Hangang. The miracle refers to the incredible economic growth over the past few decades which has affected the heart of the nation, symbolized by the River Hangang, Seoul's main artery. In recent years the continued development of the economy has been accompanied by the increased use of nuclear power. In 1988, 46.9 percent of South Korea's electricity was supplied by this means, making it the world's third-largest user of atomic energy for power generation. Since the advent of democracy in 1988 a fierce debate has been raging concerning the effect of the nuclear power plants on the health of the people employed by them and those living close by.

Previous page: The giant domes of the Yeonggwang nuclear power plant towering over a neighboring village.

DEFORMITIES SPAWN FEAR AND DISTRUST

Enormous trucks thundered past one after the other as we drove through forests of dark pines approximately thirty-five miles from Kwangju, the capital of Chollanam-do province. Leaving the valley, we headed for the sea, where beyond a group of farms we could see the giant domes of a nuclear power plant towering over the surrounding countryside.

With a capacity of 950,000 kilowatts, reactors No. 1 and 2 at Yeong-gwang are the largest type in use in South Korea. Just beyond the wire fence of the complex is the village of Seongsan, which has a population of three thousand. It was an incident which took place in this quiet rural backwater that started the nuclear debate in South Korea in the summer of 1989.

"Wife of Yeonggwang Power Plant Employee Miscarries Two Children Without Brains." The employee, Kim Ik-Sung, has had little peace since this headline appeared in a local paper on July 29 of that year. It sparked a wave of "radiophobia" never before seen in the history of nuclear power development in South Korea.

"I swear it's true. I really did have to work in there without any protective clothing." Hugging his knees, Kim seemed lost in thought. The psychological burden of having thrown down the gauntlet to the government and the Korea Electric Power Corporation was obviously weighing on him heavily, along with the endless visits from reporters, lengthy investigations, and being branded as "the father of deformed children."

Kim is the fifth son of a farming family, and after leaving junior high school he helped out on the family farm. While there he also did some temporary work for a subcontractor at the Yeonggwang plant straight after the birth of his eldest daughter in March 1987. He worked for three hours in one of the boron mixing tank rooms, breaking up brown clods of the mixture with a hammer. The room was within the radioactive danger zone of the No. 2 reactor.

"They stopped me when I first entered the room because I wasn't wearing protective clothing, but one of the bosses who was with me made me go in anyway. They didn't take a note of my name." At the time Kim did not know what was meant by the sign "Radioactive Zone."

For the next twenty-six days he worked outside the zone, during which time he was constantly plagued by headaches and dizziness. Kim's wife had her first miscarriage in November 1988 at the age of twenty-eight. The child, which weighed just under four pounds, had a head half the normal size. The incident became a taboo topic even within the family. The second miscarriage took place in June 1989, by which time Kim was working as a security guard at the corporation's housing estate. Once again the fetus was found to be without a brain, and it was aborted by caesarian section. According to the doctors at Yeonggwang General Hospital, these unusual miscarriages could have been caused by hereditary factors, by drug or chemical poisoning—or by exposure to radiation.

News of the second miscarriage began to spread by word of mouth until finally it became the focus of a series of articles in the Korean press. On August 1, a group of doctors from Kwangju announced that, according to the results of a health survey carried out in Seongsan, "Abnormally high levels of white blood cell reduction and anemia have been observed not just in the father of the microcephalic child but also in other residents living near the nuclear power facility." Overnight the concern about exposure to radiation reached new heights.

The Ministry of Science sent out its own survey team the day after this announcement was made. Their interviews with local residents revealed that another employee at the plant had given birth to a deformed child, and the rumors about radioactive contamination spread even further.

In the midst of the debate Kim left his security guard job and quietly took his wife and daughter to the outskirts of the village to live. "If only I hadn't done that work at the plant . . ." he said, falling silent once again.

We were shown into the boron mixing room at the Yeonggwang plant where Kim had worked without protective clothing. Once inside the plant, we had stripped down to our underwear and changed into yellow overalls as protection from radiation. On our chests we placed two types of radiation detectors. When the heavy doors opened we were hit by an oppressively warm blast of air. The needle on our geiger counter started to move and stopped at 0.05 millirems.

"The people around here are kicking up such a fuss about the plant being dangerous, they just don't know anything about radiation, that's all," commented our guide, the section chief. We just watched the needle on our counter and thought about another incident we had heard about involving Kim Dong-Pil, aged twenty-two, a distant relative of Kim Ik-Sung. Kim Dong-Pil lives with his parents, two brothers and a sister, and his wife and two-year-old daughter next to the gate of the power plant. His daughter was born with deformed ankles. We visited him at home.

"I'd really like to get a job, but I just feel tired all the time," he told us forlornly.

On August 3, 1989, Dong-Pil was thrust into the limelight after he participated in a meeting between the villagers and the medical survey team which had rushed to the area after hearing Kim Ik-Sung's revelations. Dong-Pil asked one of the doctors if his daughter's disability had anything to do with his work at the power plant. That same night the television news reported that the "daughter of an employee at a nuclear power plant had been born with a genetic defect," and Dong-Pil's case became known across the nation.

Dong-Pil went to work at reactor No. 1 in July 1986, just before it began commercial operations. Like Kim Ik-Sung, he was working for a subcontractor, lured by the 90,000 won (approx. U.S. $140) per day, ten times the usual wage. He met the other seven workers in the area for the first time the day he started. They received no safety instruction. The men worked in the radioactive area for two fifteen-minute stretches a day for two days, a total of one hour, the work consisting of changing pipes in the pressurizer. For the first fifteen-minute stretch they carried a pocket radiation detector which measured up to 200 millirems; for the second a device which measured up to 500. Unable to bear the stifling heat Dong-Pil took off his mask while he cleaned the welded joints in the pipes. On several occasions, after he had finished, the light on the contamination monitor would flash a warning red. Dong-Pil, however, was never told that he was responsible for taking a note of the radiation levels.

Several days after the management had heard rumors about high levels of radiation, Dong-Pil was summoned to the environmental radiation laboratory for testing. He was never given detailed results, but the figure of "seven or eight hundred millirems" uttered by the technician remained in his head. Not long after this, his hands were covered in odd swellings. A year later his disabled daughter was born.

The Korea Electric Power Corporation insists that Dong-Pil's level of radiation was 70 millirems. This is less than the level of 5,000 millirems which the International Council for Radiation Protection (ICRP) has designated a safe limit for workers at nuclear facilities, and is not large enough a quantity to cause headaches or skin diseases, according to the plant management. The corporation denies that Dong-Pil even entered the radioactive zone. In reply to the claims of these one-time employees of the company, the Ministry of Science has announced it will allow them to be examined overseas, in accordance with their wishes. As Dong-Pil told us, "As a Korean, it makes me deeply ashamed that I can't trust the medical establishment in my own country. But the corporation and the government just keep denying everything."

Dong-Pil, who once held a second dan in Taekwondo, now spends his days pottering round at his parents' restaurant trying to help out. Fellow villagers who had promised to support him have now turned against him since Dong-Pil expressed his wish to be examined overseas, and he has become the target of abuse. "I feel as if I'm up against a brick wall all the time," he confided. He grows more anxious with each passing day. "All I want is a proper examination and to know exactly what the effects of the radiation are. Until then, I'm too afraid to have any more children."

FINANCIAL INCENTIVES LURE WORKERS TO THE POWER PLANTS

Approximately twenty miles northeast of Pusan, near the village of Kori on the Sea of Japan, is the site of South Korea's first nuclear power plant, which went into operation in 1978 during the Park presidency. Three more reactors were added soon after to make it the country's largest nuclear power facility.

"The money was good, and that was the main thing," remarked Choi Dae-Young, aged twenty-eight, the mayor of Hyoam, the village next to Kori. With these words he summed up the local residents' eagerness to work as day laborers at the plant when it first opened. The region had been largely left out of Korea's economic miracle, and the people scratched out a living by cultivating seaweed.

We spoke to Song Moon-Gil and Kim Hak-Moon, two men who had worked at the Kori plant. They told us that, although they had been aware of radiation, they "hadn't thought there was much to worry about."

To the men, the daily rate of 20,000 won had seemed ample incentive to work at the plant. Song and Kim worked for the second time at Kori in 1989 for a month during a lull in the seaweed industry, conducting inspections of the pipes in the steam generators. The pair described their work and the state of their health with a surprising lack of concern:

"We used to take the asbestos lagging off the pipes and wash them in disinfectant, then scrape off the rust. Some days we had radiation levels of 90 millirems." Often it was too hot for them to wear masks. After a few days of this work, spots began to appear on their stomachs and backs, which the two men and their fellow workers diagnosed as heat rash. Neither Song nor Kim usually drank, but working at Kori left them so tired that they began to do so to alleviate their fatigue.

Hong Joo-Bo, plant manager at Kori Nos. 3 and 4, informed us that even the day laborers receive thorough training and safety instruction and insisted that "there must be some other reason for their tiredness and skin conditions."

Despite Hong's assurances, the working conditions at the plant as casually described to us by Kim and Song were somewhat different. "I used to write the radiation levels in at less than they actually were, sometimes at zero," said Song. "When I thought my level was getting too high I used to leave my detector in the changing room—nobody ever found out," added Kim.

The Korean Ministry of Science does not allow workers who register more than 1,250 millirems in three months to engage in operations within the restricted radioactive zones of power plants. According to the ministry, checks are carried out every three months and suitable measures taken to ensure that employees' readings do not go over the internationally accepted annual limit of 5,000 millirems. The ministry adds that, in 1988, of the 6,639 people employed at nuclear power facilities in South Korea, not one showed a radiation level over this amount.

According to Kim and Song, they altered their records after a month of work, putting their total radiation levels at around 800 millirems. The reason was quite simple: going "over the limit" meant no more work, and making a living was of more importance to them than possible danger from exposure to radiation.

During the period from 1988 until the start of 1989, five deaths from cancer were reported in the village of Hyoam, which has a population of 750. Of these five, the three males were all day laborers at the Kori plant. Adding to the local residents' suspicions was the discovery of gloves and other rubbish from the plant buried secretly in the village.

Amid the controversy created by these incidents came the contamination scare at Yeonggwang at the end of July, and then the health problems being experienced by Song, Kim, and several other workers at the Kori plant began to take on a new light.

After the public outcry in the summer of 1989, the corporation paid a "radiation exposure allowance" of between 60,000 and 100,000 won (approx. U.S. $90-160) to nine workers including Kim Hak-Moon and Song Moon-Gil. The mayor reproved them for "endangering their lives for such a trifling amount of money," and the pair agreed that they would never work in a nuclear facility again.

DREAMS SHATTERED BY NUCLEAR POWER

On June 9, 1989, Pang Yoon-Dong, a young worker at one of Korea's nuclear power plants, died of stomach cancer.

"I want to know what really caused his death, even if I have to go to court. But it's like trying to attack a fortress with a slingshot—it's hopeless," said Pang's younger brother, Yoon-Doo. His parents sat next to him, silently watching Yoon-Dong's twelve-month-old son playing happily with a fly-swatter. We visited Pang's family at their home in the rice-growing district of Ansong-gun, Kyonggi-do, thirty-five miles south of Seoul. The early winter sun bathed the paddy fields and a row of stately poplar trees in light. The farm in Ejook-Myon village, where Pang Yoon-Dong was born, is a typical medium-sized farm, with four acres of rice and one and a half acres of vegetables. He was the fourth of eight children. After graduating from the local high school and completing three years of military training, at the introduction of a friend from the same village he joined a company which did work on a subcontract basis for the Korea Electric Power Corporation, and started work at the Kori plant in January 1984.

"He was a hardworking boy," said his mother. A strongly built, taciturn man who neither drank nor smoked. On his rare visits home he spoke of his wish to become a full-time employee of the corporation and be transferred closer to home, but apart from that Pang hardly ever spoke about his work. His starting wage was low at 140,000 won per month (approx. U.S. $230), so his parents sent rice and vegetables to help out both him and his new wife, Choi Chang-Ran.

After several attempts Pang succeeded in becoming a qualified electrician, and he joined the full-time staff of the corporation in April 1988. When Yoon-Doo made a congratulatory visit, however, he was shocked to find his brother a haggard shadow of his former self.

"Here was I thinking he was having it easy working at this big-time power plant, when in fact he wasn't able to take any holidays, and he'd lost his appetite completely."

In June the same year, Pang succeeded in obtaining a transfer to the Pyongtek thermal power station near his home town. By this time he could hardly force food down his throat, and six months later his dreams were shattered by the discovery that he had stomach cancer. He was operated on at Seoul University Hospital, but it was too late: the cancer had already made its way into his liver. "Former Power Corporation Employee with Incurable Cancer" was the headline that the newspaper *Hangeorae* used on its first scoop of 1989. The connection with radiation exposure drew the interest of the public, and the media became the battleground for a war of words between the power corporation and the antinuclear movement.

Pang's duties at the Kori plant had included the regular inspections of reactors No. 1 and 2, and the repair of the electrical wiring and pumps on the occasions when part of the system ceased operating without warning. The power corporation insists that the most radiation Pang was ever exposed to was in 1985 when his annual total was recorded as 2,647 millirems. Pang worked at Kori for a total of four years and three months; his average total exposure to radiation was said to be 1,109 millirems, well below any level likely to cause cancer.

On the day of the funeral, a gift of one million won from the power corporation was delivered to Pang's widow, with an offer of work. Pang's brother does not believe the power corporation told the whole truth about the amount of radiation his brother was exposed to. He has asked several times to see the pertinent records, but the management refuses to disclose any information. Pang never appeared to hold any grudge against the company while on his sickbed, but whenever the power corporation's side of the debate surfaced in the media he would say: "None of those people who are saying 'it's safe' ever went into any of the danger zones."

DEMANDS FOR RESETTLEMENT

The first thing to catch our eye as we entered the village was the digital display which proclaimed a radiation level of 0.008 millirems.

"We don't know if that's the real figure or not," grumbled Nam Ki-Dong, deputy chairman of the Hyoam Resettlement Committee. The display was hurriedly erected by the power corporation in April 1989 for the purpose of monitoring radiation levels.

"Who's going to trust them when they secretly bury radioactive rubbish and then say there's no contamination?" Nam continued. The 178 households of Hyoam village, who want to move away from the Kori plant, have little confidence in the Korea Electric Power Corporation.

From the end of 1988 through to the following April, yellow drums filled with waste, protective clothing, gloves, and other rubbish from the power plant were discovered buried in the hills and in the remains of an industrial reservoir in the village. On a tip-off from one of the plant employees, the whole village turned out to dig up the secretly buried waste. The power corporation continues to insist that the material is not radioactive. This has been confirmed regarding a portion of the material; the rest of it is currently being analyzed by the Ministry of Science.

On April 12, 1989, over a thousand angry people, including those from the nearby village of Kilcheon, loaded the drums onto their tractors and held a demonstration outside the Kori plant. Five men including the chairman of the Kilcheon resettlement committee were arrested and charged with obstructing the operations of the plant.

"It's not that I oppose all nuclear power plants, it's just that I don't want to live next to one that has such a slapdash attitude to safety as this." Nam himself was found guilty and is currently appealing the verdict. The demands of the residents near Kori do not stop with resettlement. In June 1989, approximately three hundred villagers received medical examinations at the power corporation's Hanil Hospital, situated on the company housing estate. The results showed no incidence of radiation-linked diseases, but Nam dismisses the examinations as careless and far from accurate. Not only were people's weights and heights recorded incorrectly in a number of cases, but Nam also claims that results were produced for people who had not even been examined. The same animosity could be seen between corporation officials and local residents in Seongsan, where the Yeonggwang plant was blamed for a child's deformed ankles and the miscarriage of two anencephalic babies. If anything, the reaction against the power corporation was even stronger there.

"The fact is that children with defects appeared after their fathers had worked at a nuclear power plant. Everything has a cause, and in this case, we think radiation is the cause. It's the people from the corporation who are being one-sided, with their insistence on fixing compensation at a level that suits them," said Kim Sang-Il, chairman of the Seongsan Resettlement and Budget Committee.

COMMUNICATION BREAKDOWN

After the twelve thousand workers involved in the construction of the Yeonggwang plant had departed, the villagers were left with dozens of empty houses and a mountain of debt. Catches of *koolbi*, a fish for which the region is well known, were drastically reduced compared with previous years. The villagers continue to demand compensation from the corporation for what they see as the disintegration of the local economy since the plant began operating.

A deeply rooted mistrust of the government seems to be a significant factor in the people's suspicions about nuclear power in South Korea. When we mentioned to the resettlement committee that in the cases of Hiroshima and Nagasaki, no significant genetic differences had been found between those who were exposed to radiation and those who were not, the committee was ready with the reply:

"The Japanese government could be lying about the figures, for all you know."

We spoke to Choi Hong-Sik, head of the radiation department of the Science Ministry, who is fighting an uphill battle to restore the people's faith in atomic energy.

"A simple lack of knowledge lies behind all this fuss about nuclear power, combined with past history and the changes now taking place in society," he said, choosing his words carefully. He was alluding to the recent accidents, and allegations of gross negligence and cover-ups connected with the construction of nuclear power facilities on the part of the previous administration, which have rocked the national assembly ever since South Korea established a democratic government in 1988.

"We know that nuclear power is safe, but we are prepared to respond to the questions of the people in good faith," added Choi.

Following the incident at Yeonggwang, the ministry announced in August 1989 that it would conduct a medical survey of all the residents within a two-mile radius of the plant, adding that it would include a doctor to be chosen by the people of Seongsan. This was not acceptable to the villagers, who had demanded a survey team of which half the members would be chosen by them, not just one. It will be a long time before the uproar at Yeonggwang dies down and the people and their government are able to communicate on more amicable terms.

LEARNING FROM AN A-BOMB SURVIVOR

On August 6, 1945, Koak Ki-Hoon was a cadet in the Japanese Imperial Army stationed in Hiroshima. After the war he became a founding member of the Korean A-Bomb Casualties Association, and is now living in Seoul, where he has just retired from his position as a high school principal after forty years of teaching. Koak is still an avid reader of Japanese literature, and the walls of his study are lined with literary magazines and works by well-known authors.

As one of those who has experienced radiation exposure, Koak is deeply interested in the media debate about nuclear power. Irritated by the manner in which the experiences of Korean A-bomb survivors were being ignored by those involved in the debate over radioactive contamination, he was only too happy to act as our interpreter during our stay in South Korea. "I believe I'll be able to use my experiences to help," he told us.

Koak drove us around the areas on which media attention was focused, in his beloved new car, recently bought with some of his retirement money. When we visited Kim Ik-Sung and Kim Dong-Pil, the day laborers who had sparked the nuclear debate, they turned to Koak and asked whether he thought they should have any more children. Koak switched from interpreter to adviser and reassured the men that he had three sons and two daughters, saying that, although he could understand their concern, the important thing was for them to look ahead to the future, not dwell on the past.

Meeting the family of Pang Yoon-Dong, who died a painful death from stomach cancer, Koak was reminded of his own hardships and his endless efforts to obtain recognition and compensation from the Japanese government. To this day the Korean nationals who were in Hiroshima and Nagasaki at the time of the bombing have received neither apologies nor compensation from their former colonial masters.

"I suppose it can't be helped," he said bitterly, "after all, how can you fight a whole country?"

The ex-principal did not reserve his criticism for Japan, and commented that he thought the antinuclear movement seemed unaware of some basic facts about radiation. To their claims that radiation damage may be passed on in the genes he retorted, "On what basis can you make that statement?" Neither did the power corporation escape the lash of his tongue. Every time Koak heard the statement that employee radiation levels were well below the danger level, he commented that surely it would be better to make sure that employees were exposed to no radiation at all. As a *pipokja*, or A-bomb victim, himself, Koak has no time for those who argue without possessing more than a superficial knowledge of what they are talking about, nor for those who try to escape their responsibilities. The two sides of the media debate on nuclear power refuse to budge from their respective standpoints, with the result that the victims and their families have been left stranded in the middle not knowing who to believe.

Some fifteen years ago, Koak published a book in Japanese, *Korean Radiation Victims*, in which he harshly criticized Japan for ignoring its responsibilities toward the Korean victims of the A-bomb. That fight continues today. Koak now feels it is also his mission to contribute what he can to this latest nuclear debate:

"Being a victim of the Hiroshima A-bomb, I believe I am more qualified than anyone else to speak about this issue, and I feel it's my duty to do so. We can help prevent the possibility of radiation claiming future victims and enable a greater number of people to understand the victim's point of view. I believe the time has come for us to play a more active role in this debate." After clocking up approximately eight hundred miles traveling to and from nuclear power plants and the settlements near them, these were Koak's parting words.

A QUESTION OF SOCIAL RESPONSIBILITY

On our return to Seoul we spoke to doctors involved in radiation medicine. "How can I remain calm when I've been accused of being a tool of the government?" asked Koh Chang-Soon, professor at Seoul National University and chairman of the Korean Society of Nuclear Medicine. Anger and humiliation were apparent in his voice as he told us his version of the incident concerning the government survey.

In August 1989, as part of the Science Ministry medical survey team, the professor had visited Seongsan where he had told the residents that from a medical point of view it would be difficult to imagine that anencephaly could be caused by radiation. Immediately he became the target of abuse from the villagers, and all discussions in Seongsan were over in ten minutes.

"The people there won't even listen unless there's something in it for them," he said disgustedly. "A political solution is the only way to get us out of this mess. Unless we have a guarantee from the residents that they are not going to set out to find fault with any surveys we carry out, I don't see how there can be any cooperation."

Public suspicion appears to be undermining the Science Ministry's efforts to bring the radiation issue under control. "What is being questioned here is the whole issue of the medical profession's duty to society." This was the opinion of Yang Kil-Seung, who runs the Seongsoo Hospital located in Seongdong-gu, an area crowded with small factories in Seoul. Yang is a central figure in an organization of doctors concerned with promoting medical care for the people.

"Where do you suppose the people have got their suspicions from?" he said. "If nobody tells them anything except that there 'are' or 'are not' any effects from radiation, is it any wonder they've lost faith in the medical establishment? We believe that doctors must play a much larger role in educating the public than they do at present."

The group was established in November 1987 by a group of doctors at universities supporting democracy, and other physicians outside the official power structure. The organization has its main office in Seoul, and its 415 members voluntarily provide a consultancy service, carry out surveys, and treat patients with work- and pollution-related illnesses. The incidents at Kori and Yeonggwang came to light at around the time these doctors began to investigate the health of workers subcontracted to the plants. Directly after media attention was first focused on Seongsan, the Kwangju Jeon Nam branch of the organization announced the findings of its survey: that white blood cell depletion and anemia were abnormally common among the residents of the nearby villages. The results of the survey were seen as an indication that many of the residents of Seongsan were suffering from the initial phase of radiation-related illnesses.

The Seoul headquarters of the group, of which Yang is a member, quickly denied the validity of this result produced by one of their branches, saying that not enough care had been taken in carrying out the survey, and that doctors needed to be especially cautious when working in a field such as radiation because there is still so much that is unknown.

During his time at Seoul National University, Yang was imprisoned for a year for protesting against the martial law instituted by the Park regime. He finally graduated from a British university, and returned to South Korea with the idea of contributing to the improvement of working conditions in the nation's factories. In October 1989 he participated for the first time in a meeting of the International Physicians for the Prevention of Nuclear War (IPPNW) in Hiroshima.

"To be quite honest, most doctors had not paid enough attention to victims of the A-bomb in this country," he said, with a touch of embarrassment. "It may take ten or twenty years for radiation to make its presence known in the body, so we must be careful not to jump to conclusions, but just continue to do research and carry out surveys."

The Korean government aims to construct another forty-four nuclear reactors by the year 2031. The current controversy surrounding atomic energy has been spurred on by the prominence given to nuclear power since the advent of democracy, and the government will need to educate the public and obtain its support if it is to succeed in carrying out this ambitious program of nuclear power development. The group of doctors intends to continue conducting regular medical examinations and lifestyle surveys of those living around nuclear power plants. An air of secrecy still surrounds the truth about radioactive contamination, but it is Yang's hope that their perseverance will be rewarded with reliable results and the publication of previously unreleased data.

PART 5

BRITAIN · FRANCE

THE ROUGH ROAD TO NUCLEAR SUPREMACY

*F*acing the Irish Sea in the northwest of England lies the notorious Sellafield Nuclear Complex. Formerly known as Windscale, the plant played a leading role in establishing Britain as the third nation to possess a nuclear weapons capability. Today it continues to perform a vital function by engaging in reprocessing nuclear fuel. The price of development, however, has been a series of accidents which have caused incalculable damage to the environment. In 1984, the plant's name was changed in an attempt to improve the less-than-spotless image it has gained during the forty years it has been in operation.

Previous page: Rolling hills reveal the infamous nuclear complex at Sellafield in northwest England.

THE WORST NUCLEAR ACCIDENT IN BRITISH HISTORY

On October 10, 1957, Arthur Wilson glanced up from the instruments he was checking to be confronted with a horrifying sight. He had been doing his regular round of the gauges in the special reactor used for plutonium manufacture, when he saw flames shooting up from around the fuel rods. After a second, when he realized that his eyes had not deceived him, he yelled "Fire!" For a short while there was no reaction; everybody was quite confident that such an accident would never occur at Windscale.

This is how the worst nuclear accident in Britain's history began. The story of the fire at Windscale is only too well known by people all over the world closely involved with the problems of nuclear power generation. Wilson and his workmates quickly turned their attention to putting out the fire. But the blaze, rather than subsiding, steadily increased in intensity. Finally it was decided to pour water on the reactor, although they were aware that this could cause an explosion. For a day and a night, a constant stream of water was leveled at the reactor, and, by the afternoon of October 12, the fire was at last put out.

Along with smoke and steam, vast quantities of radioactive material were released from the reactor, spreading around the plant and contaminating the surrounding farmland. Wilson, at that time an up-and-coming young technician, was exposed to radiation as were the other employees. "Before then," he told us, "there had been a number of minor accidents, but that one was terrible. I heard later on that we only just escaped meltdown on that occasion."

Wilson had worked at the plant since the first reactor was put into operation in 1950. Four years later he began to have problems with his right foot, and after the accident his left foot began to trouble him, too. Five years after the accident he found himself unable to work, and he had no choice but to retire. He received no compensation of any kind. Widowed and in a wheelchair, Wilson has lived by himself for the last twelve years in the village of Millom, twenty-five miles from the complex.

Windscale's No. 1 reactor, radiation from which had caused his disability, was the pride of the British nuclear weapons development program, which had sprung up in response to the American monopoly of the field at that time. Plutonium processed in Windscale was used in the manufacture of Britain's first atomic bomb, which was successfully exploded in 1952 at Monte Bello Island in Australia. In 1956, a year before the accident, the world's first reactor to be used for commercial power generation had been completed. The company promised it would make electricity "too cheap to meter." While the reactor supplied power to the surrounding district, plutonium for military use was extracted from the used fuel.

At one time Wilson felt proud of his contribution to these achievements.

"On the other hand," he said, lying back on the sofa bed, "look what Windscale has done to me. All I can move is my right hand." After Wilson was forced to leave the plant and live on a small pension, Windscale continued to expand its activities into the areas of nuclear power generation and fuel reprocessing. The road has not always been a smooth one, though, as this list of accidents shows:

November 1963: Radiation leakage from advanced gas-cooled reactor. Six employees exposed.

August 1970: Accident at fuel reprocessing plant involving plutonium solution.

April 1979: Radioactive waste at fuel reprocessing plant found to be seeping into the ground.

July 1979: Fire at fuel reprocessing plant.

On each of these occasions, the surrounding area of land and sea was contaminated by radiation, and the local residents became anxious about their own safety.

After the disastrous fire of 1957, two of the reactors which separated plutonium from spent nuclear fuel were shut down forever.

CONTAMINATION OF LAND AND SEA

"It all started when the Irish Sea was found to be contaminated by radioactive material," explained Jean McSorley, a founder member of CORE, or "Cumbrians Opposed to a Radioactive Environment," a group set up in January 1980 to monitor contamination in the district.

"The contamination got rapidly worse in the 1960s," she continued, "particularly since a large-scale nuclear fuel reprocessing plant was completed in 1964." Enormous amounts of radioactive waste were discharged out at sea via a pipeline approximately one and a half miles long. Contamination reached a peak in the 1970s when the plant was running at full strength, and every day over two and a half million gallons of nuclear waste were spewed out into the ocean.

More than thirty different kinds of radioactive substances, including plutonium and cesium, were detected in this waste liquid.

"What makes this contamination special is that the materials released, such as plutonium-239, which has a half-life of 24,000 years, and americium-241 with a half-life of 400 years, are all those which give off alpha rays," McSorley explained.

Although alpha rays can be blocked even with thin paper, once these substances enter the body, they have a more harmful effect than gamma or beta rays.

Despite the seriousness of the contamination, the local residents only started to become concerned in 1976, when a proposal was made to build a facility for reprocessing used nuclear fuel rods from overseas as well as those from domestic facilities.

Objections to the plant have been voiced by Ireland as well, which is understandably nervous about the contamination of plankton, shellfish, and other marine life in its waters. In 1980 the Irish government demanded that the British close Sellafield, and in 1985 it submitted evidence of contamination to the European Parliament and called for a resolution that would result in immediate closure. The first demand was ignored. The second ran into fierce opposition from the British government, which blocked its adoption.

McSorley showed us a bar chart published in 1984 by the National Radiological Protection Board which showed the levels of plutonium-239, plutonium-240, and americium-241 detected in ordinary household vacuum cleaner dust from houses on the Cumbrian coast and from houses in Oxford. Of the twelve bars representing twelve locations on the graph, one extended far beyond the others. The village of Ravenglass, a few miles to the south of Sellafield, recorded levels of plutonium five hundred times the figure for Oxford. A comparison of the levels of americium showed that houses in Ravenglass were twenty-six thousand times more contaminated than those in Oxford. Explaining the reason for these results, McSorley said. "Ravenglass is situated on an estuary, so naturally mud and sand carried in on the tide accumulate on the shore. When the tide goes out the sand is blown into the villagers' homes."

DESTRUCTION OF A NATURAL PARADISE

We went for a walk along the Ravenglass estuary. It was difficult to believe that, twenty years ago, the area had been a wildlife reserve, with up to twenty thousand sea birds nesting on the beach at any one time. Now only the odd seagull was to be seen, swooping down onto the vast stretch of sand.

When Christopher Merlin and his wife, Christine, moved into their new home overlooking the Ravenglass estuary, little did they know that in the course of time they would find it unsafe to live there. Unwittingly, they had bought a house which was highly radioactive. When we made inquiries at the village, we were informed that the Merlins had left and gone to live in the hills five years previously. Trying to find their home was no easy task; it took us two hours of traveling along a narrow hill road before we came upon an old stone house nestled in the hills, miles from other human habitation.

Two friendly dogs ran out to greet us at the door, followed by the Merlins and their two sons. A stream ran in front of the house, beyond which we could see a dense forest of pine trees. The house commanded fine views of the surrounding countryside.

The Merlins were originally from the suburbs of London. Christopher Merlin had often been taken to the beach at Ravenglass as a child, and in 1973 he and his wife decided to move to the area. The Merlins have many happy memories of those first few years after they moved; the kindness of the villagers, and the flocks of sea birds on the shore. At that time, they knew little about the Windscale nuclear complex, situated only a few miles to the north of what seemed like a natural paradise.

This happy state of affairs continued until 1976, the year before their eldest son was born. That spring, a man came to the house introducing himself as an employee of the National Radiological Protection Board and asked if he could set up a radiation monitor in their garden. The board, having told the Merlins that there was "nothing to be concerned about," was oddly reticent on the matter of possible contamination. A friend advised them to have the inside of their house checked for radioactive material, but the board was reluctant to cooperate. By this time the Merlins were more than a little concerned, so they sent a sample of dust from their vacuum cleaner to Pittsburgh University to be analyzed.

The results showed they had every reason to be worried. Plutonium and americium were detected in the dust, and radioactivity was recorded at a level of 13.5 picocuries per gram. The report from Pittsburgh added helpfully that, "in the United States, building permission is not given in areas where the level of contamination in the ground is one picocurie or more."

The couple eventually decided that, for the sake of their children, they had no choice but to leave. There was little prospect of selling their home on the estuary, and it took two long years before they could take out a loan and it wasn't until 1984 that they were finally able to move from the coast to the hills. During this period they appeared in a television documentary about the problem of radioactive contamination in Windscale. This earned them the hatred of the villagers, who complained that they wouldn't be able to sell their fish and that tourists would disappear.

In 1985, deciding they had had enough of the endless financial and emotional strain, the Merlins began procedures to demand compensation from British Nuclear Fuels, the public corporation which operates Sellafield. They are confident of winning, they say, because the company has no way of denying that it kept the truth about radioactive contamination hidden from the public.

SELLAFIELD AND LEUKEMIA

The radioactive material accumulated over the years in water and on the land is not only having drastic effects on the traditional way of life on the Cumbrian coast, but is also threatening the health of the locals, plunging them into a state of panic about leukemia and cancer.

"Mum, I'm going to die, aren't I?"

Janine Allis-Smith will never forget the day her son Lee, now aged seventeen, made this sad remark. It was the summer of 1984. Lee was in hospital and had just been told he had leukemia. "You'll be all right. You can fight it," she told him as she sat next to his bed, trying to hide her own fears. The Allis-Smiths live in the village of Broughton Mills in the southwestern part of Cumbria, an area that consists mainly of sheep farms.

"I'm starting to think that maybe it wasn't such a good idea to try and bring the kids up in a natural environment," Mrs. Allis-Smith said ruefully. The family had always spent their summer holidays swimming, fishing, and generally taking it easy at a beach on the Irish Sea coast. Little did they know that only just over a mile away the Sellafield nuclear complex was discharging radioactive waste into the sea.

Lee, a keen sportsman, first began to notice there was something wrong with his health at the end of 1983. In August the following year he broke out in blisters all over his body. He was taken to hospital in Manchester where he was diagnosed as having acute lymphatic leukemia and hospitalized immediately. He went through nine months of intensive treatment until May 1985. At first Janine did not make the connection between her son's illness and radiation from Sellafield. However, as his stay in hospital lengthened into months, she realized that in the same ward there were a number of other children with leukemia. She got talking to their parents and was surprised to find that all the leukemia patients had one thing in common: some connection with the Cumbrian coast. They were all children who had enjoyed swimming and playing on the beach.

Soon after Lee was discharged from hospital his mother followed up on the suspicions which had formed in her mind. By inquiring at the district health authorities and reading what specialist publications had to say about the effects of radiation on the body, she gradually built up a picture of the connection between Sellafield and leukemia. Her next task was a careful investigation of all the leukemia patients in the area and the circumstances surrounding their illnesses, including those children who had already died. To do this, she built up a network of parents of leukemia patients in her spare time, sending out a six-page questionnaire to the parents of any new cases she heard of. The questions were concerned with matters such as parents' health, the mother's pregnancy, the child's everyday habits, the details of their illness, and so on, a total of thirty questions in all. The thirty-five replies she has received so far all point to a connection with the nuclear complex.

"I know there are other patients," she said. "But they have family working at the plant and they're afraid of being laid off, so they don't reply."

The thirty-five families who replied are united in their aim to prove in court that their children's illnesses were caused by exposure to radiation from the nuclear facilities at Sellafield. To this end the families applied for legal aid to enable them to sue British Nuclear Fuels (BNF). Their first applications were dismissed, although after an appeal in March 1989, eighteen families were granted financial assistance to go to court. This initial victory has given a great deal of encouragement to Janine Allis-Smith and the other parents, and at the time of writing they were busy gathering and organizing evidence for the case. Their action is the first such case in the world to be filed against a nuclear power plant on behalf of people suffering from leukemia.

"Sellafield has hidden too many things from the public, and it's marvelous to get this opportunity to force BNF to account for their actions in court," Janine told us. "It just makes me so angry when I think of my son and all those children living in fear, never knowing when leukemia is going to strike them down again."

DOUBLE EXPOSURE

The farms around Sellafield were also on the receiving end of contamination from the plant. Those that we visited had suffered doubly, having also been affected by fallout from Chernobyl. James Phizacklea stood over six feet tall and was solidly built—it was not difficult to imagine that he was a former rugby player. He was the very picture of health. Or so it seemed. "These last few years I've started having all sorts of aches and pains," he told us. "And it's not just me but my daughter Jennifer, too; she's got leukemia."

The Phizacklea family owns a sheep and dairy farm five miles east of Sellafield. James recalled that his father had been forced to dump milk for months after the fire at Windscale in 1957. James took over the running of the farm with his wife, Ann; they have two daughters: Laura, aged seven, and Jennifer, aged five. Their peaceful life-style was first disrupted in 1986:

"I remember it was just after New Year. James got these big lumps on his arms. And he was tired all the time—he'd go out to work on the farm, but come back soon after and sit down saying how exhausted he was. He had a thorough examination, but we're still not sure what caused it," recalled Ann, a former nurse.

Later in the year, the area became contaminated by cesium-137 from the accident at Chernobyl in April.

"Five days later, on May 1, it rained. The pasture needed a bit of rain, so I was happy as anything of course . . . If only I'd known." Phizacklea looked tired all of a sudden as if the memory was too much for him. The level of cesium contamination on the farm reached 17,000 becquerels per square meter. The animals recorded equally high levels.

Under British law, meat with a reading of 1,000 becquerels or more per kilogram cannot be sold. Every one of Phizacklea's stock is over this limit. Before the accident, he had one hundred milking cows. A year later he reduced the number to twenty; it was too difficult to get hold of un-contaminated feed, and the amount of milk consumed had decreased drastically due to the public's fear of radiation since the accidents. The farm was suffering yet again from the effects of radiation; but this time from a nuclear power plant not five but 1,350 miles away, and the government refused to provide any compensation.

In the summer of that same year came the last straw. Jennifer, only two at the time, was found to have leukemia.

"When I heard it was leukemia, the first thing I thought of was Sellafield," said Ann. "The smoke from that place passes over our house all the time. Plus there was Chernobyl, of course. I know it's almost impossible to prove, but you can't deny that having a nuclear fuel reprocessing plant on your doorstep must have some effect."

Her husband had always believed that as long as a nuclear power plant was run properly, there would be no problems. In 1976 he had even worked as a turbine operator at Sellafield himself. Now, however, he occasionally wonders whether he was exposed to radiation during that twelve-month period, although there is no way he can prove that the illness which has now spread from his arms to his legs was caused by radiation.

Jennifer's leukemia is in remission after two and a half years of treatment. However, the uncertainty of not knowing when she will be struck down again, combined with James's mysterious illness and the cesium contamination of the farm, add up to a terrible burden for the family. Bitter experience has left them firm in the belief that nuclear power plants are far from safe. "As far as we're concerned, Sellafield and Chernobyl have committed the same crime. How are farmers supposed to make a living when they can't even produce food that people feel safe about eating?"

THE 'NUCLEAR VILLAGE'

Just to the south of Sellafield lies a small town known locally as the "nuclear village." Its real name is Seascale, and it is home to two thousand people, most of whom are employed at the Sellafield complex or in related businesses. Dr. Barrie Walker was born in Seascale and spent his childhood there. Ten years ago, out of a desire to live an unhurried life in natural surroundings, he returned to open his own practice in the village. What he found in Seascale soon shattered this illusion. As he began to examine and treat the townspeople he noticed a disproportionate number of leukemia and cancer cases amongst his patients.

According to a survey he has carried out, there have been eleven cases of leukemia in the village since 1955. This is ten times the national average in Britain, where leukemia occurs at a rate of once in every 100,000 people. Moreover, the cases are concentrated mainly in the 1960s and 1970s. This corresponds to the period of expanded production at the nuclear fuel reprocessing plant and the occurrence of a number of accidents. Dr. Walker believes there is a definite connection.

In 1983, Yorkshire Television produced a special documentary, "Windscale: the Nuclear Laundry," which dealt with the issue of radioactive discharge from the nuclear power plant. Thanks to this, the nuclear village of Seascale became known all over the country. The following year, a government committee set up to investigate the situation acknowledged that, up until 1983, there had been seven cases of leukemia. It denied, however, any connection with the plant at Sellafield, insisting that only a small quantity of radiation had been released.

Dr. Walker strongly disagrees with this conclusion. "The committee believed all the data Sellafield submitted to them, most of which was actually extremely suspect. The residents here don't have an ounce of faith in their findings." The doctor has been criticized by the plant management and local union bosses, but believes he has the backing of the local residents. Since he publicized details about the high incidence of leukemia in the area, parents have stopped letting their children play at the beach. "They put out all this P.R. about the plant being safe, but even the employees don't take their families to the beach. It's obvious they don't trust Sellafield, so how can they expect anyone else to?"

Prior to meeting Dr. Walker, we went on a tour of the complex. The huge site contained an impressive array of nuclear facilities: the world's first magnox reactors producing plutonium for military purposes, the fuel treatment plant thought by the local residents to be the main "culprit," the gas-cooled reactor closed down nine years previously, the storage facilities for radioactive waste—the complex was like a nuclear department store.

It is forty years since the plant began operations to process plutonium for military purposes. The development of nuclear reprocessing since the war has reflected the increasingly diverse ways in which atomic energy has come to be used throughout the world. As the number of nuclear power facilities has grown, Sellafield has placed increasing emphasis on the establishment of facilities for reprocessing used nuclear fuel. At the present time, a new facility is being built which, it is hoped, will be capable of reprocessing twelve hundred tons of fuel annually. There are only two facilities for the commercial reprocessing of used nuclear fuel rods in the world; Sellafield is one and the other is in France. Used fuel will be transported from nuclear power plants in seven countries to Sellafield for reprocessing; ten-year contracts have already been signed in the hope that the nuclear department store will be able to keep a lid on the world's nuclear waste.

Dr. Walker acknowledges the importance of the complex to the local economy, but at the same time he is determined that, whatever the financial benefits, the health of the people of Seascale and the surrounding districts must not be sacrificed. Dr. Walker's fears are not unfounded; the 1980s have seen a steady increase in cancer in Seascale, including eight cases of malignant lymphatic tumors, as well as cancer of the bladder, kidney, and uterus.

"The leukemia and cancer here can only be thought of as legacies from Sellafield," he said. "As a doctor I'm charged with saving lives, so I feel it my duty to continue speaking out on this matter." His concern for the environment and the local people left a lasting impression on us as we left the nuclear village.

FRENCH DUPLICITY

A long with the United States, Britain, and the Soviet Union, France may be considered a developed nation in the world of atomic energy. More than any other country, France relies heavily on this form of energy: seventy percent of its electricity is supplied by nuclear power. Yet despite this dependence, little is ever heard of accidents involving radioactive substances. Does this mean that there are none? With this question on our minds, we visited France in pursuit of the truth, and spoke to some of those living with the effects of exposure to radioactive materials.

Previous page: A walking stick and a heavy limp—the results of exposure to carbon-14.

THE IRRESPONSIBLE HANDLING OF RADIOACTIVE MATERIAL

Gèrard Noury, aged forty-three, who is physically disabled, and his wife, Annick, came to visit us at our hotel in a working-class area of Paris. Noury looked to be in a great deal of pain as he leaned on a walking stick for support, dragging his crippled leg.

The couple had traveled to Paris from their home in the port city of Le Havre, approximately 150 miles away on the Channel coast. After a short rest, Noury began to tell us about the accident he had been involved in and its effect on his life. In June 1970, he had been working at a factory under contract to the French Atomic Energy Commission when he accidentally came into contact with a liquid containing the radioactive material carbon-14.

"It was about ten in the morning. One of the pipes burst and the pressurized liquid began to spray out. My boss told me to shut the valve closest to the break, so I did. At the time I was wearing protective gear, but large quantities of the liquid still managed to get in through gaps in my clothing and the corners of my mask."

By the evening Noury's arms had swelled up, and he was overcome by nausea. The next morning he visited the factory doctor, who dismissed his fears, saying that radiation had nothing to do with his illness. Noury had his doubts about the doctor's assurances, but three days later he was back on the job.

Two months later he got married. The swelling on his arms had gone down and he appeared to have recovered completely. Then, toward the end of the same year, two of his ribs broke while he was asleep. Noury was in hospital for nine months after that, during which time he lost his job. There was no mention of compensation.

Four more ribs broke after that, and in the early 1980s he lost the use of his left leg, at one stage having an operation on his knee. The Nourys went to Paris in an effort to find out the cause of Gèrard's ailment, but to no avail—every doctor they saw told them the same thing: that it had nothing to do with radiation. No tests were ever conducted. In 1988, the couple, still clinging obstinately to their belief that Gèrard's troubles had originated in that accident of 1970, were dealt a further blow. A rumor went around that the medical establishment was being reticent about Noury's illness because he had AIDS.

"Even our children's friends didn't want to come round any more," Gèrard told us, his voice strained with emotion.

Ostracized by his neighbors, Noury decided to fight back. He attached a placard to his clothing with the words "I am not an AIDS patient. I am a victim of radiation," written on it, and began a silent vigil in one of the city's shopping centers. His protest was in vain. "We have only got ourselves now," his wife murmured. Recently her husband has begun to feel pain in his right leg as well. "I want to prevent my body from deteriorating any further. We've decided to buy a geiger counter to try and establish once and for all the relationship between my illness and radiation," he said. This had been their reason for traveling to Paris. We were at a loss for words.

HAZARDOUS SMOKE DETECTORS

Our next stop was the resort of Nice in the south of France, where we spoke to Nicole Jammet in her apartment on the sixth floor of a high-rise block overlooking the sea. Mrs. Jammet had lost her husband, Yves, to leukemia seven years previously, and was now living alone.

"Where shall I start?" she began, gazing out of the window at the azure sea. "My husband was a pilot in the air force. He was a military man through and through—even if he had felt the slightest bit of dissatisfaction with the military he would never have said so."

In contrast to her slight frame, the man in the photo was tall and well built. After leaving the air force he had worked as an electrician in a private company for five years, and in 1972 he went to work at the navy missile research facility in Chateauroux in central France, where, according to his widow, he had been exposed to radiation when he was made to clean smoke detectors.

The smoke detectors in question used americium-241, which gives off alpha rays. The alpha rays cause an electric current to be set up which is broken by contact with smoke, thus acting as an alarm. However, when this substance with a half-life of 433 years makes its way into the human body, it accumulates in the bones and bloodstream and is likely to cause cancer.

Yves Jammet knew that opening the detectors and cleaning them was dangerous. He also knew that they were supposed to be sent back to the manufacturers for repairs. No matter how many times he told his superiors that it was not only dangerous but against the law for the detectors to be opened, he was continually ignored.

"It was three years after he started work there, that he began to complain of being tired all the time. Yves had never had a sick day in his life up until then," his widow continued. "Two years after that we found out that he had leukemia." After several months spent in and out of hospital, Yves Jammet died in February 1982. That same day his wife discovered the connection between the smoke detectors and her husband's death. She found his work schedule on the bookshelf next to the bed.

"It had written in it which officers had ordered him to do repairs and things like that. When I read that book I realized that smoke detectors had killed my husband."

The Ministry of Defense recognized Yves Jammet's death as being work related, yet they urged his widow to sign a document stating that his death was "nothing out of the ordinary." Shocked by such blatant deceit on the part of the military, Nicole Jammet took the Ministry of Defense to court. A verdict was handed down in her favor in 1988. However, her husband's former employers have appealed this decision, and she has yet to receive any compensation.

Mrs. Jammet's lawyer, Vladimira Giauffret, whom we talked to in Nice, had harsh words of condemnation for the ministry's actions.

"The reason they ignored Yves' pleas to take him off dangerous work was that they were more concerned about their budget than the health of their employees. Their refusal to pay out compensation springs from the same motive: if they pay one lot they will be swamped with other claims."

Giauffret then told us about another case which concerned a man who came into contact with radioactive substances when he was in the army. Like Yves Jammet, this exposure to radiation eventually caused leukemia and he died leaving a wife and three children. Also, as in Jammet's case, the army recognized his death as work related but refused to take responsibility. Giauffret summed up the situation succinctly: "The military gets nervous at any mention of radiation."

Until her husband's death Nicole Jammet had never doubted the military's judgment on anything. The last seven years have changed all that. "If Yves had not left that work diary, I would have been none the wiser," she said. "Now I feel I must continue the fight for the sake of those in the same position as myself."

THE DANGER OF LOW DOSES OF RADIATION

Bella Belbeoch, a nuclear physicist, has firsthand experience of the changes that even low doses of radiation can make in the human body. We visited Bella and her husband, Roger, also a nuclear physicist, and spoke with them at some length about the effects of exposure to low doses of radiation. Bella had worked for the Atomic Energy Commission analyzing the effects of radiation absorption on the structure of materials. She was involved in the experiments themselves, using X-rays, over a four-year period from 1956 to 1960.

"When I was working with the X-rays I always seemed to be tired," Bella told us. "And my periods were irregular as well." She turned to her husband for confirmation. "That's right," he laughed, "she used to think she was pregnant all the time . . ."

After Bella had been working in the same section for a while, her condition deteriorated from lethargy to anemia, and lumps appeared at the base of her fingers. The doctor told her that her white blood cell count was down. "I had a feeling then that it was because of the X-rays," she told us. After a short stay in hospital she returned to work, this time in the data analysis section, away from the experiments. Gradually her health returned to normal. Through her experiences, Bella realized that there are often marked differences in the way people working with radiation are affected. Many of the women doing exactly the same work that she was noticed no changes in their bodies whatsoever.

The Atomic Energy Commission was established under government auspices at the end of the Second World War for the purpose of developing not only nuclear weapons but also the commercial uses of nuclear power. According to figures supplied by the Confédération Française Démocratique Du Travail (CFDT), the labor union to which all commission workers belong, sixty cases of illness caused by exposure to radiation were officially recognized between 1946 and 1985. Bella Belbeoch was one of these. "They told me I had the initial symptoms of leukemia. At that time even the researchers took the effects of radiation pretty lightly and it wasn't until one of the younger ones died of cancer in 1968 that people began to be more cautious." Her husband nodded in agreement and added, "If it was like that in a research institution among scientists, I hate to imagine what it was like at factories and power plants."

As a result of Bella's experience, the couple became interested in the effects of low radiation dosage. They were surprised to find that there was no research being done on the subject whatsoever in France. The unions and the media also showed a profound lack of interest, which in the Belbeochs' eyes was inexcusable. They had no choice but to visit specialists in Britain and the United States and to make their inquiries there.

Roger showed us some data published by the government in 1988, detailing the causes of death for French uranium miners. The figures showed that this group has a rate of lung cancer 2.7 times the national average. "The funny thing about this data is that it was presented at a conference overseas. You can't find it here in France," he said. "I got straight onto the media and the unions about it, but there wasn't even a flicker of interest. They didn't even bother to come and see the data. That's typical of the attitude here," he added disgustedly. His wife continued. "In this country, disease caused by radiation is treated just like any another illness. The people are told nothing. This problem really needs to be dealt with by the medical establishment—it shouldn't be physicists like ourselves giving out warnings, but until doctors get more interested we don't really have any choice," she concluded with an air of resignation.

THE FRENCH COVER-UP IN CORSICA

The battered car, which served as a mobile medical center, had definitely seen better days. As it wound its way slowly up the twisting Corsican mountain road, the driver, Dr. Denis Fauconnier, informed us over the din of the engine that in the next village on his rounds there was a large number of people suffering from thyroid conditions. According to the doctor these illnesses had been brought about by the accident at Chernobyl in 1986.

The village of Speloncato lies in the northwest of the island, three miles from the converted monastery that serves as Dr. Fauconnier's home and clinic. It has a population of 170. As we approached, we could see a group of stone houses clustered together around the top of the mountain. As the physician responsible for providing health care in nine such villages, Fauconnier makes regular visits to patients suffering from thyroid problems and has the complete trust of the residents.

The island of Corsica, approximately 2,250 square miles in area, has a population of 220,000. When it rained six days after the disaster at Chernobyl on May 2, 1986, the tourist paradise was covered in radioactive fallout. The news of contamination came not from the French government but via Italy.

"The government continued to insist that there had been no ill effects, even after the rain," the doctor said. "But when I called an Italian friend he told me that everyone was in a panic there because milk and vegetables had been contaminated. It really gave me a fright, I can tell you."

Fauconnier went round all the villages as fast as he could, warning people not to eat any vegetables or meat, or drink cows' or goats' milk. During that period the government was sticking to its "no negative effects" line in the newspapers and on television. However, as the doctor told us, "There was no reason why France should be safe when the rest of Europe was flying into a panic and taking all sorts of countermeasures." On May 12, exasperated by the government's attitude and wanting to know for certain the extent of the damage, he sent a sample of goats' milk to be analyzed by the Radiological Protection Board in Paris.

The results were just as he had expected. Iodine-131 was detected at a level of 4,400 becquerels per liter. The half-life of iodine-131 being eight days, he calculated that the level in Corsica on the day after the accident when it rained would have been 70,000 becquerels. "The EC level for safe consumption is set at 500 becquerels, so it was a hell of a shock when I heard the results." Disappointed with the government, which had not even bothered to carry out any kind of analysis until he sent the sample to Paris himself, Fauconnier continued his careful observation of the villagers' health. His fears were realized. In an area which already had a history of thyroid problems caused by viral infections, there was a sudden increase in the number of enlarged thyroid glands among children, and large numbers of the elderly also began to complain of sore throats. Thyroid problems increased threefold in the two years after Chernobyl.

Fauconnier was concerned that the next effect to make itself felt might be cancer, and with this in mind he wrote a letter to the authorities requesting a thorough medical survey of the local residents. The reply was simply a repetition of the well-worn phrase "there is no need to worry about radioactive contamination."

Fauconnier found it difficult to believe that the French government could be so indifferent to the issue of contamination. For the first time he realized just how heavily France relies on nuclear power. With fifty-three nuclear reactors, 69.9 percent of its power produced by atomic energy, and two out of every three homes running on nuclear-generated power, it was clear that the government was anxious to avoid any criticism of its own nuclear policies following from the accident at Chernobyl. For this reason, Fauconnier believes the government showed a marked lack of official interest in radioactive contamination, even to the extent of suppressing information.

It is just over two hundred years since the tricolor was raised to shouts of "liberty, fraternity, and equality." As far as nuclear policy is concerned, however, these ideals seem to have been lost along the way. "It's going to be some time before I can feel at all confident about the islanders' health," commented Dr. Fauconnier, as he got back into his car to continue his rounds.

ACCUSER OF THE MOTHERLAND

In Copenhagen, Denmark, we met a woman, Martine Petrod, whose father had worked at a nuclear weapons plant as well as at a bomb test site. Martine told us that her father had subsequently died of cancer. Although French by birth, Martine had taken up Danish citizenship ten years previously at the age of twenty-seven, and she now worked as an education consultant in Copenhagen. Her reason for giving up her French citizenship was, she told us, because she "couldn't stand the system there anymore."

Martine's father, René, became an electrician for the Atomic Energy Commission in 1966 and was employed at a nuclear weapons plant on the outskirts of Dijon, 185 miles southeast of Paris. It was during this period that France was forging ahead with its atmospheric testing program in defiance of world opinion. In 1966, the same year that René started work, the first nuclear test was carried out at Mururoa Atoll.

"My father's main job at the factory was general maintenance—one of his jobs involved installing electric safety devices," Martine told us.

"I also heard that he sometimes had to work in the hot zone—that's the radioactive zone."

In 1972 Martine graduated from university and left for Denmark. In 1978 she was told that her father had cancer of the kidneys.

"He was sent to Mururoa twice, once in 1977 and again in 1978. Soon after he got back the second time, he found out that he had cancer. He was fifty when he died." Martine's tone was unemotional.

Her father had received double pay while working at Mururoa and had enjoyed the added bonus of living in the South Pacific. Whenever he had any free time, he would go off snorkeling. Like the other French workers sent out to Mururoa, René had been told nothing of the dangers of radiation and the true nature of the work they were engaged in. When Martine first heard this from her mother, she started to change her attitude toward France.

"Well, wouldn't you?" she asked "Can you imagine allowing workers to swim in waters that you knew were contaminated with radioactive material from bomb tests? It just shows how ignorant and insensitive the French can be."

Martine's mother had heard about former colleagues of her husband's who had met a similar fate. "My mother is not the type who would get together with other families in the same situation and fight against the government for compensation and recognition," said Martine. "What's more worrying is that the vast majority of French people know next to nothing about the dangers of radiation."

She believes the media is to blame for this situation because of its tendency to turn a blind eye to criticism of the government's nuclear policy. The French media, she claims, is so caught up with vague notions of "national honor" and the image of France as the "policeman of Western Europe" that it has lost the ability to look objectively at nuclear issues.

Since her father's death she has acted on her own initiative helping those suffering from radiation-related illnesses. Using the FFr 150,000 (approx. US $27,000) compensation paid out to her as a surviving family member by the French government, she established the Copenhagen Foundation against Nuclear Tests.

Interest earned on this fund (between $2,000 and $3,000 per year) is sent directly to those victims most in need. Although she admits herself that it is not a great sum of money, Martine is happy to be able to do something to show her support for victims of radiation. In Denmark she has given lectures, spoken at rallies, written to newspapers, and generally done everything within her power to encourage public debate on France's nuclear policy. Largely as a result of her efforts, the island of Mururoa and French activities there have become well known among Danish people.

"It really is time for the French to wake up and face the facts. We shouldn't have to tolerate this 'see no evil, hear no evil, speak no evil' attitude of the French media any longer."

In spite of the fact that Martine has changed her nationality, it would seem that she still feels a strong sense of duty to try to prevent further accidents involving radiation and to inform the public of France's irresponsible handling of radioactive substances.

SUBVERSION OF THE TRUTH

In France, the Institut Curie, named after Marie Curie, the discoverer of radium, has long been at the forefront in the treatment of radiation-related diseases. At this institute, the world's first bone-marrow transplant was carried out to save the life of a victim of an accident at a nuclear reactor. The institute also acts as the mouthpiece for the medical side of France's atomic energy policy.

The institute is also the workplace of Dr. Roger Gongora, France's leading authority in the field of radiology. Dr. Gongora has been involved in researching cancer and other radiation-related diseases for the past thirty-five years. His dislike of the media is legendary, but he agreed to be interviewed on condition that we would not take any photographs. We spent two hours discussing a number of issues with Dr. Gongora through an interpreter. The following is an excerpt from that interview:

Reporter: How many people have you treated for radiation-related diseases until now?

Dr. Gongora: About five hundred. Eighty-five were in critical condition when they arrived here; twenty of them were from overseas. They had been exposed to large doses of radiation, either from medical equipment or through misuse of machines for detecting metal fatigue. Most of them had burns; some died after only a short period of treatment because they had been exposed to such massive doses of radiation.

R: Had any of your patients been involved in accidents involving radiation at nuclear power plants?

G: In 1958 I treated five Yugoslavian scientists who had been exposed to large doses of radiation while working on an experimental reactor. I have treated other patients from overseas in similar circumstances, but there haven't been any from this country. Power plants here have stringent safety precautions, you know.

R: What is your opinion of the relationship between exposure to low doses of radiation and the incidence of cancer?

G: In developed countries, between twenty and thirty percent of all deaths are caused by cancer, so it is impossible to say if exposure to radiation is a determining factor. From experience, I would say that there is no connection between cancer and exposure to low doses of radiation.

R: But aren't people who work in the field of nuclear energy more susceptible to cancer?

G: This is probably going to disappoint you but in France we've found it's just the opposite. Statistics show that those working in nuclear-related industries are less likely to suffer from cancer than other people. The best way to avoid cancer is to work in a nuclear power station.

R: Have you ever treated any people who were involved in or who lived near the nuclear testing sites?

G: No. Small quantities of ash probably did fall after the tests were carried out, but all possible precautions were taken and no one has ever been affected.

R: Don't you think it's possible that the military could be covering up the existence of such victims?

G: If that were the case, I'm sure journalists like yourselves would have found out pretty quickly. We work closely with the military here, and if they were carrying out treatment in secret we would soon know about it.

R: We heard that Polynesians have been treated in Paris for diseases caused by exposure to radiation.

G: That's impossible. Rumors like that are purely political propaganda.

The interview with Dr. Gongora left us with a bad taste in our mouths. The next day we spoke to Madeleine Briselance, the leader of the antinuclear testing group SOS Tahiti.

"Take a look at this," she said, taking out a photograph.

The picture showed a young Tahitian girl and her mother in a Paris hospital. The girl was receiving treatment for leukemia.

"These people are relatives of my husband, so the hospital reluctantly allowed me to visit her—that was when I took the photo. The poor little girl has died now, though. And she wasn't the only one—lots of patients were brought out here from Polynesia."

Listening to her story, we were reminded once again of the difficulty of breaching France's "nuclear defenses."

PART
6

BRAZIL · NAMIBIA

CESIUM CONTAMINATION IN GOIÂNIA

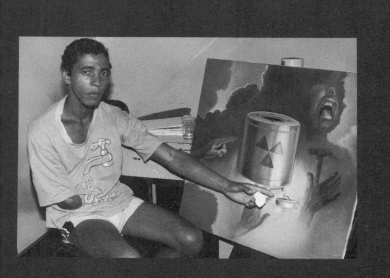

*I*n September 1987, a cylinder containing cesium-137, a radioactive substance used in medical equipment, was removed from an abandoned hospital in Goiânia, central Brazil. As a result, over two hundred people were exposed to radiation. Four died, and the survivors are still suffering from the tragic effects of the "glittering powder."

A GLITTERING POWDER

"When we broke open the cylinder a little capsule the size of a matchbox fell out," said Robert Alves, as he pointed listlessly to a painting of the cylinder done by a local artist. We were visiting the Leide Foundation set up by the Goiás state government to help the victims of the accident in Goiânia.

It was Alves who had unwittingly caused the cesium contamination in the city. His right arm had been amputated to prevent the effects of handling the radioactive substance from spreading to the rest of his body.

On September 13, 1987, he and his friend, Wagner Ferreira, set out for an abandoned cancer hospital in search of scrap to sell. The three doctors who had originally run the hospital had moved elsewhere in 1984, and the site was overgrown with weeds. Entering the grounds, the two men saw a small concrete hut. There was no fence around it, and the lock was broken. Inside lay a white metal container.

The two young men lived from day to day never knowing where their next meal was coming from, so to them the container spelled much-needed cash. They loaded it onto their light truck and took it home, intending to dismantle and sell it. The white outer shell was easily broken, but the cylindrical container inside proved much tougher. Alves and Ferreira attacked it with hammers and screwdrivers for three days before finally succeeding in breaking it open. Unfortunately, they were unaware of the meaning of the three black triangles painted on the outside of the container.

The fruit of their labors was a small capsule which the men took along with the broken container to a scrap dealer, Devair Ferreira. In exchange they received a small amount of cash.

We attempted to interview the scrap dealer, but he refused to speak to us unless we paid him. "All the media attention has gone to his head," explained Halim Girade, director of the foundation.

According to Girade, Ferreira took a hammer to the mysterious capsule, curious to find out what was inside. It broke on impact, and a sparkling blue powder, not unlike the sequins used at carnival time, flew into the air. The dealer then proudly handed out the glittering powder to all his friends and relatives in the neighborhood, spreading contamination from house to house and person to person and causing 249 confirmed cases of exposure to high doses of radiation and the loss of four lives. As a result of the careless disposal of four ounces of cesium-137, combined with the multiplying effects of poverty and lack of education, the lives of Robert Alves and the others exposed to the "glittering powder" will never be the same again.

PLAYING WITH THE DEADLY POWDER

On the wall of a room in the Leide Foundation headquarters hangs the smiling photo of the little girl called Leide Ferreira for whom the foundation is named, and who, at six years old, became a victim of the blue powder.

Leide's father Ivo was the elder brother of the scrap dealer, Devair Ferreira, and one day he brought a small amount of the powder home from work and showed it to the family.

"The powder glowed in the dark when you turned out the light," Leide's mother said. "Leide put it on her face and hair and looked in the mirror. If only we'd known that it was dangerous . . ." Her voice trailed off. At eight o'clock that evening, the family of five sat down to dinner. Leide began to eat bread and boiled eggs with the same hands she had used to play with the cesium powder. After consuming only half her egg she collapsed and started to vomit. Continuing to vomit all through the night, she lay in bed crying, her small body racked with pain.

By the next morning, however, Leide had recovered enough to eat breakfast and go out to play. Her mother heaved a sigh of relief. That same day, the hands of Wagner Ferreira broke out in blisters and a rumor went round the neighborhood that the "bones were visible underneath." Those who had come into contact with the cesium-137 from the hospital site were beginning to show symptoms of acute radiation sickness. Many visited their family doctors, but for a while the local doctors were mystified by their condition. Edson Fabiano, a car painter, was one of those whose fingertips swelled up after touching the powder—his doctor told him that he had probably been stung by a bee. It wasn't until two weeks after the cesium was first removed from the hospital site, and four days after Leide Ferreira became sick, that the true nature of the "glittering powder" came to light.

Fabiano observed the skin inflammation, nausea, and hair loss among his neighbors and was suddenly reminded of the pictures of victims of Chernobyl that he had seen on television. He traced their illnesses back to the powder and the scrap dealer, Devair Ferreira. The families who had been struck by the strange sickness took the powder to the state health authorities for appraisal, and as Fabiano had predicted, it turned out to be radioactive.

Even after the truth about the powder was made public, there were very few people who understood the nature of cesium, and this ignorance only served to exacerbate the suffering of those affected.

FEAR OF CONTAMINATION INCREASES WITH A VENGEANCE

The Brazilian government and armed forces swung into action when it became clear that there was a case of cesium contamination in Goiânia, and fourteen people, including the scrap dealer, Devair Ferreira, his brother, and his niece, Leide, who had put the powder in her mouth, were flown to a hospital over five hundred miles away in Rio de Janeiro. For some of them, medical treatment arrived too late, and a month after their hospitalization, Devair's wife Maria, his assistant Israel Santos, Leide, and a young man by the name of Admilson de Souza were all dead.

The four deaths were a shock to the people of Goiânia, who vented their growing fear of exposure to radiation on the bereaved families. Leide's father, who still bears a painful scar from the time he handled the cesium, gave us an account of what occurred after Leide's death.

"I was too ill to go to Leide's funeral myself, but from what I heard it was terrible. Although she was buried in a lead coffin it didn't satisfy the people living around the cemetery. They claimed the cesium contamination would spread, and some people even threw stones at the coffin during the burial." He wiped away a tear at the thought.

The graves of the four victims lie on a small hill approximately thirty minutes' drive from the center of Goiânia. In contrast to the other graves marked by simple crosses, their graves are monumental. Even Leide's grave, the smallest, measures six by twelve feet. Halim Girade, who was guiding us, told us that, to prevent contamination, the bodies were wrapped in sheets of lead two and a half inches thick, then covered with another layer of bronze. Each of the coffins weighed over thirteen hundred pounds. Preventative measures did not stop there, however; each of the graves was lined with a layer of concrete a foot thick and the coffins were covered with a further layer after they had been lowered in.

Despite the incredible precautions taken, the nearby residents still complained. Girade brought out some slides of the funeral which showed local residents linking arms around the truck carrying the coffin and young boys throwing stones while police tried to fend the crowd off with shields and truncheons, forming a human barrier as Leide was placed in her final resting place by crane.

According to Girade, over three hundred people including tenants from the nearby housing estate and local landowners took part in the demonstration at the funeral. Many were genuinely afraid of contamination, while others were more concerned that the value of their property might drop.

OUTCASTS OF SOCIETY

After the four victims of cesium contamination had been buried, the local people's attention turned to the survivors. Ostracized by their neighbors and uncertain in their own minds about their health, they became increasingly isolated from the rest of the community. The unpretentious concrete building in central Goiânia that houses the headquarters of the Leide Foundation seems to be the survivors' only refuge from the vilification of their fellow citizens.

The twenty staff members of the foundation include six doctors, who not only treat those affected by the cesium but also provide food rations and assistance in finding housing and work. People pour into the building every day with worries about their health and their future. For many of the victims, the ignorance of their neighbors has made it extremely difficult to lead a normal life.

Sitting dejectedly on a bench in the foundation's offices was Madalena Goncalves, a black woman aged fifty-two. "I've been on TV so many times in connection with the contamination that now my neighbors are too frightened to talk to me," she confided.

Goncalves is single and was working in the home of Leide's family when she came into contact with the glittering powder. Her hands swelled up and came out in blisters, and her health has never been the same since. After Goncalves's shack was torn down for fear of contamination, the foundation found her new accommodation, but her new neighbors will have nothing to do with her. She comes to the offices every morning at seven and whiles away the hours until they close at six.

Odesson Ferreira stood in the entrance to the foundation offices playing with her two-year-old daughter. Her husband had been given some of the cesium powder by the scrap dealer, and as a result he had had to have the swollen fingers of his right hand amputated. He is unable to find work because of his connection with the cesium contamination. The family's house and all its contents, including the six pigs they kept, were packed into drums and taken away to prevent further contamination. The Ferreiras' new neighbors abuse them whenever they step out the door, and as Odesson told us, "The foundation is the only place where we can go."

At the foundation they receive food and a living allowance. The amount that victims are entitled to receive range from 55 cruzeiros (approx. U.S. $30) to 165 cruzeiros per month, depending on a number of factors, such as the income of the family. The foundation also rents houses to those whose own had to be destroyed to prevent secondary contamination, although the victims would prefer homes in their own names rather than rental accommodation. The foundation also provides food rations every fifteen days. The recipients claim, however, that the allowance is insufficient and that the food is like "pig swill."

Edson Ferrari, head of public relations for the foundation, retorted:

"The allowance is not below the minimum wage, and the food is the same as that served in municipal and state hospitals. If we increase the amount, they'll just sell it, and if we give them houses rather than rented accommodation, they'll do the same."

At present twenty-one families, a total of ninety-six people, are totally dependent on handouts from the foundation. These, however, represent only some of the victims; others are cut off from all such assistance.

VICTIMS OF SECONDARY EXPOSURE IGNORED

When it became known that cesium contamination had occurred on an unprecedented scale in Goiânia, the Brazilian government, the army, and the state government loaded radiation detectors onto helicopters and into vehicles and embarked on a comprehensive check of the city. First of all, they listed eighty-one contaminated areas, then narrowed these down to eight with particularly high radiation levels. All the homes within a one-hundred-and-fifty–yard radius of these eight "hot spots" were checked individually, and any residents found to have cesium-related symptoms were taken to hospital for further examination. The resulting data led to the demolition of all the homes within a thirty-yard radius of Devair Ferreira's house, and the registration of 249 victims who had come into direct contact with the cesium powder.

Teresa Fabiano hugged her two-year-old daughter, Natasha, and told us angrily, "My husband and daughter both show symptoms of cesium contamination, but they will only register my husband. Have you ever heard of anything so ridiculous?"

At the time of the accident, the family was living in the house behind Devair Ferreira's. "Devair's wife loved children, and she was always hugging and kissing Natasha, who was two months old at the time. The poor little thing had diarrhea for eight months after the accident. And look at these blisters under her nose. She gets them all over her body."

The state government insists that Natasha Fabiano's symptoms have nothing to do with exposure to cesium.

"It doesn't make any sense to recognize only those who actually touched the cesium—my daughter is suffering from secondary exposure." The doors of the foundation thus closed to Fabiano, she has no way of obtaining medical treatment for Natasha.

Jasil Andrade is another woman pushing for the widening of the foundation's jurisdiction. Doctors there refused to recognize her husband's skin cancer as being related to the cesium contamination, and she believes the government is trying to cover up the true extent of the damage.

The Andrades lived forty yards from Devair Ferreira's house, and they helped to carry people with skin inflammation, hair loss, and other symptoms of radiation sickness to hospital after the accident. Not only was Jasil's husband left off the official register of victims, but the couple had to pay to move house because they lived more than thirty yards from the center of the contamination. They feel the figure of thirty yards to be an arbitrary one with no real significance in terms of the effects of the cesium.

A group of those dissatisfied with the measures taken by the state government got together in December 1987, three months after the accident, and formed the Cesium Victims Association. Jasíl became the chairperson. When we spoke to her she had just returned from a trip to Brasilia to petition the federal government for medical assistance for victims not covered under the present system. She showed us a list of the association's members.

"Our members include the 249 victims recognized as such by the state government. In total there are about five hundred names on our list; this shows you just how much the authorities are trying to downplay the incident."

Edson Ferrari's response to the association's claims was cool: "The leaders are all overreacting—most of the victims are perfectly satisfied with the assistance we are providing."

At the present time it would seem there is no way that Jasil Andrade, frantically busy with work for the association while taking care of her husband after his operation for skin cancer, or Teresa Fabiano, worried by her daughter's mysterious illness, will ever make it through the door of the foundation's office.

THE UNKNOWN SYMPTOMS OF CESIUM CONTAMINATION

"Shall we talk outside?"

Dr. Maria Curado of the Leide Foundation beckoned us to follow her out of the second-floor surgery. A young doctor in the same room had just finished telling us that there were no problems with the health of those exposed to the cesium powder. As we went down the stairs, Dr. Curado began to speak in a low voice.

"No problems? Who are they trying to kid? That's what they tell the media, but I know better. I'm always arguing with the rest of the staff about the foundation's policies."

We drove to a restaurant in downtown Goiânia where she elaborated on the situation of cesium victims in the city.

Of the 249 people recognized by the state government as having been exposed to cesium, the treatment of 120 consisted of showers to wash off the substance. The remaining 129 were hospitalized, and 50 of those were feared to have actually absorbed cesium-137 into their bodies. Fourteen of the worst cases from this last group had been taken to the naval hospital in Rio de Janeiro, where four died.

Eighteen months after the accident, ninety-six patients were still going to the foundation's clinic for regular checkups.

"Rather than there being no problems, we're encountering symptoms we've never seen before," Curado told us, leaning across the table. A year after the accident, burnlike marks began to appear on the skin of those exposed to the cesium, regardless of the amount involved. At present there are twenty-eight known cases with these symptoms. Despite this, the foundation insists that it can help only those who are officially registered.

"I'm always telling the staff they should examine anybody who shows these symptoms, regardless of whether they're on the official register or not. But they won't listen. It's not me who decides the foundation's policies, and I can't see them changing their ideas in the near future."

Dr. Curado is also carrying out her own research on cancer, reading papers on the effects of radiation in an effort to broaden her knowledge. "There's still so much that we don't know about radiation . . . but even so, I never thought I'd be treating patients with symptoms like this."

When we spoke to Dr. Curado, she had just been invited to the International Physicians for the Prevention of Nuclear War (IPPNW) conference in Hiroshima, and was greatly looking forward to speaking with fellow doctors there concerning the treatment of radiation victims. A myriad of questions face the doctors dealing with the aftermath of the cesium tragedy. Why is it, for example, that the group with the highest level of exposure of between 620 and 700 rads survived, while four of those in the next group who were exposed to between 450 and 600 rads died? What conclusions should be drawn about the relationship between dosage and damage to health? The available literature warns that cancer is likely to appear between two and five years after exposure, but what concrete measures may taken to counteract this? What can be done to alleviate the depression suffered by cesium victims? The list goes on.

"Whether it is officially recognized or not, people are suffering from the effects of exposure to cesium-137 in Goiânia, and I have a feeling that those effects are going to become even more apparent over the next few years. If only that cancer clinic had disposed of the cesium properly— as a doctor myself, I feel so ashamed. We must do all we can to help the victims."

THE BURDEN OF FOUR OUNCES OF CESIUM

We found it hard to believe that a mere four ounces of cesium-137 could have such horrific effects on the residents of a city. We became interested in the fate of the vast amount of goods and material that were declared contaminated by radiation after the Goiânia accident. By chance we met Weber Borges, a freelance journalist investigating the accident, who urged us to visit the storage site.

The site was located in some hills fourteen miles from the center of Goiânia. Through the barbed-wire fence we could see shipping containers and drums piled haphazardly on top of each other. The entrance was guarded by an armed soldier.

As we walked around the site, our guide, who was carrying a radiation detector, reeled off the numbers of waste containers. "There are 4,250 oil drums, 1,327 small containers, 12 large containers, and 8 large concrete-filled drums."

When the true nature of the cesium contamination came to light, the Brazilian government mobilized six hundred workers, including two hundred army personnel, to demolish houses in the affected areas. The pile of waste we could see was the result of three months of this decontamination activity. As we approached the concrete-filled drums, the needle on our guide's radiation detector reacted violently.

"This drum contains a dog that belonged to one of the men who took the cesium from the abandoned hospital. That row of drums over there contains the house of Leide Ferreira and all its contents, including a sixteen-inch layer of earth from underneath it. You want to know if it's safe? Of course it is; I've been working here for a year and a half now, with no problems at all."

That same night we met Borges at Dr. Curado's house, where he showed us a video he had taken of the contaminated houses being demolished on December 6, 1987. Water was being poured on the houses as they were knocked down.

"That's to prevent contamination spreading via dust," the journalist explained. "But as you can see, the water is just running off into the street; some scientists in São Paulo are starting to get worried about the possibility of secondary contamination from the water." In another film, we saw workers demolishing houses again; some were wearing protective gear reminiscent of spacesuits, but others were dressed in T-shirts.

"This is the kind of slapdash waste collection that was carried out for three months," Borges said angrily. Dr. Curado nodded in agreement. Borges was fired from his job at the local television station only a week after the accident.

"I happened to criticize the government's cleanup operation on the national news, so the next day I was fired—that's not uncommon here in Brazil." Since his dismissal Borges has continued to conduct his own investigation into the cesium tragedy.

The accident has left an indelible scar on the minds of the people of the peaceful provincial city of Goiânia, and as yet they cannot feel completely confident that further tragedies will not occur. Already four of the drums storing contaminated material from the accident have corroded, and their contents have been moved to other containers. Moreover, the present site is only temporary and will soon need to be vacated; another has yet to be decided on.

Borges commented, "Money buys technology, but it doesn't necessarily buy good management. The tragedy of Goiânia has proved this, but neither the doctors responsible for abandoning potentially dangerous equipment nor the government which was supposed to be supervising their activities have been questioned about their part in the accident. How can we believe that the same thing won't happen again?"

PARALLELS WITH HIROSHIMA

During our stay in Goiânia we spoke to Yokoyama Toshiyuki, a survivor of the Hiroshima A-bomb.

"When I read about the accident in the paper, Hiroshima immediately sprang to mind. I said to my wife that I could just imagine the terrible things that would be happening. The article said that some of the victims were taken to the naval hospital in Rio with skin conditions and hair loss—that's just how it was in Hiroshima. The papers also said they would be cured in three days, but we know that radiation is not that easy to get rid of."

In August 1945, Yokoyama was a junior high school student who, like his classmates, had been mobilized for the war effort and was working in a factory. When the bomb exploded above Hiroshima he was saved from death by crawling under his workbench, but his back and arms were hit by flying glass, covering him in blood. As he fled from the factory he noticed swollen bodies floating in the nearby river. A month later his father died, after losing all his hair.

In 1953 Yokoyama emigrated to Brazil, where for many years he supported his seven children by growing vegetables. He is currently employed by the city. "I'd like to do something for the cesium victims in the city, but being first-generation immigrants it's hard enough just trying to give the children a decent life," he said, his shoulders drooping in a gesture of resignation.

In October 1988, Yokoyama traveled to São Paulo to be examined by a group of doctors from Hiroshima including Kuramoto Kiyoshi, vice director of the Hiroshima Red Cross and Atomic Bomb Survivors Hospital. Yokoyama invited the group to come out to Goiânia to examine the cesium sufferers there, but unfortunately the team was not able to fit a visit into its schedule. Yokoyama has not lost hope of getting a medical team from Hiroshima to visit the stricken city, however.

"Judging by the photos my relatives have sent me, Hiroshima has made a remarkable recovery. It would be marvelous if it could establish a sister-city relationship with Goiânia and do something to help the cesium victims . . . People here don't even know what radiation is."

One doctor from Hiroshima who did visit Goiânia after the accident is Hirofuji Michio, who worked for eleven years from 1952 at the Hiroshima Memorial Hospital. We interviewed Dr. Hirofuji on our return to Japan:

"I read about the accident in the paper and sent some information on the treatment of radiation-related illnesses to the Brazilian Embassy in Tokyo. They replied by asking me to go out to Goiânia to help the people there."

Dr. Hirofuji left for Brazil three months after the accident in December 1987, and stayed there three weeks.

"The symptoms of the cesium victims in Goiânia are basically the same as those observed in Hiroshima after the bomb, except without the effects of the heat and blast. When I told the local doctors this, they pressed me for methods of treatment. There aren't any particular methods, and I wished I could have told them more. As it was, I taught them what I did know, about stimulating the patient's cells by electrotherapy and the kind of illnesses which were likely to appear a few years after exposure to radiation.

"Although radioactive materials are used for medical treatment all over the world, we are still a long way from having a fail-safe cure for people affected in this type of accident. Prevention is better than cure, and my experiences in Brazil have convinced me that the proper management of these substances is by far the best way to prevent further tragedies of this kind."

NAMIBIA'S URANIUM MINES

*O*n March 21, 1990, the end of colonialism in Africa was celebrated with the independence of Namibia from the Republic of South Africa. However, few people are aware that for many years a United Nations decree banning the export of uranium was ignored by the South African government in order to capitalize on the world's fourth-largest resource of the mineral. The predominantly black and Coloured miners in Namibia have been forced to work under atrocious conditions with no knowledge about radiation whatsoever.

Previous page: Eight hundred feet deep and nearly a mile wide—the open-cast uranium mine in the Namib Desert, Namibia.

DEFYING THE UNITED NATIONS

The Namib Desert, stretching for eight hundred miles along Africa's Atlantic coast, is home to the Rossing Mine, one of the largest opencast uranium mining operations in the world.

In 1968, the multinational London-based corporation Rio Tint Zinc (RTZ) obtained the rights to develop the area from the South African government, bringing the Rossing Mine under its jurisdiction. Preparations for mining began two years later in 1970 when companies such as the Mitsubishi Corporation and the Kansai Electric Power Co. signed long-term contracts for the purchase of uranium.

However, in 1974 the United Nations issued a decree banning the mining, refining, and export of uranium from Namibia, in an effort to forestall a plundering of its natural resources. The Decree No. 1 for the Protection of the Natural Resources of Namibia invalidated all mining rights granted by South Africa, as well as viewing all exported raw materials as stolen goods for which a post-independence Namibia would be entitled to seek compensation.

Despite these explicit instructions from the U.N., mining began in March 1976. RTZ has taken a great deal of care to devise an export route making it possible to ship uranium despite international criticism. The route the product takes to Japan has been traced by African affairs expert Kitazawa Yoko.

A subsidiary company formed by RTZ in Switzerland is responsible for the sale of the uranium. RTZ sends the intermediate product, uranium oxide (yellowcake), to the British Nuclear Fuels processing plant, where it is converted into uranium hexafluoride. This is then used in the uranium enrichment process in the United States whereby the proportion of uranium-235 in the fuel is increased. Before being exported to Japan, it is mixed with uranium from Australia and Canada along the way, so by the time it arrives at its final destination, the country of origin is unclear.

Uranium mined in Namibia is supplied to seven of Japan's nine nuclear power companies, which, in deference to the U.N. decree, have vowed not to renew their contracts after they expire. However, the uranium they have already purchased under the terms of their previous contracts continues to be transported to Japan to drive the turbines of nuclear power stations.

The Rossing Branch of the Mine Workers Union of Namibia (MUN) has demanded wage increases and improved working conditions on a number of occasions, but when it comes to the issue of uranium export, the union's position is a little more complex. "Ethically it's probably not correct, but there are 2,200 workers here who rely on the mines to keep their families alive, and there are no other industries nearby of a comparable size," was the comment of Winston Gruenewald, president of the union.

LOW WAGES AND LOW SAFETY STANDARDS

The company is equally well aware of the weakness of the workers' position, and conditions at the mine are inferior, with almost no protection against radiation.

When mining began in 1976 the workers were provided with accommodation less than three miles from the mine, in the middle of the desert. We spoke to Clement, who had worked at the refinery's acid plant ever since the mine opened. Holding his hand to his throat, he spoke in a husky whisper. "Our rooms as well as our bodies were constantly covered in dust. It would've been bad enough if it was just from the desert, but there were huge clouds of it from the mine as well."

At the time the workers' living quarters were segregated: in total there were 1,500 black workers, 1,000 Coloureds, and only 200 whites. All the buildings were brick, but there were clear differences in the areas allotted according to race. The white workers had large kitchens and living rooms, while the black and Coloured workers camped in small rooms housing between six and eight men. Moreover, the accommodation for black and Coloured workers was surrounded by a wire fence and guarded by patrols, making it seem more like a prison than company housing.

"The whites lived like kings compared to us. All we got was a bed and a chest of drawers. The married men had to leave their wives and children at home, of course; the place couldn't really be called 'company housing,' it was more like a camp." Clement showed us a photo taken in his room in 1976, and sure enough, the only extra piece of furniture to be seen was a portable radio.

The miners now work eight hours a day and get two days off a week, but when the operation first started they were working twelve-hour days. Despite these long hours, their wages were still less than half of those of the white workers. At that time wages were paid on an hourly basis, so if the black and Coloured workers wanted to increase their incomes they had no choice but to work themselves to exhaustion. This hourly rate was calculated according to experience, and ranged from about fifty cents to U.S. $1.20. Even Clement, who was a fit worker, was only ever able to earn $135 a month. Although prices of everyday items were low, it was still far from enough to support a decent standard of living. Compared with other workers in Namibia, the miners were relatively well paid, but most of the men were sending a large part of their pay home and scraping by on very little themselves.

In addition to the inferior accommodation and low wages allotted to them because of their color, the workers at Rossing were kept completely in the dark concerning the dangers of radiation. They were told that X-rays and gamma rays penetrate the body, but were assured that uranium did not contain sufficient quantities of these to make it dangerous. The company only made the wearing of film badges compulsory in 1979, three years after operations began, and then only in the final stages of the uranium oxide extraction process.

A HIGH INCIDENCE OF RESPIRATORY DISEASES

For the past three years, Clement has been worried by an increasing tightness in his chest; a number of his fellow workers have the same problem. He introduced us to some of these men.

"Often at night I feel sharp pains in my chest, and it gets difficult to breathe," said Harry, a heavy machinery operator, clutching at his chest. He has been at the mine for nine years and is concerned that his nose and throat problems are caused by the dust. While on the site he is often overcome by nausea, yet the company doctor sent him away with assurances that there was nothing seriously wrong with him.

"That doctor can't be trusted—he wouldn't even tell me the name of my condition," said Harry, his face clouded with uncertainty. Reed is another worker with health problems that he believes were caused by working at the mine. He works at the uranium recovery plant, and several years ago was hospitalized with a "throat condition." Reed is still not certain what is wrong with him; he knows there is something not quite right with his thyroid gland, but did not seem certain about what the gland actually was when we spoke to him. These two men were just two of the cases we heard about of workers having problems with their noses, throats, and lungs. The majority had never used masks or film badges during their work.

"The company just tells us to wear our protective glasses and boots, and to shut the windows of vehicles when we're on the site," said James, a worker introduced to us by the union. At the bottom of the opencast pit, the wind rarely blows and the men work in stifling heat, constantly surrounded by irritating clouds of dust. "The only rest we get is while waiting for the next truck. We have about two or three minutes to gulp down our sandwiches—that's our lunch break. The dust gets into the bulldozers and shovels we drive, through the air conditioning, so the sandwiches as well as our hands are covered in filth," continued his companion, Morris.

Whether the technique used for extracting uranium is opencast or ordinary mining, exposure to radiation poses a serious threat to miners, because radioactive materials are absorbed from the dust into their bodies. At the present time the respiratory ailments prevalent at Rossing are generally seen as being caused merely by the dust itself, rather than any harmful substances contained within it. There is no room for complacency, though, for as surveys at uranium mines in New Mexico have shown, as long as there is uranium in the dust, the internal exposure of the miners will progress to increasingly harmful levels. When we suggested this to the Namibian miners, they turned to each other and began to talk in worried tones, recalling a coworker who had died of lung cancer a few years previously, and wondering if his death was caused by the radioactive dust.

The president of the MUN, Gruenewald, told us regretfully that in spite of numerous attempts to talk with the company, the RTZ management was continuing to insist that such illnesses are the concern of specialists, and had refused to allow them to be discussed during any labor negotiations.

RADON CHECKS CARRIED OUT IN SECRET

The company town of Arandis lies seven miles to the north of the Rossing Mine. Workers began to move into accommodation there at the end of the 1970s, and at present it is home to nine hundred households with a total of more than 2,500 people. All the homes are detached and have a living room, three bedrooms, and a solar water heater providing a constant supply of hot water. The settlement has schools, a hospital, a church, and a supermarket, and it is surrounded by greenery, earning it the title of "the new oasis."

"It looks great, doesn't it?" remarked our guide, Hylton Villet, vice secretary of the MUN. "But actually it's only the unskilled black and Coloured workers who live here."

White workers and skilled black and Coloured workers are housed at the resort of Swakopmund, forty miles to the west on the Atlantic coast. "A lot of the residents of Arandis suffer from throat conditions caused by sulfuric gases from the mines. We've taken the issue up several times but to no avail; the company just keeps saying there is no problem. The environment at Swakopmund is clean, though; it's a textbook case of discrimination," he added, shaking his head irritably.

The greatest problem facing the residents of Arandis, which to the outsider appears to deserve its title of "the new oasis," is that the town is located downwind from the mine and thus is constantly exposed to harmful substances released into the atmosphere during the mining and refining processes. Walking around the town, we came upon a number of odd plastic containers which turned out to be proof that the mine owners were worried about the possibility of harmful substances being emitted from the mine. We first encountered these when Paul Rooi, vice president of the MUN, took us to visit the home of a friend. The man was out, but his wife, Margaret, was happy to speak to us.

"What exactly is radon gas?" Her opening remark caught us off guard.

Margaret told us that two employees from the mine had visited in November 1989, saying they wanted to check for radon gas. She showed us the two small plastic pots they had left behind. Shaped like inverted cones, they were about four inches high and inscribed with the numbers 989 and 990. We took off the lid of one to find a white paper filter inside. Radon, a radioactive gas, is produced from the decay of uranium-238 or thorium-232. The gas is released during mining, and radioactive particles attach themselves to the dust. When the dust is inhaled those particles are absorbed through the lung leading to an increased risk of lung cancer. Rooi and Villet were both surprised; neither of them had ever seen the pots before.

"I'm not sure, but it seems that the filter absorbs the radon," Margaret told them. "They come to change them sometimes, and I just do what they say."

The radon checks had begun with only a scant explanation about what they were for, and no information about the possible effects of exposure to radiation. There is no doubt the company discovered that radon gas was being released into the atmosphere and was trying to find out discreetly the seriousness of the contamination. "Is radon really that dangerous?" Margaret asked with a worried frown.

MINE PROPAGANDA

During our stay at a hotel in the town of Swakopmund, where the white workers and black and Coloured skilled workers were housed, we noticed a poster advertising tours of the uranium mine. These operated every Friday and cost a mere five rand (approx. U.S. $2.50). At the time we were still waiting for a reply to our request for access to the mine to gather material, so we decided to take part in a tour to furnish ourselves with some extra background knowledge.

A few days later we arrived at the meeting point near the hotel at eight in the morning to find a group of fifty or so tourists had already gathered. Together with the sightseers, most of whom seemed to be German— perhaps not surprising considering Namibia was once a German colony—we climbed into a bus, emblazoned with the company slogan, *Working for Namibia*.

Fifty minutes later we arrived in the company town of Arandis, where our guide, Beth Volshenk, related the history of the Rossing Mine and its operations. However, no mention was made of the United Nations decree banning the export of Namibia's natural resources, or of the fact that Arandis was home to black and Coloured workers only.

After a brief drive around the town, we arrived at the mine itself just after ten o'clock, and were first taken to see the opencast pit, which was eight hundred feet deep and nearly a mile wide. We peered down into the pit, the sides of which were cut into terraces, and marveled at the machinery which from above looked more like toys. After only fifteen minutes walking around, our glasses were covered with a thin layer of powder. This was the dust the workers were so afraid of.

Our next stop was the plant where the ore is broken up to produce uranium oxide. During the tour the guide explained about levels of radiation at the mine, saying that the average level for workers at Rossing was 0.3 rems per year, well below the internationally designated safe exposure limit of 5 rems.

We had discovered that everyday hygiene standards were not being met, let alone radiation safety standards, so the figure of 0.3 rems hardly seemed credible. After completing the tour we asked some workers about this figure; without exception they replied they had never heard it before. The mine management was obviously doing its best to impress upon visitors how safe its operations were, but was less concerned about informing its employees.

"That's how they do things at Rossing," one of the workers commented wryly. "If we want to find out anything about radiation, it looks as though we'll have to join a tour as well."

A few days later, after much negotiation, we finally managed to meet Dr. Steve Kesler, the general manager of the mining operation. We quizzed him about the workers' radiation levels, the high incidence of respiratory diseases, and the measurement of radon gas in the town of Arandis, but his only reply was that the company was "doing its utmost for the welfare of the workers and their families." To our final question regarding the employees' concern about cancer, he answered confidently that there was no cause for concern about exposure to radiation, either at present or in the future.

THE MUN: BUILDING A FUTURE IN NAMIBIA

During our stay in Namibia we went along to observe a MUN meeting at Arandis. Five hundred mine workers had gathered in the town hall, and the topic under discussion was the proposed return to work of one of the union officials who had been involved in SWAPO (South West African People's Organization) activities. After a three-hour debate it was decided to take action to force the company to reinstate the man, and the meeting ended with a rousing cheer in support of the decision.

The MUN has been in existence for over four years, despite efforts by the South African government and the mine management to suppress its activities. When first established, it had a mere twenty members; the union is now supported by over 70% of the workforce with a membership of over fifteen hundred workers, including twenty whites. A vocal supporter of SWAPO, the MUN has not been daunted by four years of harrassment and imprisonment and is committed to continuing the fight against the company and the South African government. Gruenewald sees the MUN's struggle as "a fight to make the authorities realize that whites are not the only humans."

The union's original demands for improved working and general living conditions were consistent with the wider aim of abolishing apartheid and directing the country toward independence, SWAPO's principal goal. However, since SWAPO gained the greatest number of votes in the Constitutional Assembly elections in November 1989, the MUN has begun to direct its efforts toward matters closer to home.

Of the many issues vying for the union's attention, the most urgent is that of its members' health. Not only the increasing incidence of respiratory ailments but also the possibility of exposure to radiation during the various stages of the mining and refining process pose a great threat to the workers' well-being. MUN officials themselves have only a sparse knowledge of radiation, and most of the ordinary workers have none at all. The company has never given out any basic information on the subject, and even if the men want to find out for themselves, there are no books available on the topic, even in the capital of Windhoek.

Each time we met with mine workers during our investigation, we were questioned about Hiroshima and Nagasaki, about nuclear testing and weapons factories, and about accidents at nuclear power plants. Without exception the men would fire anxious questions at us about their futures and plead with us to tell them anything we knew about the situation at other uranium mines. Fourteen years after the establishment of Namibia's most vital industry at the Rossing Mine, there is still an almost complete dearth of information on radiation levels there, caused in part by the apartheid policies of the South African government. Independence will without a doubt bring radical changes to this state of affairs.

Workers will have access to information about radiation that may make them more fearful for their health than they are now. They will also discover that the demand for uranium has decreased since the accident at Chernobyl.

Namibia relies on its natural resources for eighty percent of its income from exports, and after independence uranium will continue to be the mainstay of the nation's economy. How the new nation fares on its own will be influenced by demand for the ore. For the miners, and for the new government, the aftereffects of the monopoly held on information by the South African government and the British multinational mining corporation will continue to loom large in any discussion on Namibia's future.

PART 7

NO MORE VICTIMS

THE FUTURE OF NUCLEAR POWER

*D*uring the sixties and into the early seventies, America, the Soviet Union, Britain, and France engaged in a desperate race for supremacy in the field of nuclear weapons. The late Kanai Toshihiro of the Chugoku Newspaper, a tireless critic of this destructive contest, was deeply concerned about the way in which the power of nuclear weapons was expressed in kilotons and megatons, rather than in terms of environmental destruction and loss of human life.

It would seem doubtful whether any lessons have in fact been learned from the victims of radiation in Hiroshima and Nagasaki. Despite the warnings from Kanai and many others of the suffering caused at every stage of the nuclear development process, uranium mining, weapons manufacture, nuclear testing, nuclear power generation, nuclear fuel reprocessing, and radioactive waste storage still continue.

In this, the final section, we consider what path should be taken by Japan and the world in order to avoid further destruction by radiation in the future.

Previous page: Residents of Semipalatinsk campaign for a halt to nuclear testing and an end to official secrecy.

THE PRICE OF NUCLEAR DEVELOPMENT

In their efforts to develop sophisticated nuclear technology, the world's leading nations have been left with a legacy of problems not likely to be solved in the near future. The most serious of these problems concerns the release of radioactive substances into the atmosphere and their consequent absorption by humans. Anyone who experienced the explosions in Hiroshima and Nagasaki would be aware of their incredible destructive power in terms of searing heat and the force of the blast itself, even if they were not aware of radiation. On the other hand, most of the damage caused by nuclear materials since 1945 has been caused by exposure to radiation itself.

There is no way of knowing when radiation enters the body, and unless a person is subjected to a massive dose in a short space of time, the effects are not immediately obvious but may take years to manifest themselves. Added to this is the fact that radioactive contamination does not produce a distinct set of symptoms, making it difficult even for experts to judge whether a particular medical condition has been caused by radiation. When a person has been exposed to radiation even the most advanced medical techniques are unable to remove it. The effects of exposure to radiation may be passed down to the next generation, and this is the main reason why radiation is the object of so much fear.

As we started to investigate victims of radiation in other parts of the world, we realized that most of these people did not have access to anything like the medical care or welfare services that the victims of Hiroshima and Nagasaki were able to benefit from. Instead they were living from one day to the next in constant uncertainty about their health. The most disturbing discovery was that the vast majority of radiation victims are not recognized as such by the very governments which are to blame for their suffering.

The Chernobyl disaster in 1986 was the catalyst for an increased interest in nuclear issues all over the world. Ordinary people began to demand that governments take responsibility for the damage they had allowed to happen over the years, and previously unknown cases of suffering caused by radiation were uncovered one after another.

A typical example of this growing awareness of the dangers of radiation is the recent revelations concerning the Soviet nuclear testing site near the city of Semipalatinsk in Kazakhstan, where for a long time it was forbidden to even mention the existence of damage caused by radiation. The renewed interest in nuclear issues after the Chernobyl disaster, however, coincided with the era of *glasnost*, with the result that investigations into radiation damage could be carried out with relative ease. Through journalists' reports the Soviet people became aware of the extent of radiation contamination at the Semipalatinsk test site, and the Nevada-Semipalatinsk organization to oppose nuclear testing and assist radiation victims became known throughout the world. By exposing the lies perpetrated over the previous forty years, the popular movement eventually forced the Soviet government to announce in July 1990 that the site would be closed in 1993.

The growing interest in the problems of radiation was also felt on the other side of the world in the United States, where it was revealed around the time of the Chernobyl disaster in 1986 that radiation had been both intentionally and unintentionally leaked from the nuclear weapons manufacturing complex in Hanford, Washington. This revelation led to another: that there were abnormally high incidences of cancer and thyroid conditions among the residents of the nearby towns. The Department of the Environment (DOE), which had insisted that there were no effects from radiation leakage or experiments, was eventually forced to retract these statements when the local residents obtained incriminating documents under the Freedom of Information Act.

The uncovering of careless and irresponsible management at Hanford was the signal for a series of similar discoveries at weapons facilities in Oak Ridge, Tennessee; Rocky Flats, Colorado; and Savannah River, South Carolina. In the former uranium mining areas of New Mexico, radioactive waste abandoned in mines and refineries became an issue, with the result that, one after the other, nuclear-related facilities all over the country were persuaded by the DOE to release the results of medical surveys carried out on workers and residents.

As a result of the Chernobyl disaster the voids in the history of nuclear development are gradually being filled in, but there has been little progress made in provision of support for victims of radiation. In most cases this suffering has still not been publicly acknowledged by the governments concerned. Even in the case of American ex-servicemen involved in nuclear tests, who have recently become eligible for compensation, the amount is awarded in a lump sum for certain specific types of cancer, but no allowance is made from public funds for the day-to-day health care of these men. A law providing for compensation for the residents of towns downwind of the Nevada test site only passed Congress in October 1990, and like that concerned with ex-military personnel, it makes too little provision for their future medical care. The medical expenses of A-bomb victims in Japan are mainly, though not completely, provided for under two laws, the *Hibakusha* (A-bomb survivors) Medical Law and the *Hibakusha* Special Welfare Law. Using rates applied in Japan we worked out the cost of supporting victims of radiation in the United States and the Soviet Union. In 1990 there were approximately 352,500 registered *hibakusha* in Japan. The annual budget for *hibakusha* medical care works out at ¥358,000 (approx. $2,750) per person. According to our calculations, we estimated that 855,000 people in the United States were affected in some way or other by radiation, including ex-army personnel, employees of nuclear weapons facilities, and residents of the surrounding areas. In the Soviet Union the number of people affected by the Chernobyl and Ural disasters comes to almost two and a half million. Basing our estimates on these figures we arrived at an annual total of $2,344,670,000 for the United States and approximately three times that amount for the Soviet Union. What must be remembered is that these figures cover only medical care and welfare allowances for radiation victims and do not include other costs such as those for cleaning up contaminated areas.

Already claims are being made against the U.S. government. In July 1989, a court ruling ordered the federal government to pay $73 million in compensation to residents near the Fernald nuclear weapons plant in Ohio, on the grounds that property values had declined due to radioactive contamination from the plant. Similar instances of contamination are coming to light all over the United States, and it is becoming increasingly difficult for the government to defend its policy against concerned groups claiming vast amounts of compensation.

Two other pressing problems faced by the U.S. government are the dismantling of aging nuclear weapons facilities and the disposal of almost a half-century's worth of nuclear waste. According to estimates from the DOE, the cost of these operations alone would amount to $200 billion.

The Soviet Union has already been landed with an enormous bill for its nuclear development program. By the end of 1989 the Soviet government had spent over 9 billion rubles on cleaning up after the Chernobyl disaster alone. A member of the Supreme Soviet, Yuri Shcherbak, who has been studying the aftereffects of Chernobyl, has estimated that the total cost of the accident including material damage and the cleanup operations could come to as much as 250 billion rubles, roughly equivalent to Japan's government expenditure for the fiscal year 1990. Shcherbak's estimate does not include the damage caused to other nations in the region by the disaster.

The British government is also facing charges of negligence and demands for compensation from those affected by their testing in Australia in the fifties and sixties, and before long France will be forced to count the cost of its nuclear testing policies in the South Pacific. Governments all over the world are beginning to pay the price for not encouraging more research into safer methods of harnessing the energy that nuclear scientists had succeeded in releasing from the atom. Unfortunately, the cost of negligent management is likely to place a heavy burden not only on the present generation but on our descendants well into the next century.

THE CONTINUING NUCLEAR DEBATE

The tragedy of Chernobyl and the escalation of the suffering of victims in the surrounding areas has without a doubt influenced the decisions of other nations to build nuclear power facilities.

In 1986, the Yugoslavian government announced that the construction of nuclear power plants would be postponed until the formulation of a long-term electricity plan. Switzerland announced the abolition of all nuclear power plants within forty years. The Austrian government announced the dismantling of the newly completed Zwentendorf power plant.

In 1987, the Mexican Department of Mines decided not to put the Laguna Verde plant into operation until safety could be guaranteed. Spain abandoned plans for an experimental radioactive waste treatment site. A referendum in Italy, which revealed that almost eighty percent of its citizens oppose nuclear power, led to the announcement of a moratorium. The Netherlands and Finland also postponed plans for new facilities.

In 1988, the Swedish government promised to close two reactors by 1996. The Swiss General Assembly canceled the construction of a nuclear power plant. Belgium also canceled plans for new nuclear power facilities.

In 1989, West Germany abandoned plans for the nuclear fuel reprocessing facility at Wackersdorf. In Sacramento, California, local people voted to close the Rancho Seco facility. New York State bought the Shoreham plant for one dollar with the intention of dismantling it.

The accident at Three Mile Island occurred several years before Chernobyl, and since then no orders for new reactors have been made in the United States. Three Mile Island provided the impetus for Sweden's decision to shut down all nuclear power plants by the year 2010. The accident at Chernobyl merely served to hasten this reversal in nuclear policy all over the world, and in many countries the prevailing attitude toward nuclear power is one of caution.

A visit to any bookshop leaves no doubt that the general public is more concerned than ever before about the earth's environment: a vast array of publications warn of the imminent destruction of the earth and inform us of ways to avoid it. However, almost without exception, they ignore the environmental problems caused by radioactive contamination from nuclear tests, weapons factories, fuel reprocessing plants, reactor accidents, and the careless disposal of radioactive waste.

Having seen firsthand the destruction caused by radiation, we find it incomprehensible that the issue of radioactive contamination should be left out of the environmental debate.

A glance at world history since the end of the Second World War shows that there have been only two periods during which the contamination of the earth's environment by radiation has been a widely debated issue. The first period was during the 1950s when the United States, the Soviet Union, and Britain carried out atmospheric tests of megaton-class bombs in an effort to maintain their position in the race for nuclear supremacy. The Japanese term *shi no hai*, "ashes of death," an apt description of nuclear fallout, was coined after a hydrogen bomb was detonated at Bikini. The American movie *On the Beach,* based on the Nigel Shute novel, painted a realistic picture of the end of the world brought about by a nuclear war. It was also during this period that scientists discovered that strontium-90 could make its way into the human body via the food chain.

The second period of reaction against nuclear technology was after the accident at Chernobyl. In Europe there was a rush on iodine, children could no longer be heard playing outdoors, and women decided to delay having children.

During both these periods contaminated food posed an immediate threat to ordinary citizens, who felt the effects of radiation far more intimately than those of global warming, the destruction of the ozone layer, or deforestation. Seen in this light it is difficult to see why it has been left out of the debate as the issue of radioactive contamination would seem the obvious starting point for any discussion on the environment.

In spite of the dangers of radioactive contamination, the idea of nuclear power generation has been experiencing a resurgence in popularity in recent years, for the reason that nuclear power plants do not discharge carbons into the atmosphere. Some groups have advanced the argument that nuclear power plants are kinder to the environment than power plants which use fossil fuels. In Sweden, a number of people have been calling for a reappraisal of the plan to abolish all nuclear power facilities, and the argument supporting this type of power generation as a solution to the problem of global warming is gathering force in other countries as well. This trend is most apparent in France, which relies on atomic energy for 69.9 percent of its power. The Soviet Union and Japan are similarly dependent on nuclear power.

France has not altered its policies of further expanding the use of nuclear power generation and is aiming at maintaining its status as Europe's main atomic energy producer before EC unification in 1992.

The Soviet Union, or rather the Soviet government, has been most keen to revive the flagging fortunes of nuclear power generation. However, because of the fierce opposition to nuclear power that was generated after the accident at Chernobyl, further construction of nuclear facilities has become impossible. Power plants in Krasnodar, Minsk, Odessa, and Armenia have been closed, and plans for future plants have been canceled; in March 1990 the Ukrainian parliament demanded that the three remaining reactors at Chernobyl be shut down.

Japan, with its lack of natural resources, continues its policy of decreasing reliance on fossil fuels. The notion of nuclear power as the savior of the environment is widely accepted among officials of the Ministry of International Trade and Industry (MITI). From MITI's point of view the sudden enthusiasm for protecting the environment is seen as a means to a quite different end: by persuading the public that nuclear power offers a viable alternative to traditional forms of power generation, new reactors may be built without provoking storms of protest. The same applies for those other nations eager to revive the fortunes of atomic energy as a power source. If the dangers of radioactive contamination were to be widely publicized, considerable damage would be done to the case for nuclear power. Consequently, one is forced to the conclusion that this is the main reason why radiation is conspicuously absent from the environmental debate.

This is not to say that the pronuclear governments have been completely successful in promoting nuclear power: in Japan, for example, there is a great deal of public opposition to the government plan to increase the percentage of electricity generated by nuclear power from the present 26.2 percent to 34 percent by 1999.

During our investigations we visited both Chernobyl and Three Mile Island, and came to understand the hollowness of the popular belief that nuclear power is safe. In the book *Genpatsu wa naze kiken ka* (Why is nuclear power dangerous?), Tanaka Saburo, a former Japanese power-plant engineer, questions the safety of nuclear power and gives several examples of work he has done at reactors to avert potentially dangerous situations. He also points out the wide discrepancy in terms of safety between new and long-established facilities, where the pressure vessels are likely to have become brittle.

The economy myth as embodied in the slogan "Electricity too cheap to meter" has recently been under attack in the same way as the safety myth. In the case of Three Mile Island, for example, the initial construction cost of the Unit-2 reactor was $700 million, and the cost of the cleanup operation after the accident was $1 billion. If the drop in share prices and compensation to local residents are included, the total cost comes to $4 billion.

When something goes wrong with a nuclear reactor the resulting damage is far from minimal. The Chernobyl disaster has shown that the destructive force of radioactive contamination can affect wide areas. The high financial, environmental, and human costs of that particular accident will be a burden on Europe for many years to come.

These stark realities have brought about a change in attitudes toward nuclear power generation all over the world. It is common knowledge that the techniques associated with the various uses of atomic energy have yet to be perfected. It could almost be said that the disaster at Chernobyl has given us the opportunity to make a choice: whether we should delay the construction of further nuclear power plants while we reevaluate their worth, or whether we should press on with building more facilities and think about it as we go.

Having seen firsthand the suffering caused by exposure to radiation in many different parts of the world, we hope that all nations, including our own, will have the courage to choose the former alternative. Japan, unfortunately, seems to have chosen the latter path, contrary to trends in the rest of the world.

THE PROBLEM OF NUCLEAR WASTE

In addition to the dubious safety and high price of nuclear power, a major cause for concern is the problem of how to dispose of waste from nuclear power plants. Most of the used fuel produced at nuclear power plants in Japan is sent to Britain and France, where it is reprocessed and sent back to be used again. However, along with the reusable fuel comes highly concentrated, highly radioactive waste material, for which no satisfactory method of disposal has yet been found. There is one fuel reprocessing plant operating in Japan, but due to various technical problems its output is only a fraction of what was originally anticipated. Others have been planned but have been delayed due to widespread public opposition.

As Japan's record in the field shows, the development of fuel reprocessing facilities is not as advanced as other aspects of nuclear technology. The United States has already closed one of its reprocessing plants, and has moved out of the field. Only facilities in Britain, France, Germany, and Japan remain. In Part 5 we reported on the high incidence of leukemia near the British nuclear waste disposal facility at Sellafield. This tragedy is not only the responsibility of Britain, but of all the countries who ease their worries about dangerous nuclear waste by sending it abroad for disposal.

Advocates of atomic energy claim that one of its major advantages is that nuclear fuel can be recycled. This, however, ignores the fact that a safe and reliable method of carrying out this recycling process is not yet available. Even supposing that an effective way of reprocessing spent nuclear fuel were to be developed, the problem still remains of how to dispose of highly radioactive concentrated waste, an unavoidable byproduct of the recycling process. The use of atomic energy has been described quite accurately as the equivalent of living in an apartment without a toilet.

In the United States, for example, the DOE's plan to reprocess spent nuclear fuel at an experimental plant at Carlsbad, New Mexico, was canceled when the state government banned the import of radioactive waste. As a result, several tons of highly radioactive waste have become stranded as the facility would have taken waste not only from nuclear power plants but also from weapons facilities.

Atomic energy has been lauded by some as the answer to protecting our environment from further damage. However, it seems hardly realistic to believe that nuclear power will save the earth from further destruction when we are faced with a future of ever-increasing piles of abandoned waste.

TAKING ACTION

When we set out to investigate the damage caused by radioactive substances in various parts of the world, it had never occurred to us that we would be considered experts on radiation. Wherever we went we were confronted by people anxious about the lumps on their throats, the burns on their arms, restrictions on drinking milk, and a host of other matters. Many expressed a loss of faith in the assurances of their governments and military authorities, and many wanted to know if doctors could be sent from Hiroshima to help them. In every area we visited, the local people had suffered a great deal before managing to breach the wall of official secrecy to ascertain that radiation was the cause of their diseases. Even when the residents succeed in obtaining damning evidence of the harm done to them and revealing it to the general public, governments and businesses still, on the whole, dismiss the matter and refuse to acknowledge their responsibility. By the time the claims are recognized as legitimate, it is usually too late to do anything for the majority of the victims.

Even when qualified physicians and scientists embark on their own surveys and publish results, their efforts are largely ignored. Local doctors have played an especially vital role in the village of Seascale, near Britain's infamous nuclear facility, and in Malaysia's Bukit Merah, where radioactive waste was irresponsibly dumped. In both these cases the governments and companies concerned have refused to take the results of independent surveys seriously, preferring instead to criticize their methods and motivation. The present situation, therefore, is one of a stalemate between those who allege they have suffered from the negligent handling of radioactive substances, and those who counter that all their fears are based on ignorance and unscientific methods.

Surveying, examining, and confirming damage caused by radiation is an expensive and time-consuming business involving specialized knowledge. It would seem that this work could best be carried out by an independent international research organization, which would also provide neutral ground for all concerned parties to discuss their differences in a scientific manner. Such an organization could dispatch survey teams to any area where radiation damage was alleged to have taken place, assess the situation, and recommend appropriate countermeasures where necessary.

The accident at Chernobyl demonstrated that radioactive contamination has no respect for man-made borders, and that there are limits to what one nation can do to respond to the problems of contamination over a wide area. If an international research organization could compare the effects of radiation damage in different regions, the results of such a survey could assist greatly in unraveling the remaining mysteries in the field of radiation medicine. Moreover, the knowledge that such an organization could swiftly dispatch survey teams to any region where contamination was suspected would no doubt make those dealing with various radioactive materials think twice before indulging in any dangerous practices.

Efforts have already been made to this effect by established organizations: in the fall of 1989 the International Physicians for the Prevention of Nuclear War (IPPNW) formed a team to survey nuclear test sites and weapons facilities, and in April 1990 the International Atomic Energy Agency (IAEA) sent an international team of experts to the Soviet Union to study the effects of the Chernobyl disaster. In reality, however, both organizations are subject to the whims of their host governments, and do not have a free rein in conducting surveys. To avoid these problems, a solution would be to form a new organization under the auspices of the

World Health Organization, which has wide experience in conducting health surveys and which also has been carrying out research on the possible effects of a nuclear war ever since the "nuclear winter" theory was first debated in the early 1980s.

One of the problems in urgent need of research by such an organization is that of the effects of exposure to low doses of radiation. Many radiation-linked diseases are caused by low-level exposure to radiation, yet far too little is known about it.

The experiences of Hiroshima and Nagasaki are the starting point for any study of radiation-linked diseases, and the data collected during the treatment of A-bomb survivors in these two cities has become a textbook for the world's radiation researchers. During our investigations in various regions of the world, however, we came across problems which were inexplicable even after referring to this information.

At testing sites, nuclear weapons manufacturing plants, uranium mines, and refineries, we met people who had been exposed to levels of radiation far lower than those recorded in Hiroshima, yet the incidence of leukemia, cancer, and other radiation-related diseases was often unusually high. In addition, even though no genetic defects have been confirmed in the children of A-bomb survivors, large numbers of deformed children have been reported near the Semipalatinsk test site in the Soviet Union. These facts contradict much of what we have so far assumed to be the effects of exposure to radiation.

Governments and businesses have been known to quote data from Hiroshima and Nagasaki to back up their claims that there are no harmful effects from low doses of radiation, but it is becoming more and more a matter of debate whether the knowledge gained from the experience of the A-bombs is applicable to all levels of exposure.

In Hiroshima and Nagasaki, radiation-related illnesses were caused by exposure to radiation at the actual instant of the explosion and for a relatively short period after the blast. In contrast to this, people living near nuclear test sites since 1945 have been showered with radioactive fallout on several different occasions, while those near nuclear weapons manufacturing facilities have lived with radioactive contamination continuously over long periods of time. It would seem that more attention needs to be paid to the differences in the circumstances of exposure and to the warnings of those researching the effects of low doses of radiation.

As more information comes to light concerning the effects of low doses of radiation, there appears to be increasing cause for pessimism. In 1977, the International Commission on Radiological Protection (ICRP) calculated that if ten thousand people were exposed to 1 rem of radiation, one case of cancer would result. This figure, however, is only an estimate and was obtained by calculating back from what was then understood to be the danger level of 100 rems based on data from Hiroshima and Nagasaki. Questions have been raised concerning this method of evaluation, and in November 1989 the American Science Council recalculated this figure using the latest information from Japan. It subsequently announced that the risk of cancer from 1 rem of radiation was actually over ten times that estimated by the ICRP. This startling reevaluation demonstrates that the data concerning Hiroshima and Nagasaki itself is far from being immutable, and that different conclusions may be drawn with each addition of new information. Defining, estimating, and verifying the effects of exposure to radiation is an exercise fraught with difficulty—precisely the reason why action should be taken now at an international level to research the effects of exposure to low doses of radiation.

THE ROLE THAT JAPAN CAN PLAY

At every United Nations General Assembly or round of arms reduction talks, Japan emphasizes its special position as the only nation to have experienced an atomic attack. Over the last forty-five years Japan has proclaimed its commitment to the abolition of nuclear weapons and the establishment of a permanent peace in the world. Yet at the same time it has poured huge sums into the expansion of its armed forces, thus inviting the suspicion of both developed and developing nations. To maintain its standing in the world it is crucial for Japan to translate its words into action and use its special position to provide tangible assistance to victims of radiation in other countries.

Japan has become the world's largest provider of overseas aid, even surpassing the United States. However, the form which this aid has taken has drawn harsh criticism from many countries, which allege that instead of improving the day-to-day existence of the people of the recipient nations, Japanese aid contributes to the destruction of the environment and appears to be motivated by a desire for profit rather than altruistic aims. While aid from Europe and the United States is concentrated mainly on improving the education and general welfare of the people, Japan's contributions have tended to consist of dams, roads, and other construction projects.

Our travels in areas contaminated by radiation impressed upon us the need for drastic change in Japan's aid policy: Japan should make more contributions toward the health care of victims of radiation, particularly as the country has had the unique experience of dealing with the medical treatment of the survivors of Hiroshima and Nagasaki. A more humanistic aid policy would also help to improve Japan's image in the world. We had heard that after the cesium contamination incident in Brazil a Japanese doctor, who had worked with A-bomb survivors in Hiroshima after the war, had rushed to the scene of the tragedy. When we later visited this doctor in Tokyo he told us that some Japanese immigrants in the area had been expecting a team of Japanese specialists in radiation medicine to visit after the accident occurred. "I was so ashamed, I didn't know what to say to them," he told us.

In response to our article on Brazil, which mentioned that some Brazilian doctors were keen to study in Hiroshima, we were pleased to hear the announcement that the governor of Hiroshima Prefecture, Takeshita Toranosuke, had decided to invite the Brazilian doctors to study at the Hiroshima Red Cross and Atomic Bomb Survivors Hospital from August 1990.

Our hope that Hiroshima will one day become a world center for information on radiation damage and the treatment of victims is beginning to be realized in other ways as well. Once again on Takeshita's initiative, a committee to explore all the possibilities for international cooperation in the treatment of radiation sufferers was formed by eleven organizations involved with the treatment of A-bomb survivors and related research. In response to the efforts being made in Hiroshima, the Ministry of Foreign Affairs signed a joint Japanese-Soviet agreement on the occasion of Foreign Minister Shevardnadze's visit to Japan in September 1990, which pledged Japan's support for victims of the Chernobyl disaster.

This agreement marks the first time that the Japanese government has embarked upon a program of aid for victims of radiation in another country. We believe there is ample scope for Japan to extend aid to other nations. For example, Japan could offer assistance to the Marshall Islands, which is still suffering from the effects of American nuclear testing in the 1950s. The people of this region are deeply suspicious of the United States but relatively friendly toward Japan. The fact that the crew of a Japanese fishing boat became victims of the same hydrogen bomb test is also a factor, and the people there have great expectations of Japanese cooperation in providing medical assistance. To date the only such aid forthcoming has been from private organizations rather than the government itself. In addition, Japan's image in the region has been further tarnished recently with its support of a proposed nuclear waste dump, so the offer of medical aid would be one way of restoring the country's reputation in this region.

Japan could also play an important role in the United Nations to urge other countries to participate in the establishment of an international radiation research organization, which would become the basis for the dispatch of medical teams, the acceptance of overseas doctors to study at medical facilities, and technical cooperation in the form of medical equipment and knowledge. This type of activity would not only strengthen Japan's position in the international community, but also serve to increase the respect given to its opinions by other nations at the arms reduction talks in Geneva, and in the United Nations. Above all, at Japan's initiative, action would at last be taken to promote the exchange of information in an effort to alleviate the suffering of thousands of radiation victims around the world.

RADIATION AND ITS VICTIMS
A CHRONOLOGICAL TABLE

15th century   Appearance of lung disease among workers in present-day Germany and Czechoslovakia engaged in mining pitchblende, a uranium-rich ore containing silver and other precious metals.

1895   German physicist, Wilhelm Röntgen, discovers the X-ray.

1896   An American physicist becomes the first person to be treated for the harmful effects of X-rays after conducting the same type of experiments with fluorescence as Röntgen. X-rays are used medically for the first time in the treatment of breast cancer.

1897   *March 1:* French physicist, Henri Becquerel, discovers the radioactivity of uranium.
Thomas Alva Edison experiments with X-ray fluoroscopy. His assistant suffers from hair loss; Edison himself complains of sore eyes. Skin damage also reported.

1898   Pierre and Marie Curie discover the naturally radioactive substances radium and polonium.
A survey of the harmful effects of X-rays is proposed at English academic conference.

1899   Ernest Rutherford identifies alpha and beta rays.

1902   X-rays are found to cause skin cancer.

1903   Rutherford announces his theory that radioactivity is associated with a natural transmutation of the elements.
Radium is brought to Japan and used for medical purposes.

1905   Low sperm counts are noted among male X-ray assistants.

1911   Rutherford discovers the nucleus of the atom.
The illness suffered by pitchblende miners is diagnosed as lung cancer.

1913   A cafe in Tokyo, The Marie Curie Cabaret, serves water spiked with radium and invites customers to inhale radon gas.

1915   Report on the safety and protection of X-ray technicians is given at a British conference on X-ray techniques.

1921   Formation of the National Radiological Protection Board in Britain.

1922   A warning about the danger of X-rays is issued at an American medical conference.

1923   A total of one hundred radiation specialists are reported to have died of work-related illnesses.

1924   Uranium found to be the cause of lung cancer among miners at the Schönberg mines in the Erzgebirge region of Germany.
High incidence of anemia, bone cancer, and leukemia noted among female workers making fluorescent paint for clock faces using radium at the U.S. Radiation Corporation factory in New Jersey.

1925   Formation of the International Congress of Radiology (ICR), forerunner of the present-day International Commission on Radiological Protection.

1927   Genetic defects found in the offspring of fruit flies exposed to X-rays.

1928   ICR issues its first warning about the dangers of radiation.

1929   Birth defects observed in the children of women who had received large doses of radiation.

1932   James Chadwick discovers the neutron.

1934   *July 4:* Marie Curie dies of leukemia.

1938   Otto Hahn and Fritz Strassmann split uranium atoms and discover that nuclear fission is possible.

1939   *August:* Albert Einstein sends a letter to President Roosevelt urging the development of an atomic bomb.
September 1: World War II begins.
October: Roosevelt forms the Advisory Committee on Uranium to study the development of an atomic bomb.

1940s   A high incidence of lung cancer is noted among miners excavating uranium for the Manhattan Project.

1941   *December 8:* Japan attacks Pearl Harbor.

1942   Inauguration of the Manhattan Project.
The world's first atomic reactor, designed by Enrico Fermi of Chicago University, reaches critical mass.

1945   18 patients each with less than ten years to live are injected with plutonium as part of the Manhattan Project. The experiment continues until 1947.
July 16: The United States tests the first atomic bomb at Alamogordo, New Mexico.
August 6: An atomic weapon is used for military purposes for the first time when the United States drops an A-bomb on Hiroshima.

1946   *August 9:* The United States drops a second bomb on Nagasaki.
August 21: Accident involving plutonium at Los Alamos, New Mexico. One employee dies; a security guard suffers from radiation sickness.
May 21: Accident at Los Alamos during experiment with beryllium. One employee dies; six experience severe radiation sickness.

1949   *July 1:* The United States begins nuclear testing in the Marshall Islands.
August 29: The Soviet Union tests its first atomic bomb in Kazakhstan.
December 2: 7,780 curies of iodine-131 are released into the atmosphere at Hanford in a nuclear fission experiment.

1950   *January 31:* President Truman authorizes the development of the hydrogen bomb.
July 13: B-50 bomber carrying nuclear weapons crashes in Lebanon, Ohio. Crew of 16 killed.
August 5: B-29 bomber carrying nuclear weapons crashes just after takeoff at Fairfield Air Base in California. Nuclear weapons are not detonated but other explosions kill 19.

1952   *October 3:* Britain becomes the third nuclear power when it conducts its first nuclear test at Monte Bello Island, Australia.
November 1: America conducts its first hydrogen bomb test at Eniwetok Island in the central Pacific.

1953   *August 12:* The Soviet Union conducts its first hydrogen bomb test in Kazakhstan.

1954   *January 21:* The world's first nuclear submarine, the USS *Nautilus*, is launched. Crew subsequently harmed by exposure to large doses of radiation.
March 1: Crew of Japanese fishing boat, *Daigo Fukuryu Maru,* exposed to radiation from the hydrogen bomb test in the Marshall Islands.
September 23: Daigo Fukuryu Maru crew member Kuboyama Aikichi dies.

1956   *August:* Sodium used for cooling on the submarine USS *Sea Wolf* leaks out while the vessel is berthed in Connecticut. Seven crew members exposed to radiation.

1957   *May 15:* Britain tests its first hydrogen bomb at Christmas Island.
May 22: B-36 bomber drops nuclear weapons by accident near Cartland Air Base in New Mexico. The surrounding area is contaminated by radiation.
July 28: American C-124 transport plane jettisons two nuclear weapons into the Atlantic after engine problems. The weapons still remain unrecovered.
September 29: Storage tank for nuclear waste explodes at the Kyshtym Nuclear Weapons Complex in the eastern Urals in the Soviet Union. 10,700 residents are evacuated from the surrounding area.
October 10: Huge quantities of radioactive substances are discharged into the atmosphere after a fire in Plutonium Pile No. 1 at the Sellafield (formerly Windscale) nuclear complex in Britain.

1958   *January 31:* American B-47 bomber carrying nuclear weapons has accident during emergency landing exercise at an unspecified overseas base. Radiation dispersed over a limited area.
February 5: B-47 bomber drops nuclear weapons in a midair collision above the mouth of the Savannah River, South Carolina. Weapons still not recovered.

March 11: B-47 bomber mistakenly drops nuclear weapons near a residential area in Florence, South Carolina. Medical examinations are carried out on local people.

March 31: The Soviet Union announces a halt to nuclear testing and urges other nations to do the same.

June 16: Accident occurs in atomic reactor at the Oak Ridge nuclear weapons complex in Tennessee. Eight employees suffer from diarrhea and fever after exposure to enriched uranium.

October 15: Accident occurs at an experimental reactor in Yugoslavia. Six people receive doses of 400 rems or more; one dies four weeks later.

November 26: A fire occurs in a B-47 bomber at Chennault Air Base, Louisiana. Nuclear weapons catch fire; surrounding area contaminated.

December 30: Accident occurs during treatment of plutonium at Los Alamos research center. Five workers exposed to radiation; one dies 35 hours later.

1959   *January 18:* F-100 fighter plane carrying nuclear weapons bursts into flames at an unspecified American base in the Pacific. (At the time the United States Air Force had bases in Okinawa, Korea, Taiwan, the Philippines, and Thailand.)

April 18: USS *Sea Wolf* jettisons its atomic reactor in mid Atlantic.

August 15: Breakage found in cooling system pipe on USS *Nautilus*, the twenty-fourth breakdown since the submarine's launch in 1954.

September 25: American antisubmarine scout plane makes emergency landing in Puget Sound, Washington State. One nuclear weapon lost.

October 16: Leak of fission products at chemical treatment plant in Idaho. Two employees exposed to radiation.

October 28: Leakage occurs from heat exchangers at the Oak Ridge plant. Highly radioactive liquid contaminates nearby river.

1960   *February 13:* France conducts its first atmospheric test in the Sahara Desert, becoming the fourth nuclear power.

June 7: Explosion at missile launching site at McGuire Air Base, New Jersey. Nuclear weapons are destroyed by fire, the surrounding area is contaminated.

1961   *January 3:* Reactor explodes at experimental site in Idaho. Three die from radiation exposure. Sabotage by disgruntled employee found to be the cause.

1963   Accident involving U.S. Navy satellite in skies above Indian Ocean. Atomic batteries are dispersed and plutonium enters the stratosphere. Five ounces of fragments scattered over 12 countries.

April 10: Nuclear submarine USS *Thresher* sinks off Boston. All 129 crew members drown.

August 5: The United States, the Soviet Union, and Britain sign a treaty pledging to halt atmospheric testing. France and China refuse to sign.

November 13: 56 tons of explosives used in nuclear weapons explode at Medina Base, Texas, dispersing radioactive material. Three people injured.

1964 *July 24:* Tank explodes at uranium reprocessing plant in Wood River, Illinois. Three people are exposed to radiation; one dies 46 hours later.
October 16: China conducts its first atmospheric test in the western part of the country to become the fifth nuclear power.
December 8: B-58 bomber carrying nuclear weapons catches fire at Bunker Hill Air Base in Indiana. One of the five weapons catches fire, contaminating the surrounding area.

1965 *October 11:* C-124 transport plane carrying nuclear weapons catches fire during refueling stop at Wright Patterson Base in Ohio.
December 2: High incidence of thyroid conditions noted among young people in Utah, downwind of the Nevada test site.
December 5: A4E assault plane carrying nuclear weapons falls off the aircraft carrier USS *Ticonderoga* off the coast of Okinawa. The fact that weapons had gone missing not revealed until May 1989.
December 30: Explosion occurs at Belgian experimental reactor. One employee exposed to radiation.

1966 Soviet nuclear submarine leaks radioactive material into the sea near the Kola Peninsula. One member of the repair team dies.
January 17: American B-52 bomber carrying four hydrogen bombs collides during midair refueling off the coast of Spain. A wide area is contaminated.
September 2: Fission products at the Nuclear Fuel Service Company in Tennessee accidentally enter a separate part of the production process, causing contamination.

1967 *May 6:* Japanese scientists record radiation 20 times the naturally occurring level in the vicinity of the nuclear submarine USS *Swordfish* berthed in Sasebo, Japan. The cause is found to be leakage of cooling water.
June 2: Abnormally high levels of radiation are recorded after the nuclear submarine USS *Snook* leaves Yokosuka Base in Japan.
June 5: France starts nuclear testing at Mururoa Atoll.
June 17: China conducts its first hydrogen bomb test.
December 10: America carries out experiments to test the commercial use of the atomic bomb. The aim is to excavate natural gas using underground nuclear explosions. The surrounding area is contaminated.

1968 Soviet submarine carrying nuclear missiles explodes off Oahu Island, Hawaii and sinks killing all 70 crew members.
January 21: American B-52 bomber carrying four nuclear weapons crashes near Thule Base in Greenland. Large-scale radioactive contamination occurs.
April 11: Soviet nuclear submarine sinks near Hawaii with nuclear torpedoes on board.
May 21: The nuclear submarine USS *Scorpion* sinks off the Azores carrying nuclear weapons. 99 crew members drown.
May 24: Brookhaven National Laboratory finds thyroid abnormalities in 90% of children in the Marshall Islands.

August 16: At a Rotary Club meeting in New Zealand, residents of French Polynesia confirm the appearance of radiation-related illnesses among people in the south Pacific region.

August 24: France carries out its first hydrogen bomb test at Fagataufa Atoll.

1969   The C.I.A. reports the sinking of a Soviet nuclear submarine off the Kola Peninsula in the Soviet Far East.

January 14: Bomb accidentally dropped on deck of the nuclear powered aircraft carrier USS *Enterprise*; 25 crew members killed and 85 wounded.

1970   *February:* Explosion occurs at nuclear submarine construction yard west of the Soviet city of Gorki. Several workers killed; Volga River contaminated by radioactive material.

March 5: Nuclear Nonproliferation Treaty (NPT) comes into effect. The NPT is regarded as a breakthrough in slowing down the race for nuclear supremacy. Signatories include the United States, the Soviet Union, Britain, and a number of nonnuclear countries.

April 11: A Soviet submarine is reported as missing 340 miles southwest of England; 88 are alleged to have died.

December 18: Huge fissures appear in the earth near the Nevada test site, and a mushroom cloud rises 10,000 feet into the air. Evacuation procedures implemented too late and 86 people are exposed to radiation. The families of two who subsequently died initiate legal procedures against the government.

1971   *January 18:* Two of three pilots who flew a survey plane over the Nevada test site during the fifties die of leukemia; the other dies of cancer. Abnormally high levels of leukemia reported in Utah and Arizona by an American magazine.

October 8: Revelations are made that, at the direction of the Defense Department, 111 cancer patients at Cincinnatti University were given whole-body radiation treatment over an eleven-year period.

December 7: A group campaigning for nuclear disarmament dispatches six doctors to examine casualties of American testing in Micronesia. The U.S. government refuses them entry to Rongelap and Utirik Island near the Bikini test site.

1972   *February 25:* A Soviet nuclear submarine surfaces and drifts for 20 days 600 miles northeast of Newfoundland after its reactor breaks down.

December: Several crew members die and others are seriously injured after radiation leaks from torpedoes on a Soviet nuclear submarine.

1973   *June 8:* Approximately 100,000 gallons of radioactive waste liquid leak from a tank at the Hanford nuclear complex.

September 26: Nuclear fission products leak at Sellafield nuclear plant in Britain, exposing 35 workers to radiation.

1974   *March 14:* 2,500 gallons of highly radioactive material leak at Hanford, bringing the amount leaked since 1958 to over 420 million gallons.

1974   *April 15:* A worker at a Japanese nuclear power plant sues the Japan Atomic Power Company for inflammation of the skin caused by working at a nuclear reactor.

May 18: India conducts its first underground nuclear test, becoming the sixth country in the world to test nuclear weapons.

September 1: Japanese nuclear-powered vessel, *Mutsu,* leaks radiation when running at 2% of potential output during tests in the northern Pacific.

November 13: Karen Silkwood, who possessed proof of lax safety standards at the Kerr-McGee Cimarron plutonium plant in Ohio, is killed in a car accident. Foul play suspected.

1975   *January 15:* It is revealed that trial evacuations in case of radiation leakage were carried out from 1959-1971 by the U.S. Navy at the Sasebo base in Japan—but only among the American inhabitants.

August 15: Radical group is thought to be behind the two explosions at the Brennelis nuclear power plant in France which damaged cooling tanks and other facilities.

April 4: Report reveals that the crews of several Soviet submarines have been exposed to radiation.

June 29: Local newspaper reports that 25 workers died of cancer in the previous five years at the Rocky Flats nuclear weapons plant in Colorado.

August 30: Explosion occurs at Hanford. One person injured; at least ten exposed to radiation.

October 25: Underground nuclear explosion occurs at a Soviet naval base on the Baltic coast. A Swedish journalist claims over 40 people died.

October 27: The Oak Ridge nuclear weapons complex catches fire; 200 employees are evacuated.

November 6: Soviet dissident Zhores Medvedev reveals details of an explosion at a nuclear weapons complex in the eastern Urals in 1957.

December 28: A former KGB officer reveals that Soviet soldiers were ordered into an area east of Lake Baikal known to be contaminated by radiation after nuclear testing. 70% of the men succumbed to radiation-related diseases.

1977   *April 14:* High incidence of leukemia is noted among the 170,000 American army personnel who participated in nuclear tests in Nevada. The U.S. government starts procedures to compensate ex-servicemen suffering from leukemia.

May 27: American newspaper reports several cases of leukemia among 40 Canadian army personnel who participated in a test at the Nevada site on August 31, 1957.

September 2: The area around the La Hague nuclear fuel reprocessing plant in France becomes contaminated after a valve breaks.

October 5: A truck carrying 19 tons of powdered uranium oxide collides with a horse on a Colorado highway. The surrounding countryside is contaminated.

December 30: For the first time the United States orders medical checks of 3,224 army personnel who took part in the nuclear tests of 1957.

1978   *January 24:* A Soviet satellite, Cosmos 954, which was carrying a nuclear reactor, crashes into a lake in northeast Canada, causing contamination of the surrounding area.

January 25: Scientists testify before Congress that exposure to radiation during the Nevada nuclear tests has caused a high incidence of leukemia among ex-army personnel.

January 27: 34 of the 174,000 soldiers who took part in maneuvers at the Nevada test site claim compensation from the government for radiation-related illnesses. The claims of six are recognized. At the same time it is revealed that 900 local residents were also exposed to radiation.

February 7: The U.S. government hands out compensation to 12 ex-servicemen who claim they got cancer after participating in nuclear tests in the Pacific and in Nevada.

February 10: The Defense Department announces that it will begin a survey of radiation-related illnesses among the 300,000 American servicemen who participated in the nuclear tests.

February 19: American newspaper reports that the incidence of cancer among workers at a nuclear submarine construction yard is twice the national average.

February 26: 10,000 army and ex-army personnel, who may have been exposed to radiation rush to take advantage of the Defense Department's medical examinations over a two-week period; 140 are found to have cancer.

April 12: American magazine reveals that atomic equipment set up in the sixties by the CIA in the Indian Himalayas to observe China was abandoned resulting in the contamination of the Ganges River.

May 10: A leak at the La Hague nuclear fuel reprocessing plant in France causes radioactive contamination of the surrounding area.

May 22: Incident involving radioactive materials takes place on the submarine tender USS *Fulton* at the New London naval docks in Connecticut, forcing the docks to close.

August 4: Ex-serviceman Donald Coe, who suffers from leukemia caused by participation in nuclear tests at Nevada in August 1957, is awarded compensation by the U.S. Veterans Agency.

August 15: A high concentration of plutonium is detected in three women who worked in the laundry at the top-secret Aldermaston atomic weapons complex in Britain. A further nine are suspected to have been exposed to radiation.

August 24: Fuel leaks from an underground ICBM (inter-continental ballistic missile) silo at Cornell Missile Base in Kansas. Four officers die, and at least 29 local residents are exposed to radiation.

September 28: The family of a deceased ex-serviceman sue the U.S. government for over $10 million in compensation.

October 28: The head of the Polynesian Liberation Front reveals details of radiation-related illnesses in French Polynesia.

November 14: According to a report by the Utah State government, the high incidence of leukemia in certain areas of Utah may be attributed to nuclear tests and the mining of uranium.

December 15: Utah residents demand compensation from the U.S. government for damage caused by nuclear fallout from Nevada.

December 21: 100 residents living downwind of the Nevada test site in Utah demand compensation from the Department of Energy.

1979   *January 7:* A report prepared by the Department of Health, Education, and Welfare in 1965 noting the deaths of 28 people from leukemia near the Nevada test site is made public.

February 22: A professor at the Utah University Medical School announces that the rate of leukemia in children living downwind of the Nevada test site is 2.44 times the national average.

March 28: Accident involving core meltdown occurs at the Three Mile Island nuclear reactor in Pennsylvania.

April 6: Three plastic explosives are detonated by accident at the La Seyne sur Mer nuclear industrial complex in southern France, damaging a reactor being built for Iraq.

May 14: Radioactive waste being transported by truck for the Atomic Energy Company explodes and contaminates the surrounding area.

May 25: High concentrations of radiation are detected at former underground testing site in Jackson, Mississippi. 15 households are advised to evacuate.

June 19: Senator Kennedy produces government records proving that safety standards were deliberately ignored at the Nevada test site during the fifties and sixties in the interests of creating a realistic background for nuclear war maneuvers.

August 8: French newspaper reports that two explosions at Mururoa Atoll on July 6 and July 25 killed two people and injured six.

August 30: 442 people living near the Nevada test site sue the U.S. government claiming that their leukemia and cancer were caused by the nuclear tests.

September: The nuclear aircraft carrier USS *Traxton* leaks 13 gallons of radioactive water into San Diego Bay.

September 18: 20 pounds of enriched uranium found to have been dispersed at fuel reprocessing plant owned by the Nuclear Fuel Service Company.

September 25: Radioactive materials are seized from the American Atomic Company after allegations of negligence and lax safety standards are made by the Arizona State government

1980   *March 19:* Presidential committee confirms that testing in Nevada during the fifties is the cause of a high incidence of cancer among local residents. The committee recommends that compensation be paid.

March 23: Swedes vote to abolish all twelve of their nuclear reactors by the year 2010 in a nationwide referendum.

April 7: The U.S. and Japanese governments discuss a proposal to dispose of used nuclear fuel in the Pacific Ocean.

April 10: Seven ex-service personnel and two widows accuse the U.S. government of negligence on behalf of 250,000 military personnel exposed to radiation through involvement in nuclear tests and weapons development.

June 22: High incidence of cancer noted among people living near a nuclear weapons facility near Lake Ontario where radioactive waste from the Manhattan Project was dumped.

August 6: Congressional subcommittee investigating damage to residents' health near the Nevada test site uncovers secret Atomic Energy Commission documents recording the effects of exposure to large doses of radiation on local residents.

1981   *January 7:* The U.S. Navy is found to have dumped the nuclear submarine USS *Sea Wolf* off the Delaware coast in 1959—along with its reactor containing radioactive material.

January 31: The New York State assembly announces that radioactive waste from the Manhattan Project was dumped in a well in Tonawanda, New York State.

March 8: Nuclear power plant at Tsuruga, Japan, discharges radioactive waste into the sea, but the accident is only discovered a month later when high levels of radiation are detected in seaweed.

April 22: Damage suits filed by Marshall Islanders against six U.S. government departments, including the Department of Defense and the Department of Energy.

June 7: Israeli Air Force bombs one of two reactors under construction near Baghdad, Iraq. Destroyed reactor does not contain atomic fuel.

August 7: Australian government takes steps to compensate ex-serviceman whose health was damaged by participation in British nuclear tests.

August 24: British newspaper reports a high rate of cancer among people living near the Lop Nur test site in China.

September: Accident occurs aboard a Soviet nuclear submarine in the Baltic. Several crew members die from exposure to radiation.

September 21: Nuclear waste from the Manhattan Project is revealed to have been dumped off the coast of Boston in 1945.

1982   *January 4:* Assistant professor at Colorado University reveals that the incidence of cancer among residents in southwest Utah is twice the national average.

February 12: American military source reveals that several thousand members of the armed forces were exposed to radiation levels over the acceptable "safe" limit during testing in Nevada and the Pacific, and that the U.S. military authorities published false reports to conceal this fact.

April 24: The Brookhaven National Laboratory reveals that since the tests at Bikini in 1954, 17 children with growth abnormalities caused by thyroid conditions were noted among 243 Marshall Islanders.

July 30: 1,500 Utah residents sue the U.S. government for compensation for damage caused by nuclear fallout.

August 3: American ex-serviceman John Smitherman, who suffers from radiation-linked diseases after participating in the Bikini tests, undergoes an examination at a Hiroshima hospital.

August 10: The U.S. government recognizes radiation as the cause of skin cancer suffered by ex-serviceman James O'Connor.

1983   Iridium-192, a radioactive isotope found in machines used to detect metal fatigue, is discovered at the side of the road by a man in Morocco. He takes it home; all eight members of his family are exposed to huge doses of radiation and die.

January 9: British newspaper reports a high incidence of cancer among ex-servicemen who had participated in tests in Australia and at Christmas Island.

February 18: The Radiological Protection Board in Britain produces a list over 260 people suffering from thyroid conditions which may be linked to the Sellafield accident; at least 13 people are reported to have died of cancer.

April 6: The results of a referendum among Wisconsin residents reveal that 89% are against the construction of a nuclear waste storage facility.

May 24: The U.S. Defense Department reveals that of the 139,000 army personnel who were stationed in Hiroshima and Nagasaki after the bombs were dropped, or who took part in nuclear tests, 1,139 showed radiation levels above the acceptable limit.

June: Soviet submarine sinks near the Petropavlovsk base on the Kamchatka Peninsula. 90 crew members drown.

November 30: The Department of the Environment in Britain reports radiation levels of between 100 and 1,000 times the norm on the coast near the Sellafield complex.

December 5: An accident at an atomic bomb manufacturing plant in the desert region of northwest China in 1969 is reported in the Chinese press. The surrounding area is believed to be heavily contaminated and the factory is temporarily closed.

1984   *May 1:* About 1,000 former residents of Bikini Atoll file a collective suit against the U.S. government demanding the decontamination of their former home to make repatriation possible.

May 1: In Wallis, Texas, radioactive materials used in medical treatment are found to have been mixed with scrap iron and sold in the United States and Mexico. At least 200 people are believed to have been exposed to radiation.

May 10: Nevada residents win their case against the government. In Salt Lake City, Utah, the district court recognizes the relationship between radiation and the high incidence of cancer and orders the federal government to pay compensation.

October 22: The Environmental Agency in South Korea reports that the level of radiation in the sea around the country's first nuclear power plant at Kori is three times the international "safe" level.

1985   *January 10:* According to a CIA report, six Soviet nuclear submarines have been reported missing since the mid-sixties, with a loss of approximately 500 crew members.

January 14: Japanese Prime Minister Yasuhiro Nakasone announces the suspension of plans to dump spent atomic fuel in the Pacific Ocean during a visit to the Pacific region.

May 22: The people of the island of Rongelap in the Marshalls, who had returned to their homes in 1958 after having been forced to leave in 1954 by the U.S. government, find themselves once again forced to leave due to a continuing danger of radioactive contamination.

June 3: The Science Council of America reports an abnormally high number of deaths from cancer among ex-servicemen exposed to radiation.

July 10: The Greenpeace protest ship *Rainbow Warrior* is sunk by explosives set by French Secret Service agents while anchored in Auckland, New Zealand, prior to a voyage to Mururoa. One crew member dies.

August 27: Collision with a freight train in North Dakota, causes a truck to spill its load of uranium oxide. Between 30 and 40 members of the police exposed to radiation.

October 15: Asian Rare Earths, a company in Ipoh, Malaysia, partly owned by Mitsubishi Chemicals, is ordered by the Ipoh High Court to halt operations and dispose of its store of radioactive waste.

December 4: According to a U.S. General Accounting Office report, 17,000 servicemen participating in the 1946 tests at Bikini Atoll were exposed to higher levels of radiation than previously reported in government documents.

December 22: Chinese students hold the first demonstration in Beijing against nuclear tests in the Xinjiang Autonomous Region.

1986   *January 4:* Leakage of uranium hexafluoride occurs at an Oklahoma atomic fuel plant. One employee dies. In terms of the amount of radioactive material leaked, this accident is second only to Three Mile Island.

January 16: Citizens' action group makes public previously restricted navy documents, revealing that, between 1965 and 1977, there were 381 accidents involving nuclear weapons.

March 20: Joint U.S.-Japan committee to reevaluate the effects of A-bomb radiation reports that, at 15 kilotons, the Hiroshima A-bomb was 20% more powerful than originally revealed.

April 26: The No. 4 reactor at the Chernobyl nuclear power plant in the Ukraine explodes. Vast quantities of radioactive substances are dispersed over many countries, making it the worst nuclear accident in history.

April 30: Contamination from Chernobyl disaster spreads across Europe. Philippine government suspends completion of its first nuclear reactor. It would have been Southeast Asia's first.

May 4: The Science and Technology Agency in Japan announces that fallout from Chernobyl has affected Japan.

May 9: Deputy chairman of China's Commission of Science, Technology, and Industry for National Defense admits for the first time that a number of deaths were noted after nuclear tests were carried out.

May 23: Residents of Hubei, China, exposed to radiation 100 times the average level after radioactive waste was illegally dumped in a disused well.

June 10: The U.S Department of Energy announces that three employees were exposed to high doses of radiation during the testing of nuclear weapons in Nevada.

August 18: One million Hong Kong residents sign petition against construction of Chinese nuclear power plant in neighboring Guangzhou.

September 23: The Austrian government announces the dismantling of its only nuclear reactor at Zwentendorf. The reactor was built in 1977 but had never been put into operation.

September 25: U.S. General Accounting Office report reveals radiation levels in soil and water around nuclear facilities in the United States are over 100 times the average level of background radiation.

October 24: Revelations are made that human experiments were carried out as part of the Manhattan Project: of 18 people injected with plutonium between April 1945 and July 1947, 13 are known to have died.

1987   *February 27:* 14 employees of a West German nuclear fuel plant in Hanau are exposed to radiation.

July 28: Congress passes a bill providing compensation for ex-servicemen now suffering from 12 types of cancer who had been stationed in Hiroshima or Nagasaki, or who had taken part in nuclear tests.

September 13: Two men in Goiânia, Brazil, dismantle an abandoned cylinder containing cesium-137, a radioactive substance used in radiation treatment. They distribute the substance among the local residents: 249 are exposed to radiation and four die.

September 26: Victims of radiation hold their first international conference in New York. The 300 participants from 30 countries include A-bomb survivors, uranium miners, people living near the Nevada test site, and residents of the Marshall Islands.

November 9: Nationwide referendum reveals that 80% of Italians are opposed to nuclear power.

November 18: Iraqi planes attack the construction site of a nuclear power plant in Bushehr, Iran.

December 8: Ronald Reagan and Mikhail Gorbachev sign the INF (Intermediate Nuclear Forces) Treaty pledging to discard all medium- and short-range nuclear weapons. The 4% reduction of the total number of nuclear weapons in the world is seen as a breakthrough in the nuclear debate.

1988   *January 21:* Construction of a nuclear power plant at Krasnodar in the Russian Republic canceled—the first in the Soviet Union since the accident at Chernobyl.

January 28: Public opposition forces the mayor of Kubokawa, Japan, to abandon plans to invite the Shikoku Electric Company to build a new nuclear power plant in the area.

February 18: The National Radiological Protection Board in Britain reports a high incidence of leukemia and bone tumors in ex-servicemen who took part in nuclear tests.

March 18: U.S. Senate rejects suggestion that establishment of a committee of specialists to investigate safety standards at nuclear weapons plants would be an "obstacle to the production of nuclear weapons" and agrees to increase tenfold the amount of compensation allocated to those affected by serious accidents at such facilities.

April 25: Senate adopts a bill providing medical care for ex-servicemen affected by radiation.

May 23: Radiation leaks from a reactor in Hamaoka, Japan: 17 employees exposed during the disposal of contaminated water.

August 15: 30 times the normal level of background radiation is detected in gravel mixed with uranium ore abandoned near a nuclear facility in Okayama Prefecture, Japan.

August 26: The GPU Nuclear Co. of Three Mile Island announces that the Unit 2 reactor where the 1979 accident occurred will remain closed for 30 years.

September 6: Construction of a nuclear power plant in Minsk in the Soviet Union is halted by opposition from local residents.

September 28: The Swiss National Council announces the suspension of construction of the nation's sixth nuclear power plant.

September 29: Container ship carrying radioactive material for use in bomb-detecting devices sinks off the North Wales coast.

September 30: Allegations are made that, since 1960, 30 major accidents occurred at the Savannah River plutonium and tritium manufacturing facility.

October 14: The Department of Energy acknowledges that radiation from the Fernald nuclear weapons plant has contaminated the atmosphere and nearby rivers since 1951.

October 17: The U.S. Centers for Disease Control commence a survey of the effects of exposure to radiation on the health of 20,000 residents living near the Hanford Nuclear Reservation.

December 5: Reports reveal that, in 1987, radioactive substances leaked from a nuclear reactor in the suburbs of Darmstadt, West Germany,

December 22: The U.S. Department of Veterans Affairs provides compensation for the widow of John Smitherman, an ex-serviceman who participated in nuclear tests and later died of cancer. By the end of 1988, 551 veterans have succeeded in receiving compensation for radiation-related diseases.

December 22: The New South Wales Supreme Court in Australia orders the government to hand out compensation to ex-serviceman suffering from radiation-linked diseases.

December 23: The Department of Nuclear Energy in the Soviet Union announces that it canceled the construction of six nuclear power plants in 1988.

1989   *February 26:* Olzhas Suleymenov, first secretary of the Kazakhstan Writers' Union, appeals to the public to protest against radiation leakages that occurred on two occasions earlier in the month.

March 20: For the first time since the accident at Chernobyl, the Soviet state meteorological service releases information on the amount of radioactive substances released and acknowledges the widespread contamination of countries throughout Europe.

April 9: A Soviet nuclear submarine carrying two nuclear weapons catches fire and sinks off the Norwegian coast; 42 crew members lost.

April 14: The West German government abandons plans to built a fuel reprocessing plant at Wackersdorf in Bavaria.

May 22: The CIA reveals information about an accident in the late sixties involving core meltdown on board the Soviet nuclear-powered icebreaker *Lenin.* Between 25 and 30 crew members are believed to have died.

June 7: Results of a referendum held in Sacramento regarding the future of the Rancho Seco nuclear power plant show that 54% of residents believe it should be closed.

June 11: The Rocky Flats nuclear weapon facility is revealed to have discharged harmful chemicals into a nearby river.

June 16: Soviet authorities acknowledge for the first time that a radioactive waste disposal facility at the Kyshtym nuclear weapons complex exploded in 1957.

June 22: In Britain, the Committee on Medical Aspects of Radiation in the Environment (COMARE) confirms that the incidence of leukemia and cancer among children living near nuclear facilities such as the Aldermaston nuclear weapons plant is higher than average.

June 23: The Shoreham nuclear power plant completed in 1984 is sold to the New York State government for one dollar and dismantled.

July 2: The Nevada State legislature adopts a bill banning the dumping of radioactive waste in the state.

July 7: The U.S. government is ordered to pay compensation to 24,000 residents living near the Fernald nuclear weapons plant for lowering the value of their property.

August 2: Department of Energy survey of workers at military nuclear facilities reveals a high incidence of cancer and also evidence of genetic defects.

August 5: English-language newspaper in China reports that, between 1980 and 1985, over 1,200 people were involved in accidents with radiation, and that approximately 30 had died.

August 6: Residents of Semipalatinsk, Kazakhstan, hold a rally to press for the closure of the nearby test site.

August 16: Soviet newspaper reports that on the Chukchi Peninsula in the Soviet Far East, where atmospheric tests were carried out during the fifties and sixties, the amount of radiation is twice the normal background level, cancer and tuberculosis are common, and the infant mortality rate is abnormally high.

August 25: The Soviet deputy prime minister reveals that radioactive materials 2.5 times the quantity released at Chernobyl were discharged into the atmosphere in accidents that took place before the nuclear disaster in the Urals in 1957.

September 11: The U.S. Defense Department abandons plans to construct a nuclear test site at Del Rio, Texas.

September 29: Allegations are made that Soviet soldiers were used as guinea pigs and exposed to high levels of radiation during maneuvers in the southern Urals on September 14, 1954.

September 30: U.S. federal court awards compensation to 14,000 people living near the Fernald nuclear weapons plant.

October 7: International Physicians for the Prevention of Nuclear War (IPPNW) holds its ninth rally in Hiroshima and establishes an international committee to investigate radioactive contamination at weapons factories and other nuclear facilities.

October 11: Soviet weekly magazine reports that radiation-linked conditions have been noted among residents of the Ukraine, such as chromosome abnormalities, lowered resistance to disease, and anemia and thyroid problems among children. These conditions are attributed to the accident at Chernobyl.

October 21: 60,000 people demonstrate against nuclear testing in the Soviet city of Semipalatinsk.

October 28: Soviet government decides to halt construction of a nuclear power plant in the Crimea.

October 29: British government cancels proposed construction of three nuclear power plants due to the rise in cost of reprocessing spent fuel.

November 2: Soviet newspaper reports that some parts of Semipalatinsk and the Kola Peninsula which were used for nuclear testing are even more contaminated than Chernobyl.

November 8: Soviet weekly reports that at least 250 former employees and workers involved in cleanup operations at the Chernobyl plant have died.

December 19: After studying the latest data from Hiroshima and Nagasaki, the Science Council of America concludes that the risk of incurring cancer after being exposed to radiation is actually three to four times the level originally predicted.

1990   *January 10:* Staff at Tokyo University Hospital are reprimanded by Science and Technology Agency for negligent handling of radioactive isotopes.

January 29: Ministry of the Environment in East Germany announces a halt to the construction of future nuclear power plants.

February 8: Researchers at Tokai University in Japan discover evidence of nuclear facilities in North Korea after analyzing satellite photographs.

February 14: Mass demonstrations lasting several days take place in Belorussiya to protest the authorities' cover-up of the dangerous effects of exposure to radiation after the accident at Chernobyl.

February 16: Research by Professor Gardener of Southampton University shows a high incidence of leukemia among children whose fathers were exposed to high levels of radiation at the Sellafield complex.

February 17: Austrian newspaper reports that 6,000 deaths from cancer of the thyroid gland at hospitals in Minsk, Belorussiya, may be attributed to the 1986 accident at Chernobyl.

February 22: Construction of a nuclear power plant at Archangelsk in the Russian Republic is halted.

February 28: Results of the first referendum on the issue of nuclear power plant construction in the Soviet Union, held in the Russian city of Nizh Chegem, show that 99% of citizens are opposed to nuclear power.

March 2: Girl with leukemia in Scotland prepares to sue British Nuclear Fuels on the grounds that her illness was caused by exposure to radiation from the nearby Dounreay nuclear reprocessing plant.

March 4: The state of New Mexico vetoes plans for construction of a storage facility which would take radioactive waste from weapons-manufacturing facilities and power plants all over the United States.

March 5: The Ukrainian parliament adopts a resolution demanding the closure of the remaining three reactors in operation at Chernobyl by 1995.

March 7: The Semipalatinsk test site is shut down, but the island of Novaya Zemlya is suggested as a future testing site.

March 23: At the request of the Soviet government, the IAEA sends an international survey team to Chernobyl and the surrounding areas.

April 4: At an international conference in Poland, Soviet scientists predict that, in the future, many thousands of people will die from the effects of exposure to large doses of radiation after the accident at Chernobyl.

April 19: The U.S. General Accounting Office reports that safety precautions at American nuclear weapons complexes are inadequate, pointing out that of 1,731 facilities contaminated in incidents since 1986, only 591 have been declared free from contamination.

April 25: The Supreme Soviet studies plan to evacuate a further 180,000–200,000 people from areas contaminated by Chernobyl by 1993.

April 25: Yuri Shcherbak, a member of the Supreme Soviet, announces that the accident at Chernobyl has so far claimed over 300 lives and that it may end up costing as much as 250 billion rubles.

May 24: International Citizens for the Abolition of Nuclear Testing holds a meeting in Alma-Ata, capital of Kazakhstan.

APPENDIX

METHODS OF MEASURING RADIATION DOSAGE

becquerel

The becquerel is a unit used to measure radioactivity. One becquerel represents the level of radiation given off in one second by one atom of a radioactive substance as it breaks down and changes to a different atom.

curie

The curie unit indicates the number of nuclear transformations per second in one gram of radium. 1 curie=1,000 microcuries=1,000,000 picocuries

rad

To denote the amount of radiation absorbed, the rad unit is used. One rad is equal to an energy of 100 ergs per gram of irradiated material. The name derives from the words "radiation absorbed dose."Rads and rems can be used interchangeably for external radiation, but as radiation does greater damage internally, rads should be multiplied by 10 to indicate the dose of internal radiation.

rem

The rem unit is used to denote the amount of radiation that would cause the same amount of damage to human tissue as a specific amount (1 roentgen) of X-rays or gamma rays. The name derives from the words "roentgen equivalent man."

roentgen

This unit indicates the amount of radiation producing in one cubic centimeter of air. One roentgen is equivalent to one rem in the case of gamma and X-rays.

THE MECHANISM OF RADIATION DAMAGE

When the human body is exposed to radiation, the first changes that take place are in the atoms which make up body cells. One such change concerns the process known as ionizing radiation by which electrons are separated from the atoms of the cell, and the other is the process by which electrons absorb the energy of radiation and jump to a higher energy orbit thereby bringing the atom into a state of excitation. The end result of this complicated process of cell alteration is a "scratch" made on the DNA which composes the cell. DNA (deoxyribonucleic acid) is the most important element of the cell's make-up and is essential to cell reproduction. However when this "scratched" cell regenerates, what is created is not a copy of the unblemished original, but a copy of its altered version. This process is repeated and the number of abnormal cells grows rapidly.

When the body is exposed to a large dose of radiation, it takes only a relatively short time for organs to be damaged and vital functions to be impaired. An example of this is the hair loss which often accompanies such large doses. This symptom of acute radiation sickness is caused by the inability of cells at the hair root to reproduce when affected by radiation.

On the other hand, when the radiation dose is relatively low, changes in the composition of cell DNA take place at a considerably reduced rate, and abnormalities are slower to appear. Combined with other factors, this type of exposure can lead to cancer and other long-term effects. It is thought that when DNA, the "command center" of cell reproduction, is exposed to radiation the process of cell regeneration becomes impaired, leading to the formation of abnormal cells which eventually become cancerous. However, the exact mechanism by which radiation exposure leads to cancer is still not known.

Experiments have been conducted on animals which prove that such alterations in the DNA structure may be passed down to the next generation, but further research is needed before the same can definitely be said for humans. Radiation may occur naturally or be artificially created by weapons or power plants; either way there is no doubt that it can seriously damage the human body.

THE EFFECTS OF EXPOSURE TO RADIATION
Among the medical conditions caused by radiation, there are those known as the short-term somatic effects which occur when exposed to a specific amount and those which appear in proportion to the quantity of radiation, no matter how small it may be, known as the long term somatic effects. Even low doses of radiation can have harmful effects.

Immediate effects
Short term effects include all the manifestations of acute radiation sickness, which appear within four months of exposure, and exclude cancer and genetic damage. Symptoms include nausea, vomiting, diarrhea, delirium, hair loss, hemorrhaging, and erythema. Once a certain threshold is reached, it appears that illness occurs without exception. Below this threshold no effects will be felt. In the case of Hiroshima and Nagasaki, those who suffered from the immediate effects had received radiation doses of 100 rads (1000 rems).

The number of these symptoms increases according to the severity of the dosage. For example, at 500 rems (100 rems=1 sievert) victims may suffer from erythema, at 300 rems a patient may experience hair loss.

Long-term effects
Exposure to radiation causes long-term effects on the body which will not be immediately noticeable. The number of red and white blood cells may be reduced, and the reproductive organs may be damaged causing a low sperm count and irregular periods in men and women respectively. Premature aging and a shortened lifespan are possible effects and genetic injury may also be observed. In contrast to the immediate effects, long-term somatic effects are particularly troublesome precisely because they have no such recognizable thresholds. In other words no matter how low the dose, once the radiation has been absorbed, the risk of incurring cancer and genetic damage is always present. The level of dosage influences not the gravity of the illness but the probability of damage occurring in a particular organ. The risk of cancer also depends on the organ.

Ikuro Anzai of Ritsumeikan University, Japan, has likened the process by which radiation causes cancer to a "cancer lottery."

More specifically, being exposed to a large amount of radiation is like buying a large number of lottery tickets; similarly a small dose is equivalent to buying only a few. If your number comes up the prize is the same whether you have bought a lot of tickets or only one. This lottery however is not drawn on any particular day, so the possibility of getting the "prize" of cancer hangs over the exposed person for their entire life.

It is easy to make the mistake of thinking that because short-term radiation effects have a threshold, there is no risk as long as the dose remains below a specified level. However, when one considers the possibility of long-term somatic effects, it is clear that unnecessary exposure to radiation should be avoided if at all possible.

EFFECTS ACCORDING TO RADIATION DOSAGE

Below 100 rems: No noticeable effects
100-200 rems: Nausea approximately three hours after exposure
300 rems: Severe vomiting, loss of hair, hemorrhaging, increased susceptibility to infections due to reduction in white blood cells. Over 50% die within two months.
800 rems: Diarrhea and other problems with digestive organs, dehydration. Over 90% die within two weeks due to failure of circulatory system.
5000 rems: Severe convulsions and failure of the central nervous system. All cases die within two days

INTERNAL EXPOSURE

After the disaster at Chernobyl, the world became aware of the possibility of absorbing radioactive substances through eating contaminated food. The widespread dispersal of radioactive fallout after the accident threw most of Europe into a panic.

Vegetables and pastureland were contaminated, and the milk of cows feeding on the contaminated grass was rendered unfit for consumption, as was butter, cheese, and meat. Strict procedures were inaugurated to check all agricultural produce coming out of areas known to be contaminated.

Once radioactive substances are absorbed, the body may be harmed in a variety of ways according to the substance ingested. Some organs of the human body are more susceptible than others to the absorption of radioactive substances. There is a tendency to panic at the thought of radioactive substances being absorbed into the body after consuming contaminated food. However, more important is the extent of exposure to radiation, not the means by which it enters the body.

RADIOACTIVE SUBSTANCES

Half-life

The time required for half of the atoms of a radioactive substance to become disintegrated is known as the half-life. Depending on the element, the natural process of radioactive decay can take a fraction of a second or millions of years. For example, yttrium-90 has a half-life of 64 hours (i.e in 64 hours half of it will have changed, in another 64 hours, half of the remainder will have changed, etc.)

Iodine-131 (half-life 8 days)
The substance released in the largest quantity at Chernobyl was iodine-131. When this substance is absorbed by the human body, approximately thirty percent is retained in the thyroid gland, and the rest is excreted. It takes about six hours from ingestion to reach the thyroid, staying there for more than 120 days. Hyperthyroidism, which sometimes leads to cancer of the thyroid was one of the first radiation-related illnesses observed among survivors of the A-bomb in Hiroshima and Nagasaki.

Directly after the accident, the government of Poland distributed an iodine preparation to children. The idea was to fill their thyroid glands with a harmless, non-radioactive iodine to prevent subsequent absorption of iodine-131.

Cobalt-60 (half-life 5 years)
Cobalt-60, which is often detected in waste water from nuclear power plants, accumulates throughout the body, although the liver absorbs four times as much as any other organ.

Strontium-90 (half-life 28.8 years)
Strontium-90 tends to accumulate in the bones causing bone cancer. It has a half-life of 28.8 years, a period of time long enough for it to be absorbed into the red bone marrow at the center causing leukemia.

Radium-224 (half-life 3.7 days)/ Radium-226 (half-life 1620 years)
Although Radium-224 only affects the surface of the bones, radium-226 is known to be absorbed more deeply.

Molybdenum-99 (half-life 66 years)
Molybdenum-99, often present in fallout from nuclear power plants, is absorbed into the kidneys (50%), liver (30%) and bones excluding the marrow (15%).

Cesium-134 (half-life 2 years)/ Cesium-137 (half-life 30 years)
Cesium-134 and -137 are absorbed throughout the body, tending to accumulate in muscle tissue. In two days about 10 percent is excreted and about half is removed in 110 days. However, it takes a long time for the body to get rid of the bulk of cesium.

Plutonium-239 (half-life 24,000 years)
Plutonium-239 affects mainly the liver and bones.

DISEASES CAUSED BY EXPOSURE TO RADIATION
cataracts
bleeding gums
stomatitis
keloids
erythema
cancer of the lungs, stomach, breasts, colon, etc.
leukemia
bone marrow damage
malignant lymphatic tumors
hyperthyroidism

ACCUMULATION OF RADIOACTIVE SUBSTANCES IN HUMAN ORGANS

The organs of the body vary in their sensitivity to radioactive substances. The kidneys, bladder, and cartilage in an adult absorb relatively low amounts while the reproductive organs, eyes, and red bone marrow are more sensitive. Although susceptibility varies in adults, exposure to radiation can be particularly harmful to children.

1. **Pituitary gland**
   yttrium-90 (half-life 64 hours)

2. **Thyroid gland**
   iodine-131 (8 days)

3. **Lungs**
   plutonium-239 (24,000 years)
   radon-222 (3.8 days)

4. **Liver**
   cobalt-60 (5 years)
   molybdenum-99 (66 years)
   plutonium-239

5. **Pancreas**
   polonium-210 (138 days)

6. **Kidneys**
   molybdenum-99

7. **Ovaries**
   cesium-137 (30 years)
   iodine-131
   cobalt-60
   krypton-85 (10 years)
   barium-140 (13 days)

8. **Muscles**
   cesium-134 (2 years)
   cesium-137

9. **Bones**
   strontium-90 (28.8 years)
   radium-224 (3.7 days)
   radium-226 (1620 years)
   phosphorous-32 (14 days)
   molybdenum-99
   plutonium-239

10. **Bone marrow**
    strontium-90

EFFECTS OF EXPOSURE TO RADIATION OBSERVED IN SURVIVORS OF THE A-BOMB IN HIROSHIMA AND THEIR OFFSPRING

Microcephaly

In 1946, a number of children in Japan were born with a condition known as microcephaly. The children had abnormally small heads and were found to be mentally disabled. Without exception their mothers had been exposed to radiation relatively near the center of the blasts in Hiroshima and Nagasaki. These tragic cases occurred when the mother was exposed to radiation between eight and twenty-five weeks into pregnancy, with the majority occurring between eight and fifteen weeks. This is the period during which the cells of the fetus are most susceptible to damage by radiation.

Cataracts

The first cases of cataracts were confirmed in the fall of 1948 in Hiroshima, and June 1949 in Nagasaki. This particular condition, which differs from the cataracts commonly found in elderly people, is radiation linked and causes the lens of the eye to become clouded, hindering vision.

Leukemia

Leukemia attacks the bone marrow, preventing it from producing the white blood cells which are vital for protecting against infection. The first cases of radiation-related leukemia were noted in November 1945 in Nagasaki and in October 1946 in Hiroshima, peaking in 1951. Today, there are hardly any cases of leukemia remaining which can be attributed to the A-bomb.

Cancer

By 1960 leukemia was on the decrease in Hiroshima and Nagasaki, only to be replaced by a rise in the number of cancer patients among A-bomb survivors. At present there are twelve types of cancer recognized as being related to exposure to radiation. Some, such as cancer of the thyroid gland, became relatively common in the late fifties and early sixties, while others such as cancer of the ovaries and the colon have only recently begun to show a marked increase. In 1988 doctors in Nagasaki began to note numerous cases of skin cancer among survivors. It is generally accepted that the younger a person is when exposed to radiation, the more likely he is to succumb to cancer.

Genetic injury

The genetic material of the forty-six chromosomes may be damaged by radiation and altered in shape. It is possible to prove that a person has been exposed to radiation by the presence of these abnormalities. However, the greatest mystery yet to be solved is that of whether genetic effects occur in the offspring of people exposed to radiation. Is there a higher than average incidence of hereditary abnormalities and birth defects among the children of A-bomb survivors? Is their mortality rate higher? Do they develop at the same rate as other children? Will the incidences of leukemia and cancer be as high among them as in their parents' generation? All these questions are inextricably linked to the future of these children, and as such are receiving serious attention from specialists. Experiments conducted on fruit flies and mice have shown that genetic effects appear in the offspring of parents exposed to radiation. Since these results were obtained doctors and scientists have expressed concern that the same may be true for humans. The Radiation Effects Research Foundation (formerly known as The Atomic Bomb Casualty Commission) has been conducting a study of mortality rates and chromosome abnormalities among 77,000 children of A-bomb survivors as well as those of parents not exposed to radiation, but so far it has not found conclusive evidence of any genetic damage. By way of explanation it has been suggested that the human body is more complex than that of flies or mice, making it more difficult for such characteristics to be passed down, or that the survey sample is too small. Others have suggested that the period of the study is still too short to produce definite results, or that a large number of miscarriages have hidden the real effects of radiation.

Present medical techniques are only capable of detecting immediate effects, such as reduction in white blood cell count, when the level of exposure is 25 rems or over. In the case of lower doses, the delayed effects rather than the immediate problems give most cause for concern. However, there is no way of predicting how or when these effects will manifest themselves. According to the guidelines issued by the International Commission for Radiological Protection, one case of cancer will result if 10,000 people are exposed to one rem of radiation.

Many A-bomb survivors received a huge dose of radiation in August 1945, so the possible effects of other factors such as radiation therapy they have received since then, for example, can virtually be ignored when studying the causes of their illnesses. However, in the case of those who received relatively low doses, it is extremely difficult to ascertain to what extent the atomic bomb has been the cause of their illnesses, as opposed to other factors.

RADIATION HORMESIS

A few scholars in recent years have advanced the theory of radiation hormesis, which contends that small amounts of radiation can have beneficial effects on organs, stimulating them into activity. However, more generally accepted is the theory that radiation can cause cancer, no matter how small the dose. It is therefore strongly advisable to avoid any unnecessary exposure to radiation.

NATURAL BACKGROUND RADIATION

Natural background radiation indicates naturally occurring radiation as opposed to radiation artificially produced from nuclear power or from nuclear bomb testing. Some radioactive substances occurring naturally are found all over the world, eg. uranium and monazite.

ENRICHED URANIUM

Natural uranium is 0.7 percent uranium-235; the rest is uranium-238. A larger percentage of uranium-235 is necessary for most nuclear reactors and so the amount is increased in a complicated and expensive procedure known as enrichment. Uranium which is approximately three percent uranium-235 is suitable for nuclear power plants; with ninety percent uranium-235 an atomic bomb can be produced.

FUEL REPROCESSING PLANTS

The process whereby plutonium and uranium are separated from used nuclear fuel is known as "reprocessing." The plutonium produced is either mixed with uranium to make fuel for nuclear power stations, or it is used in the manufacture of nuclear weapons. However, the reprocessing of spent fuel does not represent an answer to the growing mountains of nuclear waste; one cubic meter of used nuclear fuel will produce 150 cubic meters of low-level waste after reprocessing.

THE ANATOMY OF DEPENDENCE

Takeo Doi, M.D.
Translated by John Bester

A definitive analysis of *amae*, the indulging, passive love which supports an individual within a group, a key concept in Japanese psychology.

PB, ISBN 0-87011-494-8, 184 pages

THE ANATOMY OF SELF
The Individual Versus Society

Takeo Doi, M.D.
Translated by Mark A. Harbison

A fascinating exploration into the role of the individual in Japan, and Japanese concepts of self-awareness, communication, and relationships.

PB, ISBN 0-87011-902-8, 176 pages

BEYOND NATIONAL BORDERS

Kenichi Ohmae

"[Ohmae is] Japan's only management guru." — *Financial Times*

PB, ISBN 4-7700-1385-X , 144 pages
Available only in Japan.

THE BOOK OF TEA

Kakuzo Okakura
Foreword and Afterword by Soshitsu Sen XV

The seminal text on the meaning and practice of tea, illustrated with eight historic photographs.

PB, ISBN 4-7700-1542-9, 160 pages

THE COMPACT CULTURE
The Japanese Tradition of "Smaller is Better"

O-Young Lee
Translated by Robert N. Huey

A provocative study of Japan's tendency to make the most out of miniaturization, that reveals the essence of Japanese character.

PB, ISBN 4-7700-1543-3, 196 pages

THE JAPANESE NEGOTIATOR
Subtlety and Strategy Beyond Western Logic

Robert M. March

Shows how Japanese negotiate among themselves and examines case studies, providing practical advice for the Western executive.

PB, ISBN 0-87011-962-1, 200 pages

THE JAPANESE THROUGH AMERICAN EYES

Sheila K. Johnson

A revealing look at the images and stereotypes of Japanese produced by American popular culture and media.

PB, ISBN 4-7700-1450-3, 208 pages   Available only in Japan.

JAPAN'S LONGEST DAY

Pacific War Research Society

A detailed account of the day before Japan surrendered, based on eyewitness testimony of the men involved in the decision to surrender.

PB: ISBN 0-87011-422-0, 340 pages

MANGA! MANGA!
The World of Japanese Comics

Frederick L. Schodt
Introduction by Osamu Tezuka

A profusely illustrated and detailed exploration of the world of Japanese comics.

PB, ISBN 0-87011-752-1, 260 pages

NEIGHBORHOOD TOKYO

Theodore C. Bestor

A highly readable glimpse into the everyday lives, commerce, and relationships of some 2,000 neighborhood residents of Tokyo.

PB, ISBN 4-7700-1496-1, 368 pages   Available only in Japan.

THE INLAND SEA

Donald Richie

An award-winning documentary—part travelogue, part intimate diary and meditation—of a journey into the heart of traditional Japan.

PB, ISBN 4-7700-1751, 292 pages

THE THIRD CENTURY
America's Resurgence in the Asian Era

Joel Kotkin and Yoriko Kishimoto

Argues that the U.S. must adopt a realistic and resilient attitude as it faces serious competition from Asia. "Truly powerful public ideas." — Boston Globe

PB, ISBN 4-7700-1452-X, 304 pages
Available only in Japan.

THE UNFETTERED MIND
Writings of the Zen Master to the Sword Master

Takuan soho
Translated by William Scott Wilson

Philosophy as useful to today's corporate warriors as it was to seventeenth-century samurai.

PB, ISBN 0-87011-851-X, 104 pages

THE UNSPOKEN WAY
**Haragei, or The Role of Silent Communication
in Japanese Business and Society**

Michihiro Matsumoto

Haragei, a uniquely Japanese concept of communication, affects language, social interaction, and especially business dealings.

PB, ISBN 0-87011-889-7, 152 pages

WOMANSWORD
What Japanese Words Say About Women

Kittredge Cherry

From "cockroach husband" to "daughter-in-a-box," a mix of provocative and entertaining words that collectively tell the story of Japanese women.

PB, ISBN 4-7700-1655-7, 160 pages

WORDS IN CONTEXT
Takao Suzuki
Translation by Akira Miura

One of Japan's foremost linguists explores the complex relationship between language and culture, psychology and lifestyle.

PB, ISBN 0-87011-642-8, 180 pages